NGOS AS NEWSMAKERS

Reuters Institute Global Journalism Series

REUTERS INSTITUTE GLOBAL JOURNALISM SERIES

NGOs as Newsmakers

The Changing Landscape of International News

Matthew Powers

Columbia University Press   New York

COLUMBIA
UNIVERSITY
PRESS

Columbia University Press gratefully acknowledges the generous support
for this book provided by Publisher's Circle Chair Anya Schiffrin.

Columbia University Press
Publishers Since 1893
New York   Chichester, West Sussex
cup.columbia.edu

Library of Congress Cataloging-in-Publication Data

Names: Powers, Matthew, author.
Title: NGOs as newsmakers : the changing landscape of international news /
    Matthew Powers.
Description: New York : Columbia University Press, [2018] | Series: Reuters Institute global
    journalism series | Includes bibliographical references and index.
Identifiers: LCCN 2017047191 (print) | LCCN 2017058233 (ebook) | ISBN 9780231545754
    (electronic) | ISBN 9780231184922 (cloth : alk. paper) | ISBN 9780231184939 (pbk.)
Subjects: LCSH: Foreign news. | Reporters and reporting. | Non-governmental
    organizations—Influence.
Classification: LCC PN4784 .F6 (ebook) | LCC PN4784 .F6 P69 2018 (print) |
    DDC 070.4/332—dc23
LC record available at https://lccn.loc.gov/2017047191

Columbia University Press books are printed on permanent and durable acid-free paper.

Printed in the United States of America

Cover design: Noah Arlow

Contents

Acknowledgments

This book was made possible in large part because nongovernmental organization (NGO) professionals and journalists took time to talk with me about their work, and for that opportunity I am deeply grateful. Special thanks to Kimberly Abbott, Steve Ballinger, Louis Belanger, Carroll Bogert, and Jean-Marc Jacobs, each of whom put me in touch with US and European colleagues early on in the research process and whose professional insights helped me better understand the world of NGO communication. My close friend Kirk Prichard also let me pick his brain about all things NGO related, especially at the outset when I was just getting my bearings.

I began this project as a graduate student, and I benefitted greatly from having multiple mentors. Rodney Benson trained me in the craft of research, encouraged me to be analytical without sounding obscure, and supported my intellectual growth by providing the right mix of space and critical feedback, both during graduate school and in the years since. Victor Pickard is the rare person whose comments are both generous and timely, and he constantly nudged me to explain why the research matters. Michael Schudson grasped the central idea for this project before I understood it fully myself, and his questions throughout helped me rethink what I thought I knew. Radha Hegde and Brett Gary offered critical input at key moments in the project's development.

At the University of Washington, several colleagues helped improve the project and bring it to completion. My department chair, David Domke, made sure I had the time and resources needed to do research. Lance Bennett offered extremely generative comments on multiple occasions, which helped me rethink specific aspects of the analysis as well as the project's broader framing. Doug Underwood checked in regularly to offer historical insight and moral support. Adrienne Russell arrived to the department as I was completing the project, and her insights and enthusiasm helped me as I brought the book to completion. Randy Beam and Patricia Moy have been important mentors since I arrived on campus.

A number of graduate students helped me review the extant literature, transcribe interviews, code and analyze data, and edit drafts of various chapters. For this work, I thank Jacquelyn Harvey, K. C. Lynch, Luyue Ma, Ruth Moon, Rico Neumann, Danny Stofleth, and Yunkang Yang. Thanks also to Winnie Cao, Wendy Durant, and Jasmine Wang for patiently helping me navigate all administrative matters at the University of Washington.

Colleagues at several institutions invited me to present aspects of this research while it was just a work in progress. For useful feedback and suggestions, I thank audiences at Northwestern University, Portland State University, Rutgers, University of Oregon, the University of Washington Jackson School of International Studies, University of Westminster, and Yale Law School. At the risk of overlooking someone, I would also like to acknowledge a number of other scholars who helped me in various forms along the way: C. W. Anderson, Mike Annany, Olivier Baisnée, Valerie Belair-Gagnon, Pablo Boczkowski, Josh Braun, Matt Carlson, Bob Entman, Lew Friedland, Andrea Hickerson, Phil Howard, Dave Karpf, Aynne Kokas, Daniel Kreiss, Seth Lewis, Steve Livingston, Ella McPherson, David Mindich, Gina Neff, Stephen Reese, Anya Schiffrin, Jen Schradie, Nikki Usher, Sandra Vera-Zambrano, Silvio Waisbord, Hartmut Wessler, Robert Wosnitzer, and Kate Wright.

At Columbia University Press, Philip Leventhal supported the project from the beginning and offered helpful advice throughout the publication process. Series editor Rasmus Kleis Nielsen and two anonymous reviewers provided thoughtful comments on an earlier version of the manuscript, and the book is better because of it. Annie Barva provided careful and insightful editing. Any remaining errors are my responsibility.

Family in both the United States and Turkey provided constant streams of humor, refuge, and love. I thank my parents, Kevin and Christine; my in-laws, Mehmet and Ülker; and my siblings and their families: Tim, Mandy, and Emily; Kate, Will, and Wilson; Tom and Inés; Beth and Ryan.

My deepest appreciation goes to my wife, Ekin Yaşin, who has listened to, commiserated with, and encouraged me in this project from start to finish. She has also shown me a world outside of work that is filled with her superlatives: the best food, the best music, the best literature, and so much more. If I thank her for being the best thing in my life, I hope she will know that I am not exaggerating in the least.

NGOS AS NEWSMAKERS

CHAPTER ONE

A New Era of NGO-Driven News?

In 2010, the photographer Platon took an assignment that brought him to the border of Thailand and Myanmar.[1] Then a photographer with the *New Yorker* magazine, Platon was paid by the Manhattan-based advocacy group Human Rights Watch to accompany a research team on a trip to the region. With elections coming later that year, Human Rights Watch wanted its researchers to gather the latest information on political repression in the country. Moreover, it wanted to relay that information to policy makers and relevant publics around the world in the hopes of generating a more robust international response to ongoing human rights violations committed by the government. Platon, Human Rights Watch believed, would prove useful to realizing the latter aim.

There on the border of Thailand and Myanmar, the group went about its double mission: researchers conducted interviews; Platon shot his photographs. Best known for his portraits of world leaders, Platon aimed to transfer the visual tactics of celebrity photography—soft frontal lighting, an absence of background or contextual imagery, a wide-angle lens centered solely on the subject's face—to photographing a motley crew of political dissidents: Buddhist monks, land-mine victims, sex workers. Asked to describe his approach to the assignment, he answered that his aim was to put the facts and figures of Human Rights Watch's reporting into terms that could render political dissidents half a world away accessible to Western audiences. "The project with Human Rights Watch," he said, "is predominantly about humanizing their statistics" (Platon 2011).

When the research team returned to New York, Human Rights Watch officials went to the *New Yorker* offices with Platon's photographs and a pitch. The magazine could use the photographs free of charge, but with a single stipulation: Human Rights Watch wanted, after a brief embargo, to send the images to other news outlets, too. According to a Human Rights Watch official, the *New Yorker* editors were keen to use the images. Platon, after all, was their photographer; the issue, given upcoming elections in Myanmar was both newsworthy and under-reported; and the financial cost to the publication of using the photographs was nonexistent. The proposal seemed like a win–win.

Yet the *New Yorker* staff had some concerns of their own. Who would get credit for the images—Platon or Human Rights Watch? Whose story was it, ultimately? Would other outlets' use of the same photographs diminish the cultivated and unique style of journalism that the *New Yorker* sought to project of itself? Both parties felt to a certain extent to be entering unchartered waters. Perhaps not surprisingly, then, unfamiliarity carried with it an undertone of anxiety concerning each other's motivations. This anxiety came to a head at one point in the negotiations when David Remnick, the magazine's editor, asked a Human Rights Watch official outright whether the organization was going to turn around right away and give the photographs to *Time* magazine.

The official assured Remnick that Human Rights Watch had no such intention. In fact, Human Rights Watch in this instance cared little about the American audience. American foreign policy toward Myanmar, in its view, was excellent. What it did care about was the prestige of being in the *New Yorker*. This prestige, organization officials assumed, would make other news outlets in countries where the group sought to change policy toward Myanmar—India, Japan, South Africa, and others—more likely to use the photographs and to draw attention to its accompanying report. It might also, they acknowledged, catch the eyes of the organization's donor base, which tended to read publications such as the *New Yorker*.

Fears assuaged, the *New Yorker* published the photographs in print and online.[2] And Human Rights Watch in turn later sent the images to news outlets in target countries around the world in the hopes of opening doors to government officials in countries where those doors had previously been closed. Months after their publication, the deputy director of external relations at Human Rights Watch told me that the photographs had reached more people around the world, in more places the organization wanted to be, than any other information product the group had ever made—be it a research report, a press release, or an online feature.[3] And yet when asked whether the publicity yielded real-world impact—that is, whether government officials in India, Japan, and South Africa changed their country's position toward Myanmar—the official acknowledged that it was hard to know.

In many ways, the Platon project was a logical extension of the advocacy work that Human Rights Watch has long conducted. Founded in 1978, the group has from its earliest days used on-the-ground reporting to identify human rights violations around the world.[4] In the 1980s, for example, the group regularly sent researchers to various countries in Central America to document war crimes by government and rebel groups (Neier 2003). Moreover, interaction with journalists has always been central to the group's "naming and shaming" strategy.[5] This strategy, which asserts that human rights violators can be publicly pressured into improving their human rights practices, relies crucially on the news media to publicize its findings. Seen from this vantage point, the Platon project simply used digital communication to amplify Human Rights Watch's existing work and reach a more global audience.

In other ways, though, Human Rights Watch's project with Platon signals a broader transformation in how the group conducts research and pursues publicity. With four hundred staff members, the group is able to conduct on-the-ground reporting in a far wider range of countries and on a broader array of human rights topics than it could with the approximately ten staffers it had for much of the 1980s. And with a larger budget, the group is able to hire journalists and photographers, such as Platon, who can produce materials that are likely to attract journalists' attention. Finally, digital technologies diversify the range of publicity options that groups such as Human Rights Watch have at their disposal. These groups can use existing media organizations, such as the *New Yorker*, to attract attention; however, they can also publish materials on their own websites and social media feeds in order to better achieve their advocacy aims. Seen from this vantage point, the Platon project is not simply an extension of past practices but also part of a larger growth and diversification of those practices that makes Human Rights Watch a key participant in the production of contemporary human rights news.

This transformation is not limited to Human Rights Watch. In recent years, a number of leading international nongovernmental organizations (NGOs) have ramped up their communication efforts. Amnesty International, which has long conducted reporting around the world, now staffs a "news unit" charged with being the online portal for human rights news (Bartlett 2011). Oxfam sends "firefighter" reporters to gather information and provide analysis in the midst of humanitarian emergencies (Cooper 2009). Médecins Sans Frontières contracts with photojournalists to boost the visibility of its advocacy efforts both in the mass media and online (Powers 2016a). In these and related instances, NGOs play an increasingly crucial role in shaping and in some cases directly producing news coverage about some of the most pressing humanitarian and human rights issues of our time.

This book provides an in-depth examination of the communication efforts by these and other leading humanitarian and human rights organizations. Drawing on interviews, field observations, and longitudinal content analysis, it charts the dramatic growth in these organizations' communication efforts, examines whether these efforts increase the organizations' chances of garnering news coverage, and analyzes the role of digital technologies in shaping the organizations' choice of publicity strategies. It asks why these groups pursue the communication strategies they do and investigates how journalistic norms and practices structure the news media's reception of these efforts. Finally, it details the consequences of these developments for the types of humanitarian and human rights news that citizens receive.

At its core, this book argues that the growth of NGO communication is a double-edged sword for both advocacy organizations and the public that consumes the information they produce. On the one hand, such efforts diversify the news. As the Human Rights Watch case suggests, the increased resources these groups commit to publicity means that they are more likely to appear in the news today than they were in the past. News consumers are thus exposed to a wider range of institutional voices, and at least sometimes these voices contrast with the views expressed by the government and business elites who have long dominated the news agenda. Moreover, NGOs can and do use digital tools to strategically shape news coverage in ways that seek to maximize their organizational objectives, as Human Rights Watch did by targeting its publicity to news media in countries where policy needed, in its view, to be changed.

On the other hand, these efforts also have costs. In their quest to garner publicity, NGOs adapt to news norms that give journalists and government officials the upper hand in defining what counts as news. This means that although advocacy groups produce information about a broad range of topics from a large number of countries, they tend to appear in places that the news media are covering and speak on issues in which the news media are already interested. Moving the media spotlight to Myanmar, as Human Rights Watch did, is thus an important exception, not an emergent rule. Moreover, despite the potential to use digital technologies to circumvent these patterns of control, NGO use of such tools centers primarily around interacting with journalists and protecting the NGOs' own organizational credibility. Exploring alternative forms of public engagement—using, for example, social media to bypass the news media and directly target relevant stakeholders—is an aim that proves secondary at best.

Beyond documenting the mixed effects of NGO communication efforts, this book also offers an explanation for this state of affairs. It argues that advocacy groups see communication as both a way to garner credibility as actors in international politics and a means to raise the funds—either directly (through public donations) or indirectly (via branding)—that are necessary for their survival and growth. NGOs hire journalists in part to help achieve these dual aims, and these journalists bring a news-making sensibility to advocacy organizations. Although the development of such sensibilities boosts these organizations' overall chances of garnering news coverage, it also ensures that advocacy groups produce information that largely accords with rather than challenges media preferences. Donors, government officials, and news organizations—each in different ways and for distinct reasons—further reinforce these tendencies by incentivizing NGOs to focus their efforts primarily on appearing in the mainstream news media. As a result, advocacy groups play less attention to using digital technologies, which might cultivate alternative forms of public engagement.

On the whole, then, this book portrays a news landscape that both offers NGOs greater opportunities to shape the news and subjects them to long-held norms of news construction. It illustrates how the expectations of donors, government officials, and journalists help to create this state of affairs and how these expectations lead advocacy groups to devote considerable resources to publicity, despite uncertainty as to whether these efforts aid in achieving their advocacy aims. Finally, it explains how the very uptake in communication efforts by NGOs helps to reproduce news norms that might otherwise be expected to change as a consequence of the legacy news media's diminished international footprint.

THE CHANGING CONTEXTS OF NGO COMMUNICATION

The growth and diversification of NGO communication have arisen amid dramatic changes in journalism, advocacy, politics, and technology. In journalism, diminished revenues and intensified profitability expectations have led many North American and western European news organizations to reduce the resources they commit to international news gathering, while the rise of satellite and online news providers has diversified the number of globally oriented news organizations. In advocacy, the professionalization of activism, the growth of the organized advocacy sector, and that sector's incorporation into governance have led NGOs to increase the amount and types of information they produce. In politics, public skepticism toward government has led many to view NGOs as credible sources of information and potential organizers for political action. Finally, the growth of digital technologies has expanded the landscape of public communication by diversifying the number of voices in the public sphere. Together, these changes have created the context in which it has become possible to explore transformations in NGOs' communication efforts.[6]

For much of the latter part of the twentieth century, international news was a prestigious, if costly, type of coverage for news organizations to provide (Hamilton 2009). In both North America and western Europe, print newspapers and television stations maintained sizeable foreign-news bureaus, and assignments within these bureaus were prized positions reserved for highly regarded reporters (Hess 1996; Sambrook 2010). As news audiences have fragmented and advertising revenues have tumbled in recent years, news organizations have cut back on the number of foreign-news bureaus they maintain and full-time correspondents they employ (Carroll 2007; Kumar 2011).[7] In the latter's place, freelance reporters and parachute journalists are increasingly common, as are satellite and online-only news providers (Hannerz 2004; Reese 2010; Sambrook 2010; Volkmer 2014).[8] These developments diversify the total number of news providers, but many remain skeptical as to whether they can offset the losses stemming from legacy media cutbacks. Thus, although scholars have long critiqued international news coverage as ethnocentric (Galtung and Ruge 1965; Gans 1979), today many wonder how news organizations—whether legacy, satellite, or online—will be able to monitor international affairs with their own network of correspondents. This situation informs what anthropologist Ulf Hannerz calls the "paradox" of contemporary international news: "In an era of intense globalizations, foreign news coverage in many media channels has recently been shrinking" (2004, 23).

At the same time, as news media have experienced these massive changes, NGOs have undergone transformations that have led them to increase both the amount and the types of information they produce. For starters, they have become institutionalized—that is, established as durable organizations rather than remaining ephemeral volunteer efforts (Keck and Sikkink 1998; Lang 2013). This institutionalization requires NGOs to produce a wide range of information materials—reports, policy statements, press releases, and so forth—for a diverse array of stakeholders that includes donors, government officials, and journalists. These groups have also professionalized. Their staff—whether researchers, advocacy officers, or communication professionals—are competitively hired in part for their capacity to produce these information materials (Powers 2016a). Finally, as the number of NGOs has grown, the whole sector has become more competitive as individual groups compete for limited funds and public attention (Cottle and Nolan 2007). Each organization therefore dedicates growing resources to managing its "brand" by maximizing its chances for positive publicity while minimizing its negative exposure (Orgad 2013). Together, these changes mean that NGOs today produce more—and more types of—information for a wider range of audiences than they did in the past.

Amid changes in journalism and advocacy, the political contexts in which both entities operate has also changed. Across western Europe and North America, notions of citizenship have expanded from infrequent participation in the political process via voting to perpetual efforts by NGOs, among other civil society actors, to hold governments—and, perhaps to a lesser degree, businesses—accountable for their actions (Bennett 2003; Friedland 1996; Rosanvallon 2008; Scammell 2014; Schudson 2015). These efforts span the gamut from street-based protests, which NGOs help organize, to advisory government fora, in which NGOs participate. These changes have led NGOs to interact more regularly with government and business officials, whether in providing services or reporting on key social issues (Lang 2013; Volkmer 2014). Beyond these interactions and in the midst of public skepticism toward government action, many view NGOs as both trusted sources of information and potential organizers of political action (Castells 2009; Lang 2013). On the whole, then, changes in politics appear simultaneously to give official legitimation to NGOs—that is, to include them within the range of official viewpoints—and perhaps to decenter government officials as the primary authority on certain topics.

Changes in technology cut across these transformations. Digital technologies potentially reshape the landscape of public communication by diversifying the tools available for producing and disseminating information. The relatively low costs associated with digital technologies make it possible for advocacy groups to produce their own audiovisual materials and to monitor issues of interest online (McPherson 2015). Sizeable budgets also give NGOs the resources to utilize more costly technologies, such as satellite imaging, to inform their reporting efforts (Aday and Livingston 2009). Furthermore, if NGOs were once reliant on the news media for visibility, today these groups have at their disposal a range of tools through which they can try to cultivate different forms of public attention (Bennett and Segerberg 2013; Chadwick 2013). Across all these settings, NGOs compete with other information-producing organizations—including businesses and governments, which often marshal far greater material and symbolic resources (Davis 2002)—for attention.

Taken together, these changing contexts raise the questions that this book seeks to answer: Do NGOs enjoy greater publicity today than they did in the past? How and in what ways do these groups use digital technologies in their communications? And what effects have these changes had on the work produced by both NGO professionals and journalists? To date, scholars have given opposing answers to these disparate questions.

NGO COMMUNICATION: BOON OR BANE?

Two primary tropes characterize the existing scholarship on NGO communication. A first argues that such groups are best understood as a boon for public communication. According to this view, NGOs take seriously the precepts of factual reporting and provide news coverage from locales or on topics that otherwise receive scant attention (Russell 2013; Schudson 2011; Zuckerman 2004).[9] Such efforts are posited to help offset some of the losses in international news coverage. Several case studies provide supporting evidence for such claims. In comparing NGO coverage of a United Nations Climate Summit with the reporting provided by American news outlets, Adrienne Russell found that NGO coverage, relative to legacy news media coverage, was "exhaustive and included the actions and comments of high-profile international and national officials, scientists, civil society and locally focused grassroots groups" (2013, 917). In fact, NGO coverage of the summit was so exhaustive that many news organizations simply directed their own readers to it for more complete coverage of the events. Ethan Zuckerman extends this point by suggesting that advocacy reportage often comes from places that otherwise receive minimal news coverage. Drawing on the example of human rights abuses in the Darfur region of Sudan, he remarks that advocacy groups produced and published reports many years before the issue ever surfaced in the Western news media. In his telling, human rights groups "did the first round of investigative journalism that news organizations failed to do" (2004, 53).

Beyond directly producing news, tropes of NGOs as a boon for public communication also stress these groups' capacity to instantiate new forms of civic engagement. One criticism of international news coverage is that it describes social problems while offering little sense of how such problems can be remedied. As a result, audiences develop a picture of the world as fragmented and frequently riven by seemingly senseless violence and hopeless tragedies (Moeller 1999). For some, advocacy groups do not merely describe social problems but also constitute the organizational backbone of what Margaret Keck and Kathryn Sikkink (1998) call "transnational advocacy networks." These networks by design seek to insert advocacy recommendations into their communication efforts. As Jürgen Habermas notes in his reformulated vision of the public sphere, advocacy groups not only have informed the public about the "great issues of the last decades" (environmentalism, human rights, feminism) but also have shown the public concrete steps to take in order to remedy these problems (1996, 381). More recently, Stephen Reese (2015), in his research on environmental groups working in China, has suggested that through this very "problem-solving" orientation, NGOs may contribute to the overall quality and transparency of public communication more generally. These and related comments suggest that in their communication efforts NGOs help instantiate a cosmopolitan vision that enlarges the perspectives of citizens both within and beyond the nation-state (Appiah 2006; Beck 2006; Silverstone 2007).

A final point made by those who see positive potential in NGOs' communication efforts pertains to their use of digital technologies. According to these scholars, such tools make it possible for these groups to improve their information gathering and refine their publicity efforts. Sean Aday and Steven Livingston (2009) describe how advocacy groups use satellite imagery to aid in their information-gathering efforts. Such tools make it possible for these groups to extend their capacity to witness human rights from afar, even when their research personnel are not directly on the ground. Dave Karpf (2012) has shown that advocacy groups can and do use digital tools to test their messaging strategies in order to identify the issues and frames that best resonate with their supporters. Finally, several authors argue that social media tools make it possible for advocacy groups to bypass the news media and directly target relevant stakeholders (Bennett and Segerberg 2013; Madianou 2013; Volkmer 2014; Wells 2015). Taken together, these authors fill out the view that NGOs' communication efforts can be viewed primarily as a positive development.

A second trope is less sanguine about NGOs' communication efforts. According to this view, NGOs' uptake in publicity work is better characterized as a bane for journalism and advocacy, respectively. From the perspective of journalism, advocacy groups are said to threaten to turn the news media into a platform for advocacy and fund-raising. Alex de Waal (1998), for example, has argued that when journalists depend on NGOs for access to news stories, they are unlikely to see NGOs as anything but part of the solution to the problems they are observing. This perspective results in a situation wherein advocacy viewpoints are uncritically passed on to news consumers. More broadly, multiple scholars stress that NGOs are not only or perhaps not even primarily principled actors; rather, they are organizations with needs and interests, and this fact sometimes leads them to act in ways that are at odds with their values and that provide misleading perspectives on global affairs (Bob 2006; de Waal 1998; Rieff 2002). They further argue that NGOs manufacture and overhype existing problems in ways that maximize the financial benefits to themselves without substantively changing the situations they profess to address (Cohen and Green 2012; M. Scott 2014; Wright 2016b). As one analyst writes, because of their fund-raising needs NGOs "tend to focus not on what has been accomplished but on convincing people how much remains to be done. . . . These pressures create incentives to present as gloomy a picture . . . as possible in order to keep attention and money flowing" (Rothmyer 2011, 18).[10] As the resources that news organizations commit to international news decline, these authors worry that journalists will unwittingly permit advocacy groups to turn the news media into a platform for their advocacy and fund-raising aims.

Skeptics also worry about the negative impacts of NGOs' newsmaking efforts on the NGOs themselves. This view shares the premise that expanded NGO communication efforts in principle boost NGOs' chances of appearing in the news. But those articulating this view argue that, in an ironic twist, rather than challenge news norms the NGOs adapt their messages to fit them. Simon Cottle and David Nolan (2007), for instance, argue that the subservience to the news media norms of timeliness and newsworthiness lead NGOs to sensationalize their causes in ways that are meant to appeal to media outlets rather than to address the deeper, more structural issues at the root of the ills addressed. Further, they see the bulk of media work itself to be indicative of the time, resources, and energy that NGOs must commit to ensuring their organizational reputations and credibility against the possibility of media-driven scandals. As such, their communication efforts are largely a necessary distraction, the result of living in a media-saturated age (Jones 2017). Relatedly, Natalie Fenton (2010) and Silvio Waisbord (2011) argue that NGOs tend to adopt pragmatic approaches to the news media. That is, although NGOs remain critical of news coverage, they prefer to cooperate with journalists out of fear that opposition will result in their exclusion from the public sphere. These authors see the importance of media coverage to be disadvantageous, in varying degrees, to the cosmopolitan project upon which many NGOs are founded.[11]

Finally, those who evaluate the uptake in NGO communication primarily in negative terms argue that it fails to enhance civic engagement. Because advocacy groups rely on media and political elites for legitimacy, they exhibit a tendency to orient their communication practices toward these entities. In Sabine Lang's (2013) evocative phrase, this orientation leads organizations to function as "proxy publics" that stand in for rather than discursively engage with diverse constituencies (see also Bob 2006). Moreover, scholars suggest that to the extent that these groups harness the affordances of online tools, they direct them primarily to enhancing this legitimacy. Accordingly, researchers have documented a range of highly targeted campaigns that seek primarily to engage political elites (Bob 2006; DeMars 2005; Lang 2013). Lost in the mix are efforts to use NGOs' communication tools to facilitate novel forms of civic engagement.

Boon-and-bane tropes thus provide different descriptions, analyses, and evaluations of NGO communication efforts. Rather than prove or disprove either, I suggest that each provides important insights into NGOs' communication efforts and these efforts' effects on public communication. Optimists correctly note that advocacy groups can and do provide coverage from places and on topics the news media routinely ignore. Moreover, these groups do indeed fuse their advocacy recommendations into their reporting. In doing so, they provide potential solutions to the problems their reporting describes. At the same time, skeptics show how the need for fund-raising and legitimacy vis-à-vis both the news media and political officials lead advocacy groups to produce communication that limits their potential for challenging news norms or cultivating novel forms of civic engagement. Skeptics also make the important point that the rise of NGO communication is no substitute for independent and rigorous reporting by news organizations.

In short, NGO communication efforts are neither wholly a boon nor wholly a bane. A better trope for capturing their mixed effects, I suggest, is that of a double-edged sword. The growth and diversification of NGO communication efforts gives rise to both the favorable consequences that optimists desire and the unfavorable ones about which skeptics warn. This book empirically shows where and how these different consequences arise. It explores which news outlets are more or less likely to feature NGOs, what types of messages are most likely to gain acceptance in the news media, which advocacy groups are more or less likely to challenge extant news norms, and how digital technologies both contribute to and detract from advocacy aims. It suggests throughout that NGOs' communication efforts are strongly marked by patterns of both change and continuity. On the one hand, advocacy groups have strongly ramped up their communication efforts in recent years, and these efforts do lead them to appear in the news more often and to use digital tools to supplement these efforts. On the other hand, journalists continue to subordinate advocacy messages to the views articulated by government officials, and advocacy groups retain a strong interest in getting their messages out in the legacy news media. In making this argument, I draw on an emergent literature that documents the mixed effects of NGO communication (Lück, Wozniak, and Wessler 2016; McPherson 2015; Moon 2017; Nolan and Mikami 2013; Orgad 2013; M. Scott 2014; Stroup 2012; Van Leuven and Joye 2014; Wells 2015; Wright 2016a, 2016b).

At the same time, I want to move beyond simply documenting the mixed effects of NGO communication. The fact that NGO communication is not neatly captured by either side of a simple binary is perhaps unsurprising. Therefore, I want also to analyze why NGOs pursue the communication strategies they do, to explain the reception of these strategies by journalists, and to explore why, despite reasonable expectations to the contrary, we see a dynamic mixture of continuity and change in NGOs' communication practices. To do this, I draw on the analytical tools provided by institutional and field theories and suggest that journalism and NGOs can be conceptualized as independent but interacting institutional fields. This perspective allows me to examine the norms and practices that shape each of these separate fields and gives me tools for better understanding the interactions within and across them. In particular, as I discuss in the next section, it offers a tool kit well adapted to making sense of the mixture of continuity and change that characterizes contemporary advocacy organizations' information efforts.

NGOS AND JOURNALISM AS INTERACTING INSTITUTIONAL FIELDS

Institutional theory begins from the premise that contemporary societies are composed of semiautonomous social fields or orders (Bourdieu 1993; DiMaggio and Powell 1991; Fligstein and McAdam 2012; Martin 2003).[12] Within any given field, actors compete for recognition and prestige according to the "rules of the game," which are enacted consciously or unconsciously by actors in the field. These actors can be individuals (e.g., researchers, journalists), groups (e.g., research departments, newsrooms), organizations (e.g., NGOs, news organizations), firms, or states. Key to each actor is that it takes into account the actions, perceptions, and practices of others within the field in an effort to accrue both resources and recognition. Institutional theory thus articulates a "meso"-level view of social life in that the actions within any given institutional field cannot be reduced to any macro social process that operates independently of social actors, nor can they be ascribed solely to individuals' preferences and idiosyncrasies.[13]

Advocacy work and journalism constitute clear examples of institutional fields. Each has some degree of autonomy from external forces. Although journalists' everyday work is shaped by commercial and political forces, decisions about what and how to publish as news cannot be reduced solely to these forces.[14] Similarly, although NGOs' work is strongly shaped by donors and government officials, decisions about what humanitarian and human rights issues to engage in and how also cannot be reduced to these considerations. There are instead constant internal struggles within any given institutional field about how and in what ways the "game" should be played. The first task for uncovering these struggles is therefore to re-create, through historical analysis, how they came to be in the first place. Moving away from the presentism of current debates, I show that NGOs developed their communication efforts initially as part of a strategy to legitimate themselves as a social field. In their earliest days, NGOs dedicated time and resources to support credible reporting about their chosen topics as a way to more effectively pursue their advocacy goals. This reporting helped these groups gain legitimacy from political officials, journalists, and donors, yet it was accompanied by recurrent debates about what form NGO communication ought to take—that is, about the degree to which communication should be used for fund-raising, branding, advocacy, and research as well as the extent to which a focus on communication distracts from other organizational aims. These debates are part of the basic struggles that inform tensions within organizations today, and they preexist transformations in journalism and technology.

Because fields are sites of struggle, different organizations within a given field pursue different paths in order to distinguish themselves from others.[15] Although communication is becoming more important to all NGOs, I use this insight to show how the pursuit of publicity varies across organizations. Whereas some organizations are interested mostly in attracting the attention of elite, agenda-setting news outlets, others spend a great deal of time and effort engaging general media. Rather than being idiosyncratic preferences, these differences are shaped by the types of funding these groups receive and the relative balance of power between different departments within any single group. This account of variation stands in contrast to sweeping statements that see all advocacy groups as moving on a similar trajectory. It also shows the divergent (i.e., double-edged) impacts that NGO communication has on public communication.

Institutions are in a basic sense social achievements. They require a great deal of effort to establish. As a consequence, there are strong incentives to protect such orders. This protective sensibility informs the pragmatic approach that many organizations take with respect to digital tools in technology. Although these groups in principle grasp the potential ways such tools could alter their relationship with the mass media, they in practice tend to use them in ways that reinforce the importance of mainstream publicity. Institutional theory helps explain why digital tools should be used in pragmatic ways rather than as some irrational approach to publicity. Established advocacy groups see digital tools to some degree as a threat. The same tools that allow advocacy groups in principle to bypass the news media also enable their opponents to attack and challenge their reporting in real time. NGOs work to preserve their organizational reputation by falling back on some of the strategies that secured their legitimacy in the predigital era (e.g., on-the-ground reporting, often based on months of research). Because this use of earlier strategies requires time and resources, it is often out of sync with the digital-news cycle.

Inertia is an outcome, one that is actively produced through institutional dynamics. For institutional theorists, a key concept in explaining this inertia is path dependence (Pierson 2000; Thelen 2002). This concept suggests that past decisions shape present actions and can lead to a sort of inertia that might otherwise seem unexpected. It costs a great deal of money for NGOs to create their press offices, and these high startup costs serve as an incentive to continue working through the mainstream media. Moreover, all NGO professionals—researchers, communication officers, advocacy officials—accumulate knowledge over time about how to interact with mainstream journalists. Semiregular contact with journalists provides feedback that further encourages NGOs to continue working with and through the mainstream news media. In journalism, too, similar dynamics prevail. Although NGOs are regularly on the ground with reporters in crisis situations, journalists for the most part continue to see NGOs primarily as "advocates" whose agenda can supplement but not supplant their own reporting.

While drawing from institutional theories, I seek also to extend them. For the most part, the concept of path dependence is used to describe continuity within an institutional field. Less attention has been paid to the role of external influences in shaping continuity of behaviors and norms. When institutions do not change, theories of path dependence mostly ascribe resilience to the power of institutions. It is when institutions do change that institutional theories focus on external pressures (Thelen 2002). Yet these external pressures are usually discussed in broad terms, as can be seen in the concepts "exogenous shocks" and "critical junctures" (R. Scott 2014; Starr 2004). This broad discussion has the unintended effect of leaving undertheorized the degree to which related institutional fields shape the behavior of a single field. In the case of NGOs, these pressures mean that publicity strategies sometimes follow in step with the strategies of those located in more powerful fields (politics, philanthropy, and journalism).

To address this shortcoming, I draw on the "field" variant of institutional theory, which situates individual institutional fields within a broader constellation of power relations. I suggest that part of the path dependence in NGOs' practices derives from path dependencies in other institutional fields. Donors still look to the news media as a signal of NGO influence, and they are relatively hesitant to fund large-scale projects related to digital technologies because of their own path dependencies: this is how they have always funded organizations, and these are the rubrics they use to understand success. Similarly, government officials still look to mainstream news coverage as a proxy for public opinion. Although occasional efforts to bypass the news media provide glimmers of hope for change, NGOs still prioritize mainstream media coverage in part because government officials want to see NGOs covered there. I suggest that these path dependencies "reinforce" one another—that is, each path dependence operates in order to ensure relative continuity in NGOs' communication practices over time. I also suggest that this argument provides a more precise account of the durability of social practices than current theories of path dependence allow.

My emphasis on NGOs and journalism as interacting fields also enables me to further understand the relative durability of news norms over time. Theorists of change have good reason to imagine that the social dynamics between NGOs and journalists might be changing (for all the reasons already mentioned). Yet analyzing the two fields allows me to identify a process that I term *field diffusion*. By this term, I refer to the process in which former (and sometimes still current) reporters gain employment in the NGO sector on a temporary or full-time basis. In their new roles, these journalists diffuse the sensibility and norms of journalism into the advocacy sector. This is a model of continuity that changes in both journalism and advocacy paradoxically enable.

Beyond analyzing NGO–journalist interactions, I utilize institutional theory in part to draw attention to the importance of institutions as such. In contrast to accounts that focus almost exclusively on what W. Lance Bennett and Alexandra Segerberg term "digitally-enabled activism" (2013, 22), institutional theory examines the social fields in which all forms of social action are embedded. Although my own empirical analysis focuses on NGOs, I suggest that such groups are merely one instance of a broader development in public-communication efforts that cuts across many other institutional fields, including but not limited to business and government. There is thus a need to understand the empirical specificity of each institutional setting as well as a need to develop a larger account of how these shifts together shape contemporary public communication. Indeed, such analyses are important in part because many of the gains achieved by NGOs that I describe could conceivably be overtaken by developments in other, more symbolically and economically powerful, institutional fields.

In sum, I draw on—and extend—the tools of institutional and field analysis in order to better explain the complex mixture of continuity and change that mark NGOs' information practices. These conceptual tools enable me to situate the current efforts of advocacy groups within a larger history related to the role of communication in the work of advocacy groups. This history helps to explain how and why NGOs have developed their capacity for providing what I refer to as "boots on the ground" coverage (Powers 2016a) as well as how these developments do not reshape NGO–journalism relations in the fundamental ways predicted by other boon-or-bane theorists. The dynamism of this relationship is instead complex, but it mostly leads NGOs to utilize their new tools in ways that reproduce—rather than challenge—basic news norms and practices.

STUDYING NGO COMMUNICATION

The term *nongovernmental organizations* refers to groups that are nominally independent of government, voluntary in nature, and interested in the pursuit of a common good (e.g., working on an issue such as human rights, gender equality, or environmental protection).[16] They can be found working at various levels (local, national, international) on a range of issues. Since the end of the Cold War, such groups have become the dominant organization form of civil society (Keck and Sikkink 1998; Lang 2013). If in the past labor unions and social movements were the primary organizations that raised social justice issues, today NGOs are, for better or worse, the primary organizers of attention to such issues and producers of related discourses.[17] In this position, they communicate to achieve a range of objectives: to boost awareness of important social issues, to lobby political and business actors to alter their behaviors, to raise funds, and to promote their organizational brands. The relationship between NGOs and communication is therefore important for understanding the organizational basis of activism, the degree to which news media are open to advocacy messages, and the role of digital technologies in the production and distribution of advocacy materials.

This book examines the communication efforts of leading humanitarian and human rights NGOs, an important subset of the larger institutional ecology of advocacy organizations. These groups provide a "most likely" research design. As some of the best-funded civil society organizations, with explicit missions to produce and publicize information that can bring attention to neglected issues, these groups are arguably best positioned to influence humanitarian and human rights news coverage.[18] If Amnesty International and Human Rights Watch struggle to get into the mainstream news and to balance the demands of publicity with their other organizational aims, it seems reasonable to imagine that smaller groups with fewer resources and less symbolic prestige face similar problems.

Historically, human rights advocacy and humanitarianism were separate discourses, with the former focused on protecting citizens against state violence and the latter centered primarily on the reduction of suffering (Calhoun 2008). These differences inform distinctive communicative functions in these organizations. Because humanitarian organizations need access to conflict and disaster zones, they tend not to speak out against the policies and politics of host governments. By contrast, human rights organizations do not provide services on the ground and so regularly engage in criticism of governments around the world. Since the end of the Cold War, though, the two fields have become increasingly intertwined, with both relying on human rights discourses to publicly justify their work. Humanitarian groups regularly evoke human rights principles, and recurrent debates among members of the field ask about the extent to which such groups ought to speak out against host governments, even if access might be cut off as a result (Kennedy 2004; Rieff 2002; Terry 2002). At the same time, human rights groups today extend their work well beyond the issue of state violence and address a range of economic, cultural, and social rights. As the historian Samuel Moyn explains, "Today, human rights and humanitarianism are fused enterprises, with the former incorporating the latter and the latter justified in terms of the former" (2010, 221). This fusion enables me to explore the prevalence of these groups within a single discourse—human rights—while also building variation into the sample. In other words, by bringing together groups with potentially different relations to media, I am able to explore in a more parsimonious fashion the factors shaping contemporary NGO communication efforts.

Central to this book is the empirical study of the following leading advocacy organizations: Amnesty International, Human Rights Watch, World Vision, Save the Children, Concern, Oxfam, CARE, International Medical Corps, Médecins Sans Frontières, Mercy Corps, and the International Crisis Group. Together, these groups constitute some of the largest and most active NGOs working on issues of human rights and humanitarian relief and thus offer a glimpse into the roles played by the field's most established organizations. These groups are also among the most active in developing staff and practices aimed at contributing to their public-communication efforts. Furthermore, by examining a relatively small number of organizations in detail, I am able to analyze the full circuit of information production—from the dynamics shaping its production within advocacy organizations to its reception by journalists and its circulation through various online distribution channels. Of course, the NGO field is far broader than these limited number of groups (Reese 2015; Waisbord 2011). It is unlikely that the findings discussed in this book can be applied wholesale to all other humanitarian and human rights groups, many of which are less interested in cultivating publicity. The degree to which these findings pertain to other thematic arenas of NGO advocacy, such as environmental groups, is also an open question. I return to the question of generalizability in chapter 7.

I bring a range of methodological tools to study NGO communication efforts. The book is based primarily on interviews with and observations of more than seventy professionals working in these organizations as researchers, advocacy officers, and public-relations professionals. These interviews were often preceded by my attendance at an organization's daily meetings, where the day's agenda was discussed and decided. Overall, I attempted to interview a cross-section of professionals, including both individuals who had been at their respective organizations for a relatively long period of time (five years or more) and those who had joined more recently. Further, I contacted both junior and senior staff to provide a cross-section of viewpoints within any one organization. Snowball sampling identified key individuals for subsequent interviews, typically by asking interviewees at the end of an interview whom else would be appropriate to speak with about these matters. I asked how and in what ways these groups pursued publicity, how these practices have and have not changed over time, and what types of opportunities and challenges have emerged from their practices. (See the methods appendix for the semistructured interview protocol.)

I supplement and contextualize these data with three additional data sources. First, I utilize primary and secondary sources—annual reports, media accounts, memoirs by key participants—to trace the growing resources that NGOs dedicate to communication efforts over time (in terms of staff size, number of research reports, press releases, advocacy campaigns, total number of countries and topics that their reporting covers, and the diversification of information formats with the advent of digital technologies). I situate these figures within a historical narrative that explains how and why NGOs decided to ramp up their information offerings. Specifically, I show how the institutionalization of NGOs in international affairs, the professionalization of NGOs' staff, and the growing competition among NGOs have led humanitarian and human rights groups to diversify their information offerings.

Second, the book presents the results of an original content analysis to analyze how NGOs' growing efforts fit into established theories of news access. Drawing on a twenty-year content analysis of humanitarian and human rights news coverage in leading US news outlets, it examines whether the reduction of foreign-news bureaus helps to open the news gates for those NGOs interested in making the news or has established patterns of news construction that minimize both the amount and type of news coverage NGOs receive. Further details on the data and methods for this content analysis—including my decision to focus on legacy news outlets—can be found in chapter 3, and the coding protocol is located in the methods appendix.

Third, I draw on interviews with reporters and editors at leading international news outlets in regard to their reporting on humanitarian and human rights issues for Syrian refugees in Turkey. This case, although possessing a multitude of unique features, contains many typical features of humanitarian and human rights situations: it occurred in a geographic setting where news outlets have few regular reporters and thus rely on stringers and "parachute" reporting efforts from journalists stationed elsewhere. In 2011, I visited the border region of Hatay, a point from which journalists conducted much of their reporting, which allowed me to meet with and observe in real time how journalists reported this story, including but not limited to their interactions with NGO professionals. Further details of this case study as well as the conditions that led to my research are provided in chapter 6.

Together, these diverse materials provide me with the empirical and analytical depth necessary to assess the roles that NGOs play in the changing news landscape and to analyze the degree to which these roles depart from established theories of news production. To be sure, these data are not exhaustive. A study of a single organization would provide more depth than is available here. Moreover, these groups' communication strategies are likely to evolve as new information technologies continue to provide new tools with which their work can be done. Nonetheless, this book aims to draw on the data I gathered to provide as clear a portrait as possible of the information efforts of leading humanitarian and human rights groups in the twenty-first century.

OUTLINE OF THE BOOK

Chapter 2 charts over time the changes in the amount and types of information work that NGOs conduct. I argue that advocacy groups' contemporary information efforts are best understood as the result of three developments: first, the professionalization of advocacy, which has led to an emphasis on credible reporting as a way for NGOs to pursue their advocacy goals; second, growing competition among advocacy groups, which intensifies the use of communication to secure donations and promote organizational brands; and third, changes in journalism and technology, which make advocacy groups more aware of the news media's norms and preferences even as new technologies allow groups to experiment with new digital formats. Together, these shifts create the conditions in which NGOs have come to be viewed as "boots on the ground" that blur the lines separating journalism, advocacy, and public relations.

Chapter 3 then examines whether NGOs enjoy greater news access today as a result of these developments. It presents the results of a content analysis of human rights coverage in a strategic twenty-year sample of leading US news outlets. On the whole, the findings reveal what I refer to as a "partial opening of the news gates" for humanitarian and human rights groups. On the one hand, NGOs—especially those with a high degree of media savvy—are more likely to appear in the news today than they were in the past, and they are increasingly able to insert human rights frames into stories that are already circulating the news media. On the other hand, how these groups appear in the news continues to follow well-established theories of news access: they tend to appear late in news stories and after other news sources, especially government officials. Moreover, efforts to drive news coverage to new issues or topics are seldom successful. Finally, despite efforts by humanitarian and human rights groups to expand their advocacy to include economic, cultural, and social rights, news coverage continues to privilege political and civic violations. Taken together, the data suggest that although NGOs enjoy greater news access today than they did in the past, the power to shape—or challenge—the rules of news access continues to exceed their grasp.

Chapter 4 asks how and in what ways advocacy groups use digital tools in their communication efforts. In contrast to arguments about a new era of direct-to-public global communication, it finds that NGOs use digital tools primarily to capture the attention of journalists and only secondarily to communicate with supporters. Moreover, advocacy groups face a conundrum in that the very visibility afforded to them in the online environment also enables politically motivated critics to launch public criticisms that aim to delegitimize the advocacy groups' role as a source of information. This criticism in turn leads humanitarian and human rights groups to be cautious about utilizing some of the Internet's more interactive features. The result is that they tend to minimize public engagement and instead utilize highly strategic forms of information management. In addition to frustrating the expectations of a new era of public communication, NGOs' publicity strategies also complicate the view that online efforts dilute their advocacy aims. These groups see online news as chaotic and thus to a certain degree permeable: they monitor the news with the hopes of grafting their advocacy reporting and action recommendations onto news flows. Although their overall rate of success in getting their messages picked up is low, they are sometimes able to insert their advocacy agenda into the mainstream news. Their highly strategic efforts thus help to diversify the news agenda by adding advocacy frames to extant coverage.

Chapter 5 questions why NGOs should continue to favor mainstream media coverage, despite new digital possibilities. Drawing on and contributing to theories of path dependence, I argue that humanitarian and human rights groups are incentivized in three ways to pursue the publicity strategies they do. First, donors continue to value media coverage as a platform to learn about NGOs and as a mechanism for measuring NGOs' impact on political discourse. They are also hesitant to fund new areas such as analytics and content management that would allow advocacy groups to further develop their online strategies. Second, political officials continue to value media coverage as a way to learn about advocacy demands. Although digital technologies create new avenues for interactions with government officials, most examples of successful advocacy are connected to mainstream coverage. Third, NGOs occupy a position that is socially proximate to journalism, which leads the former to see the latter as an ally in the pursuit of publicity. These data both confirm and extend theories of path dependence and lead to use of the term *reinforcing path dependencies*.

Chapter 6 probes why journalism norms endure despite massive downsizing in the news industry. Drawing on interviews with journalists and fieldwork at the Turkey–Syria border, I identify two mechanisms that enable these norms to endure. The first, which I call "field inertia," shows that journalists remain wedded to a view of NGOs primarily as advocates and look to NGO professionals to accomplish a prearranged set of tasks (e.g., provide on-the-ground news and analysis, respond to government statements, offer dramatic visuals), which are slotted into stories driven primarily by other sources. Editors, who remain hierarchically powerful vis-à-vis reporters, are primarily responsible for maintaining this inertia. The second process—what I term "field diffusion"—shows how the economic crisis in journalism has pushed journalists into fields such as the NGO sector. In their new roles, former (and sometimes still active) reporters bring the sensibility of journalism to advocacy groups' news-making efforts, which allows journalism norms to diffuse into other sectors, which in turn makes it more likely that advocacy groups will produce information in keeping with the news media's preferences. Paradoxically, this diffusion is enabled by the NGO sector's own efforts toward professionalization, which puts a growing emphasis on publicity.

Chapter 7 discusses the possibilities and limitations of NGO communication. I suggest that, on balance, NGO communication closely approximates representative liberal and participatory theories of public communication while frustrating deliberative and radical ideals. I situate the study of NGOs within the broader rise of "news-oriented practices"—that is, efforts by nonjournalistic actors to directly shape public communication—and I conclude with a discussion of what I see as the book's core analytical contribution: how institutions matter.

In general, my findings capture simultaneously the possibilities and limits of NGO communication efforts. Although I share with the optimists the sense that advocacy groups are important actors in contemporary news and deserve further study as such, I am also cautious about too quickly writing off the importance of an independent news media. Despite various well-chronicled problems, there continues to be a need for professional journalists to perform their gate-keeping and status-conferring roles. I therefore conclude by suggesting that although advocacy groups play an important role in shaping news coverage, their presence does not obviate the need for careful, independent reporting conducted by journalists. New developments do not obviate old problems. They multiply them.

CHAPTER TWO

The Changing Faces of NGO Communication Work

Hanging on a wall in one of Amnesty International's primary meeting rooms is a framed black-and-white photograph in which a man leans over an open newspaper. He holds a large pair of scissors in his right hand and cuts an article from one of the newspaper's sections. Beneath that image, a caption explains that the man was one of the organization's earliest volunteers. In his role as a "press cutter," the caption reads, he was tasked with coming into the organization's London headquarters to identify news articles about human rights violations that could be clipped from newspapers and then further researched by Amnesty International—with the ultimate aim of publicizing those findings in newspapers. For these efforts, the volunteer was given an annual stipend of fifty-two pounds plus another fifty-two pounds in lunch vouchers.[1] Such efforts, the caption continues, were "central to the lifesaving work" that Amnesty International undertook in its early years on behalf of individuals around the world subject to political abuse.

The man in the picture is in many ways quite different from the people who meet today in the room where his picture hangs. He was a modestly compensated volunteer; today, Amnesty International hires mostly professionals who are trained in their work and compensated reasonably well for their labor.[2] The volunteer relied on the daily newspaper for awareness of and publicity for human rights abuses; today's professionals maintain broad contacts around the world that make them aware of issues that could never have been clipped from the pages of a daily newspaper, and they have at their disposal digital tools that make mainstream media coverage just one of many targets for their publicity efforts. Moreover, many of these professionals work in the field rather than in London in the belief that being closer to events will enable the organization to respond more quickly and effectively to human rights violations. Finally, the volunteer in the picture worked at a time when Amnesty International was one of just a handful of internationally recognized NGOs; today, the organization numbers as one among many groups that work on human rights issues.

The case of Amnesty International is indicative of the broader transformation of communication work at large humanitarian and human rights NGOs. Whereas many organizations began as volunteer groups dependent on the news media for both awareness of and publicity for humanitarian and human rights issues, today they are highly professionalized and conduct a range of informational activities. Oxfam—originally the Oxford Committee for Famine Relief—was started in 1942 by a group of Oxford Quakers and academics with the aim of persuading the British government to permit food supplies into Axis-occupied Greece (Black 1992). Today, it produces research on topics related to poverty and human development around the world, and it sends communication staffers— "firefighter reporters" in the organization's current parlance—into the field to provide news and information from the scene of various humanitarian crises (Cooper 2011). CARE—originally the Cooperative for American Remittances in Europe—was set up as a way to enable American citizens to send food parcels to relatives and friends in Europe (W. Campbell 1990). Today, it employs researchers, advocates, and public-relations professionals, all of whom are tasked with producing and disseminating information across a range of platforms that seek to inform and persuade stakeholders, build the organization's brand, and raise the funds necessary for the organization to function.

How did NGOs evolve from the volunteer-driven, media-dependent work of their early days to the highly professionalized, multilayered efforts that characterize their aims today? One leading historian has written that the history of NGOs is "barely assayed" (Moyn 2010, 316), and this is true as well of their communication efforts: very little available scholarship examines the historical development of the amount and types of information that advocacy groups produce. This historical absence sometimes leads contemporary observers to view NGOs' communication efforts as the result of changes in journalism and technology. On this view, diminished newsroom resources and low-cost digital technologies have created openings in the public sphere for a range of third-party sources: as a result, NGOs, eager to exploit the new opportunities, can dedicate more resources to their publicity efforts (Bristol and Donnelly 2010; Sambrook 2010; Zuckerman 2013). This view leads to evaluations that are alternatively favorable or unfavorable of NGO communication efforts. Some see advocacy groups as providing the news that journalists would provide if they had the time and resources to do so (Gillmor 2014; Schudson 2011; Zuckerman 2013). Others worry that such efforts threaten to turn the news media into a platform for advocacy or to dilute NGOs' advocacy aims (Cottle and Nolan 2007; Fenton 2010).

These boon-and-bane views are not wrong, but they can be misleading. NGOs developed and diversified their communication efforts well before either the dawn of the Internet or the decline in foreign correspondence, and the effects of this diversification are neither wholly salutary nor deleterious. From their incipience, NGOs have sought to gain credibility as actors in international politics. Dedicating time and money to the production of credible research was viewed as a way to garner legitimacy vis-à-vis political elites. Moreover, as the overall NGO sector has expanded, these groups have also recognized the importance of publicity for raising funds and branding. These developments help to fuel a growth in both the amount and types of information work such groups utilize. Crucially, changes in journalism and technology intensify preexisting tensions between these different types of information work; they do not introduce them wholesale.

This chapter tells the story of how NGOs developed these styles of communication work. A synthetic historical account—based on organizational histories and interviews with longtime professionals—describes how and why leading humanitarian and human rights groups developed the diverse communication functions—research, advocacy, branding, fund-raising—that they have today.[3] Although such an account simplifies complex realities at individual organizations, it makes visible the basic factors driving the development and diversification of NGO communication efforts over time. Specifically, I argue that advocacy groups' contemporary communication efforts are best understood as the result of three developments: first, the professionalization of advocacy, which has led to an emphasis on credible reporting as a way for NGOs to pursue their advocacy goals; second, growing competition among advocacy groups, which intensifies the use of communication to secure donations and promote organizational brands; and third, changes in journalism and technology, which make advocacy groups more aware of the news media's norms and preferences even as new technologies allow groups to experiment with new digital formats. Together, these shifts created the conditions in which NGOs have come to be viewed as "boots on the ground" who blur the lines separating journalism, advocacy, and public relations.

This account suggests a mixed picture of the factors shaping contemporary NGO information work. In contrast to rosy evaluations of NGO efforts, it shows that competitive pressures can and sometimes do lead advocacy groups to produce information that is either inaccurate or driven primarily by the need for organizational branding. Although this concern is not novel, it has intensified in recent years due to the intensification of competitive pressures within the advocacy sector. At the same time, I also argue that NGO efforts to produce credible reports cannot be seen merely as advocacy or public relations, as critics sometimes suggest: NGO professionals view the production of credible information as the backbone of their legitimacy and as something to be defended carefully. This production does overlap with, even if it is not reducible to, some of the core aims of journalism in its focus on accuracy, pluralism, and timeliness. Moreover, it suggests a mixed picture that results not simply because of recent changes in journalism and technology. Rather, it shows that these tensions are part of the very processes of professionalization and competition that make contemporary debates about the role of NGOs possible. Whether these efforts are successful and how they might affect journalism and advocacy are questions I explore in subsequent chapters. How this situation came to be is the question that drives this chapter.

DEVELOPING BOOTS ON THE GROUND:
THE DRIVE TO PROFESSIONALIZE

The founding dates of the world's largest humanitarian and human rights groups vary—Save the Children was formed in 1919, Human Rights Watch in 1978—but each in its earliest days confronted a similar dilemma. Although their causes often generated a degree of public support, their specific claims found limited credibility among political elites. Therefore, to establish credibility, each organization had to develop policies for producing information that political elites could see as legitimate and trustworthy. They added credible research to their work not to remove advocacy from it but rather as a way to advocate more effectively. The degree to which they publicly shared this research varied, and the efforts to cultivate credibility vis-à-vis political elites were contentious, with competing factions in organizations debating the efficacy of such a development for achieving advocacy goals. Nonetheless, all organizations dedicated resources to the production of credible information about humanitarian and human rights issues—and they did so well in advance of either reductions in foreign correspondence in mainstream media or the advent of digital technologies.

The basic processes undertaken by NGOs roughly corresponds to what scholars refer to as "professionalization."[4] In using this term, scholars highlight a shift in authority toward expertise and away from other forms of authority, be they coercive or moral in nature. For humanitarian and human rights groups, professionalization took the form of relying increasingly on paid staff rather than on volunteers to conduct research, advocacy, and fund-raising work. As I discuss later in this chapter, these staff possessed educational backgrounds in law, politics, and sometimes journalism, and these backgrounds enabled them to produce information about humanitarian and human rights issues in formats that interested parties (e.g., national governments and international organizations such as the United Nations) could deem credible.[5]

Prior to their professionalization, most of the large NGOs studied here began as single-issue efforts. Save the Children and Oxfam, for example, started in war situations as part of an effort to protest British wartime policies that resulted in the starvation of civilians in Europe (Black 1992; Mulley 2009; Rootes and Saunders 2007). CARE was founded with the limited goal of enabling American citizens to send food parcels to relatives and friends in wartime Europe (W. Campbell 1990).[6] Amnesty International was initially designed to run as a year-long publicity campaign on behalf of specific "prisoners of conscience" around the world (Buchanan 2002). Médecins Sans Frontières started as a protest against the Red Cross by several French doctors volunteering for the latter organization in Biafra (Bortolotti 2004). Even Human Rights Watch, whose founding was more closely linked to political elites, had the limited aim of monitoring enforcement of the Helsinki Accords (Dezalay and Garth 2002).

Perhaps unsurprisingly given these origins, most groups relied heavily on volunteers in their earliest days. Oxfam produced newsletters that could be distributed to local churches in Oxford and the surrounding areas. These newsletters contained limited information about the effects of the British blockade on Greek civilians in World War II and provided church-goers with suggestions on what they could do to help (Black 1992). The group also relied on sympathetic allies to help promote its cause. A shopkeeper on a main Oxford street, for example, agreed to donate his window space, which the group used to display images of starving Greek civilians. This approach was in many ways typical of the volunteer-driven nature of most of these groups. At Amnesty International, for example, one early staff member remarked that in the organization's earliest days "a lot of the researchers were people that . . . had sort of walked in the office and said, 'Is there something I can do?'" (quoted in Dezalay and Garth 2002, 261).

Although NGOs enjoyed a degree of public support, they mostly lacked credibility among political elites. Oxfam was supported by church groups, but because its members were critics of the British government's wartime policy, they were derided by politicians as "fanatics, soft-heads, and sentimental idealists" (quoted in Black 1992, 9). Similarly, when Amnesty International was founded, governments around the world treated it with skepticism and suspicion. Diplomatic reports circulating in the United States suggested that the group was "a communist front organization" (Dezalay and Garth 2002, 70). Conversely, Communist countries widely believed Amnesty International to be a "front organization for western political interests" (Buchanan 2002, 588). Even those not suspicious of the group's motives thought the idea of using public opinion to address human rights violations was hopelessly idealistic. One critic went so far as to call Amnesty International "one of the larger lunacies of our time" (quoted in Power 2001, xi).

NGOs developed strategies to address these criticisms, and the production of credible information was a central component of these strategies (Heins 2008). Oxfam's early founders set for themselves a basic goal that they wrote down at their first meeting: "To obtain authentic information as to the food conditions in German-controlled or invaded countries; to promote schemes for the sending of food, vitamins, and medical aid into such countries" (quoted in Black 1992, 9–10). In order to do accomplish this goal, the group sought to "cull from all sources of information of unimpeachable veracity and circulate it as dispassionately as possible" (quoted in Black 1992, 10). In reality, this meant that it—like Amnesty International and its scissor-wielding volunteer discussed at the start of the chapter—relied on press clippings from newspapers. This approach was typical for most NGOs, where efforts to develop credibility in claims making preceded the hiring of professional staff capable of conducting research on humanitarian and human rights issues. It led groups such as Oxfam early on to conduct surveys of need in local populations as well as to develop new expert vocabularies.[7] In the 1950s, Oxfam helped bring into being the term *displaced persons*, which would become the dominant way for the international community to conceptualize the effects of war on humans (Shephard 2008, 408). This approach also necessitated the hiring of staff with technical expertise to deal with issues, not simply to provide remedial relief.

Amnesty International also developed methods for selecting cases and reporting human rights violations in direct response to political elites' suspicions. The organization's early leaders, for example, developed the notion of the "Threes Group," which required the adoption of any political prisoner from one faction in the Cold War (West, East, nonaligned) to be balanced by the adoption of a prisoner in each of the other two factions (Clark 2001). They also wouldn't allow volunteers to work with fellow compatriots; instead, volunteers had to engage with victims of human rights violations in other countries. As Ann Marie Clark notes in her history of Amnesty International, such rules were meant to protect volunteers from potential government repercussions "while enhancing their capacity to be impartial" (2001, 13).[8] In their reporting of potential human rights violations, volunteers and staffers strenuously sought to produce a credible empirical account of what happened. Indeed, one longtime staffer recalled that the organization developed a "quasi-obsessional identification with neutrality" in its quest for legitimacy (quoted in Scoble and Wiseberg 1974, 25–26).[9]

Human Rights Watch developed a similar strategy, even as the organization developed under different circumstances. Whereas Amnesty International began as a popular movement that needed to earn legitimacy vis-à-vis political elites, Human Rights Watch came into being as a result of intraelite US foreign-policy debates. In the 1970s, American political elites debated how best to manage America's role in a world riven by oil crises, inflation, the dollar crisis, and claims to sovereignty throughout the Global South (Guilhot 2005). The American Right's favored solution was a turn to the language of the free market. Milton Friedman and his "Chicago Boys"—the all-male group of young conservative economists educated at the University of Chicago—are the most prominent example of this constituency. In much of Latin America, Friedman and his acolytes established contact with local conservatives and stressed the need for free-market economic policies. This strategy garnered its first victory when Augusto Pinochet came to power in Chile, displacing the socialist regime of Salvador Allende and installing a pro-US, free-market leader (Dezalay and Garth 2002).

At the same time, the liberal wing of the American foreign-policy establishment saw in human rights a tool that could be used to publicly argue that right-wing governments needed to be held to the same human rights standards as Communist regimes (Neier 2003). For liberals, human rights formed the discursive terrain upon which they could do combat with the likes of Friedman. Arthur Goldberg, then an ambassador at large under the administration of Jimmy Carter, prevailed upon Ford Foundation president McGeorge Bundy to create Human Rights Watch. Ford's initial grant was $500,000, given to Robert Bernstein, then president of Random House publishing, to "establish liaison" with groups that could be formed following the Helsinki Accords. These groups were the various "watch" groups that would ultimately coalesce into Human Rights Watch.[10]

As for other organizations, for Human Rights Watch fact finding proved crucial to waging this battle. In the organization's earliest years,

Aryeh Neier—its first executive director—conducted public campaigns against the Reagan administration. In particular, he engaged in debates with Assistant Secretary of State for Human Rights and Humanitarian Affairs Eliot Abrams over US foreign policy in Central America (Jacoby 1986). Seizing upon the administration's nominal commitment to human rights, Neier used highly detailed, on-the-ground reporting to demonstrate human rights violations in countries receiving American support. The two debated both on television (Ted Koppel's *Nightline*) and in print (*New York Times* and *New Republic*). "As combatants go," the journalist Morton Kondracke wrote at the time, "you could not ask for a better match . . . than Abrams and Neier" (1988, 9). Years later Neier would remark on the importance of fact finding in these publicity duels: "Abrams and his colleagues made a quarrel over the facts. The style of Human Rights Watch evolved directly out of this. We started producing thick, amply documented reports. . . . Our emphasis was on providing the evidentiary bases for the claims we were making" (quoted in Rieff 1999).

As this Human Rights Watch example implies, NGOs developed their information strategies in conjunction with broader changes in the world of politics. In the post–World War II era, political elites throughout western Europe and North America dedicated growing time, resources, and energy to humanitarian and human rights issues. The United Nations, for example, was founded in the immediate aftermath of the war. From the outset, it stressed themes of human development and caring for individuals beyond national borders (White 1951; Willets 2011). State funding for humanitarian causes in particular grew in part as a result of this development (Fearon 2008). The explosion of human rights discourses came later (in the 1970s), but the growing use of such discourses created spaces in which advocacy groups could communicate with political elites (Keys 2014). Thus, although the exact trajectories of humanitarianism and human rights efforts differ, credibility was a key resource for groups that sought to involve themselves in these debates.[11] Producing research, moreover, was viewed as a way of cultivating such credibility.

Growth in organizational resources dedicated to the production of credible information was in part the result of these developments. Exact figures are difficult to obtain for all groups; however, those that are available tell a story of dramatic growth in this area. In the early 1970s, Amnesty International employed 14 researchers, each of whom was tasked with investigating human rights violations in specific countries (Hopgood 2006, 85). By the early 1980s, that figure had more than doubled, and overall staff size at the organization's London headquarters totaled 150 (Dezalay and Garth 2002, 71). By the 1990s, the group had 73 dedicated research staff (Hopgood 2006). Today, the organization has about 130 researchers, and they are supported by about 500 additional staff members.[12] Similar growth can be seen at Human Rights Watch. Throughout the 1980s, the organization employed only about 10 paid researchers (Kondracke 1988). In 1987, it published fourteen reports in the entire year, which one writer at the time described as "prodigiously productive" (Kondracke 1988, 9). Today, the group has a staff of about 400 employees (the specific number of researchers is not available), and it produces fourteen reports in a month or two.

Professionalization is often described in positive terms (though see Lebon 1996 for a critical discussion). It is important to note, though, that this development not only enabled NGOs to bolster their credibility but also forced them to make trade-offs in their quest for such credibility. The early history of Amnesty International highlights such a trade-off. In the mid-1960s, many members of the group wanted to take up the cause of Nelson Mandela, who was at the time the imprisoned leader of the African National Congress. Yet doing so was heavily contested within the organization. In the drive for credibility, Amnesty's early leadership had created the rule that in order to qualify as a "prisoner of conscience," one had to renounce all forms of violence. Because Mandela had endorsed violence against apartheid as a "last resort," the Amnesty leadership refused to take up his case (Williams 2010, 1–23). This refusal led to heated debate within the organization, and some members ultimately left the group over the decision not to endorse Mandela.[13]

Beyond specific instances of ideological disagreement, professionalization can also create tensions with the volunteer spirit that gives NGOs their initial energy. For example, Amnesty International's status as a mass movement was predicated in large part on its broad membership, institutionally organized in distinctive national sections (e.g., the United Kingdom, the United States, Canada, etc.) that organized letter-writing campaigns on behalf of prisoners. The organization's professional legitimacy, however, stemmed from research reports produced by the London-based International Secretariat. The national sections often saw the International Secretariat as being too removed from campaigning and too elitist—a worrying concern for an organization that sought to connect with individual citizens (Clark 2001; Larsen 1978; Scoble and Wiseberg 1974). Members also pushed researchers to examine new topics, which in the organization's early years revolved primarily around violations of political and civil rights (Clark 2001, 103).

If professionalization is not always positive, it is also not inherently publicly oriented. Many groups developed research functions, but they discussed the findings of such research mostly with government officials behind closed doors. For instance, although Oxfam sought information about conditions in Greece to aid in its relief efforts, it had few incentives to make that knowledge public. Ameliorating the suffering of innocent civilians was relatively popular among the populace, but the more information the Oxfam committee gathered, the more data it had to suggest that the British blockade was in part responsible for that suffering. As Oxfam's own historian explains, "To suggest, however circumspectly, that Britain's war policy was causing starvation among women and children in friendly countries was, at best, unpatriotic" (Black 1992, 10). Better, the group reasoned, to petition British leaders behind closed doors that they change course and to leave publicity to the realm of branding and fund-raising.[14]

Despite variation across the different organizational cases, it is nonetheless true that all NGOs developed research functions. Changes in journalism and technology did not initiate these developments. Rather, they resulted primarily because of a desire by NGOs to cultivate credibility among political elites, who increasingly used or interacted with the language of humanitarianism and human rights in their foreign-policy efforts. The fact that advocacy groups today conduct research that observers can view as "almost journalism" (Gillmor 2014) is in part the result of this history.

THE IMPERATIVES OF FUND-RAISING AND BRANDING

Although research brought credibility to NGOs, the provision of impartial information was never the sole aim of their communication efforts.

Since their beginnings, advocacy groups have utilized communication strategies to raise funds and to promote their organizational brands. Indeed, as the field of NGOs has grown denser over time, the imperatives of fund-raising and branding have only intensified. To differentiate themselves from other NGOs, organizations have dedicated time and money to public-relations and marketing departments. These departments are tasked with fulfilling short-term strategies related to generating donations and media impressions, and this task recurrently creates tensions with research and advocacy staff about its impact. Thus, in addition to credible information, all organizations use communication to achieve a range of organizational objectives. Like research, these efforts also precede changes in journalism and technology and stem primarily from developments within the NGO sector and the fields that immediately surround it (politics, philanthropy).

From their earliest days, NGOs have used communication to raise funds and promote their organizational brands. One of Save the Children's initial staff hires was Lewis Golden, a public-relations pioneer who lobbied the group to use pictures of emaciated children for fund-raising purposes (Mulley 2009, 263–265). Oxfam held lunchtime concerts, staged variety shows, and ran a gift shop to raise funds for its mission to Greece (Black 1992, 16). Beyond that, "it was newspaper advertising, using increasingly striking images as the 1950s progressed, which did most to familiarize the British public with [Oxfam's] name" (Black 1992, 36). CARE created promotional tie-ins with the wedding of Princess Elizabeth, setting up booths at Sears storefronts, advertising on a weekly radio show for ABC, and even getting the United Fruit Company to sponsor a contest to find the best new banana recipe in which the company would donate twenty-five cents per entry to CARE (Campbell 1990, 53). One of CARE's founding members would later remark on the organization's early fund-raising efforts, "If there was any publicity stone left unturned, I can't think what it could have been" (quoted in Campbell 1990, 113). More generally, marketing and fund-raising were the activities that were usually first to be taken away from volunteers and given to professionals because publicity departments tended to be some of the first hires (Barnett 2011, 42).

Many of these publicity efforts were controversial from the outset. Save the Children distributed "Starving Baby" leaflets, which implored citizens to give pennies in order to help save the lives of dying children (Barnett 2011, 42). More generally, the very choice of children as the organization's object of care was itself motivated not by any love for children on the part of its founder, Eglantyne Jebb, who, upon giving up an earlier career in teaching, had stated, "I don't care for children, I don't care for teaching" (quoted in Mulley 2009, 63). The decision was instead a calculated way to get donations from people otherwise reluctant to give money to "the other side" in the war.[15] Similarly, Oxfam pioneered publicity-driven clothing campaigns, whose effect in addressing humanitarian issues was questionable. These campaigns did much more for Oxfam's recognition in Britain than they did for the clothing's intended recipients in the Global South. One historian wryly notes that "the types of clothes that the wool-wearing British tended to donate hardly match[ed] the needs of, say, the famine stricken Indians in Bihar" (Barnett 2011, 43). Despite the lack of a donor match, clothing could be registered under British law as monetary equivalents, lowering Oxfam's overhead expenses to around 10 percent of its operating budget (Black 1992). In short, celebrity endorsements, advertising campaigns, and branding considerations have been with advocacy groups since their beginnings.

At the same time, as the NGO sector has grown, the drive to use communication to raise funds and boost brand awareness has intensified. In 1960, the *International Yearbook of Organizations*—a primary source for data on the nongovernmental sector—reported that 1,000 NGOs existed. By the turn of the twenty-first century, that number had risen to more than 5,500 (Cooley and Ron 2002, 10). In 2015, the *Yearbook* reported more than 12,000 NGOs. This growth is especially sharp in the areas of humanitarianism and human rights. In 1953, there were 33 human rights NGOs. That number rose steadily through the 1970s and exploded thereafter: in 1963, there were 38 such groups in existence; in 1973, there were 41; by 1983, the figure had doubled to 79 and doubled again in the next decade, reaching 168 by 1993. The most recent figure suggests there are at least 257 NGOs working on human rights issues (Thrall, Stecula, and Sweet 2014). The growth figures are similar for humanitarian groups: 3 in 1953 and 1963; 7 in 1973; 13 in 1983; 14 in 1993; and 75 by 2015 (Keck and Sikkink 1998, 11).[16] These figures almost undoubtedly undercount the total number of such groups because many organizations do not bother to register with the United Nations and are thus not captured in the available data.

This growth is driven by a range of phenomena, but chief among them are the opportunities generated by nation-states. Since the 1970s in both the United States and Europe, governments have devolved state functions to nonstate actors. In the realm of international relations, humanitarian and human rights work has been a key arena in which this devolution has occurred. Rather than directly conduct humanitarian or human rights work, nation-states fund NGOs to do it.[17] This change has been overlaid by the growing prominence of foundations, who fund the vast majority of the work by humanitarian and human rights groups. As Kim Reimann argues, the growth of NGOs is in part a response to the incentives provided by states and foundations: "It is impossible to understand the explosive growth of NGOs in the past several decades without taking into account the ways in which states, international organizations and other structures have actively stimulated and promoted NGOs from above" (2006, 46).

Public relations and marketing are used in this context as a way for organizations to differentiate themselves in a crowded advocacy sector. Concrete data on growth over time is difficult to ascertain. NGOs are not required to disclose employment figures by department, and they gain little by emphasizing the extent to which they staff public-relations and marketing efforts in contrast to research functions. Moreover, as Michael Barnett notes, "until a few years ago, the perpetual struggle of NGOs to keep their operations running was barely mentioned, conveying the impression that staff were so consumed by saintly principles that they gave little thought to earthly matters like budgets" (2011, 41–42). Nonetheless, there exists widespread agreement among observers that the use of communication to boost fund-raising and brand awareness has intensified over time (see, e.g., Cottle and Nolan 2007; Fenton 2010; Waisbord 2011; Wright 2016a).[18]

In fact, in Oxfam's case it seems public relations and marketing helped drive overall growth. With a small core of initial employees drawn from the fields of public relations and marketing, the group developed hard-hitting and often controversial advertising campaigns. It placed pictures of starving children in newspapers and hinted that failure on the part of the newspaper reader to give made the reader complicit in the children's suffering. This approach was controversial, "but any negative impact was more than outweighed in financial terms" (Black 1992, 80). In the 1950s, Oxfam reported raising five pounds for every one pound spent on advertising. In the 1960s, the ratio rose to thirty-one pounds to one pound spent on advertising. This boost was created by "bumping up the advertising budget at key psychological moments, particularly at disaster times" (Black 1992, 80). Without breaking down specific figures, the organization's own historian notes that "the rise in income enabled—indeed, forced—Oxfam to take on more staff" (Black 1992, 80).

The case of Oxfam points to one prominent strategy that NGOs developed to bring in funds and raise brand awareness: exploit emergency situations for funding purposes. One of Médecins Sans Frontières' founders, Bernard Kouchner, famously called this strategy "la loi du tapage" (the law of hype). This law states that organizations must not simply advertise the existence of a humanitarian crisis but also embellish the crisis in order to generate the maximum amount of donations (Barnett 2011, 43). Advocacy groups realized that in the early aftermath of an earthquake or a tsunami or at the height of a famine or drought, captivating visual material could bring in funds that they might otherwise struggle to obtain. This lesson was learned early and remains in effect to this day. Early in my own fieldwork, for example, one press officer explained that in emergency situations her organization makes sure to bring "visibility items"—T-shirts, hats, and stickers, all affixed with the organization's logo—with it to disaster areas in an effort to draw public attention and, it hopes, funding to its work.[19] Someone else at a different organization—Save the Children—echoed this sentiment: "A lot of the fund-raising we do during big emergencies [earthquakes, tsunamis, etc.] comes from the media profile we get at those moments. So it's absolutely critical that we build that profile in those first few weeks, or first few days even. That's why we basically just push everything else aside. . . . Fund-raising in those moments keeps our programs funded for the next few years."[20]

Beyond using emergencies to raise funds, NGOs also cultivated relationships with celebrities in an effort to boost their brand visibility. In the 1970s, groups began to experiment with organizing concerts that could be broadcast to viewers worldwide: first, George Harrison's Concert for Bangladesh (1972) and later Bob Geldof's Band Aid (1984). NGOs clamored to take advantage of such publicity events even as they came under fire for the messaging techniques used to raise funds. Band Aid, for example, was designed to address the Ethiopian famine, but its publicity referred to the entire continent of Africa. It also drew attention less to the causes shaping the famine and more to the kindness of potential donors.

How NGOs have deployed celebrities has changed over time. For example, Lilie Chouliaraki (2013) has explored the different strategies used by organizations utilizing Audrey Hepburn in the 1980s and Angelina Jolie in the 2010s: whereas Hepburn was integrated into appeals by emphasizing her commonness with others and a sense of service to distant strangers, Jolie is deployed primarily in her capacity as a global megastar. My emphasis here is somewhat more basic: simply put, celebrities have been and continue to be important for NGOs as a strategy for raising funds and cultivating brand awareness.

Perhaps the most basic aim of NGO communication is simply getting the organization's name out. "Our fund-raisers do better when we're in the media," one person explained to me. "So there is an objective in just keeping Amnesty out there."[21] Another echoed the theme: "We will sometimes speak out or communicate purely to serve our objectives: to expand operations, to open up programs. . . . Fund-raising is an objective. Communications and media coverage has [sic] a direct correlation with fund-raising support that we receive."[22]

The growth of marketing and public-relations departments within NGOs has not occurred without controversy. In his history of Amnesty International, Stephen Hopgood (2006) documents recurrent tensions within the organization about the extent to which it ought to embrace marketing and public-relations techniques. In the 1990s and 2000s, the group found itself embroiled in contentious debates about how best to promote its aims in a crowded advocacy sector. Researchers argued that their work was central to the group's core mission, and they worried that public-relations and marketing techniques would cheapen the image that the organization had cultivated. By contrast, public-relations and marketing professionals argued that the organization had become too focused on research and that it was limiting Amnesty's capacity to promote itself. As one person told Hopgood, "We are a textbook case of a lopsided organization, high on production and low on marketing. . . . The time has come for management to bring marketing in line with production so that the high quality of our product is not spoilt in stock-piling" (2006, 82).

To varying degrees, these tensions can be seen across all humanitarian and human rights organizations. Researchers sometimes see the rise of marketing and public relations as a threat to their work. Because the production of credible research takes time and money, they worry that resources spent elsewhere might reduce the resources available to them. Marketing and public-relations professionals in turn sometimes see researchers as detached from the work that is required to procure those resources. *Pointy heads* is the term that one public-relations officer used for researchers, infusing the expression with enough jest and honesty to convey both the envy and frustrations felt toward them.[23]

In organizations where the research staff holds greater sway, public-relations professionals spend much of their day waiting for researchers to give them information on which to base their work. "The day is basically structured around getting your story approved through all the different elements of the institution," explained one person. "Usually, we decide we are going to do a story, and we sit there until a researcher gives us information to base the story on." This person explained further how difficult it was to get research staff to care about reaching the general public.

> I was asking one researcher to make a call to a family of a person who had been unfairly imprisoned for a long time on spurious charges, and I asked her to help nail down the facts, which is obviously of primary importance. But they find the idea difficult to grasp sometimes of color or quotes or something that will catch the eye of the reader. And we say, "Can you ask them how they felt about it?" And they will respond: "Why should I ask them how they felt about it? Isn't it obvious how they felt? They felt bad!" And we'll say: "Can you get them to say it in their own words?" And sometimes I think they think that it is so trivial that it's not worth doing. But even if it seems trivial or cosmetic, if you can't sell the story to a shallow-minded reader who wants to identify with the person, then that information won't be read necessarily by the general public.[24]

These tensions exist because of the growth of public relations and marketing. All organizations use communication to achieve strategic objectives and not just to produce credible research. These functions, too, developed well prior to declines in foreign correspondence or the advent of the Internet. Together, the growth of research and the expansion of public relations and marketing are the major developments in NGOs' communication efforts. Although this growth preceded changes in journalism and technology, those changes have intensified the preexisting tensions.

NGOS IN A CHANGING MEDIA LANDSCAPE

Although publicity was always important to NGOs, knowing how to achieve it was part of a long-term learning process. Advocacy groups had to establish credibility not only with political elites but also with journalists. Moreover, they needed to learn about the types of stories that did and did not fit into the news media's agenda. To achieve these aims, NGOs built communication departments with staffers, some of whom possessed prior experience in journalism or public relations. As information technology made the cost of producing information less expensive, NGOs increasingly put resources into subsidizing some of the more expensive components of news production (notably, audio-visuals). Most recently, staffing reductions at news organizations have led NGOs to further increase the amount of information they produce because they see a strategic opportunity to shape the flow of international news on humanitarian and human rights topics. The sum result is that advocacy groups now produce more (and more types of) information than ever before.

Just as NGOs initially had little credibility with political elites, they also enjoyed limited credibility with journalists. Convincing reporters and editors that their information was credible required sustained and direct contact. Amnesty International, for example, initially enjoyed favorable relations with journalists sympathetic to their cause. Over time, though, they had to expand beyond this small group of contacts. One person involved in Amnesty International's early years recalled actively soliciting meetings with newspaper editorial boards: "What you had to do was convince people that you were credible; that you . . . were not pushing an agenda and that was hard to do" (quoted in Dezalay and Garth 2002, 260). Amnesty accomplished this task by being "very modest" and "very cautious" and eschewing "sensational stories." Although this approach sometimes made it difficult to get the organization in the press, it did "slowly build up a reputation and once you got that reputation then . . . news editors would say, 'Oh yeah, it's Amnesty, we can use it. We trust them'" (quoted in Dezalay and Garth 2002, 260).[25]

Credibility was established in other ways, too. The initial grant used to start Human Rights Watch, as noted earlier, was given by the Ford Foundation to Random House publishing president Robert Bernstein. The foundation sought out Bernstein because of his contacts with key figures in the elite echelons of the journalistic and literary worlds: E. L. Doctorow, Toni Morrison, and Robert Penn Warren were involved with Human Rights Watch from the outset (Neier 2003). These figures helped from the outset to ground Human Rights Watch in the upper echelons of the media world, and in that position the group aimed to establish its efforts as worthy of journalistic attention (Dezalay and Garth 2002).

Across all organizations, NGOs built communication departments whose staff increasingly comprised former journalists and trained public-relations professionals. These individuals worked not only to ensure that their work was credible but also to make that work accord with journalists' definition of news worthiness. In doing so, they managed to integrate news considerations into their organizational practices. This integration can be seen in the various descriptions given by long-serving communication professionals regarding the extent to which they had to bring their organizations up to speed on best practices for garnering media attention. "When I came in [to Save the Children]," one person who worked previously at the BBC explained to me, "a lot of press officers were issuing press releases at five o'clock in the evening"—that is, well after most news deadlines.[26] At Médecins Sans Frontières, one person discussed his role as making his colleagues better understand their relative chances of garnering media attention. "When they [the members of the organization's research wing] want to push something, they say, 'OK, this week we want to push this report on Uzbekistan.' And sometimes we have to tell them this is not realistic. There is a royal wedding or . . . [a political scandal] or whatever. Some weeks this sort of thing just isn't going to fly."[27] The integration of news considerations can be seen further in the types of cases that publicity professionals think are even worth bringing to the attention of journalists: "You can work all you like on Mauritania, but the press couldn't give a rat's ass" (quoted in Ramos, Ron, and Thoms 2007, 401).

Early efforts to attract publicity highlight the extent to which publicity considerations have shaped advocacy groups from the outset. Amnesty's largest research operation in the 1960s—investigating political torture in Greece after the military junta—is telling in this regard (Clark 2001; Nafplpioti 2005). The news media were already covering this story, and this visibility was in part responsible for Amnesty International's decision to send a lawyer to investigate alleged human rights violations. The group packaged its findings in ways that could be deemed not only credible (e.g., detailed firsthand testimonies) but also attractive to journalists. It talked about the use of torture as antithetical to a country known around the world as the "cradle of democracy" (Nafplpioti 2005). It also helped to circulate stories about how the junta altered everyday life. One report, for example, discussed forced Sunday school attendance. As a result, Amnesty International produced findings that were seen as "rigorous" while also being attractive to editors in newsrooms (Clark 2001).

Perhaps the most famous case of NGOs using news logics to attract media attention involves Oxfam. The organization played a key part in making the Ethiopian famine one of the major news stories of 1984. News of the famine had been on a sort of slow drip from western European and North American news outlets since the fall of 1983 (de Waal 1998, 122). One account, for example, recalls that the famine originally went "largely unnoticed by the Western news sources" (Barnett 2011, 156). NGOs sought to raise awareness of the famine throughout this early period. The Irish NGO Concern, for example, bankrolled the production of a documentary film about the famine. Save the Children issued a near constant stream of press releases, warning about the impending effects of the worsening conditions (Harrison and Palmer 1986, 93–99). None of these attempts, though, generated much international news coverage. Worse, the attempts largely served to anger the Ethiopian government, which viewed the attention as evidence of a Western conspiracy against a Soviet ally. As a consequence, the government restricted access to the country by refusing to issue visas to journalists (Harrison and Palmer 1986, 97).

In September 1984, Oxfam changed tack and in the process helped make the famine the major news story it would become (Black 1992, 257–265). Rather than target the Ethiopian government for being at fault, the group focused on the European Economic Community (ECC), which held vast reserves of grain stocks. If the ECC sent some of those stocks—which were otherwise unused—to Ethiopia, they could be used to help mitigate the effects of the worsening famine. To shame the ECC into action, Oxfam bought ten thousand tons of grain on the market and shipped them to Ethiopia. The group accompanied the action with a sharply worded press release entitled "Ethiopian Famine: Will Oxfam's Largest Ever Grant Shame Western Governments Into Immediate Action?" (Harrison and Palmer 1986, 112–113). One journalist recalled thinking the press release "an extraordinarily effective way of presenting the story." His editors, long reluctant to permit him to go to Ethiopia, finally gave him the go-ahead (Gill 1986, 93).

The story was provocative, implicating Western governments in the starvation of Ethiopian citizens. It also took some of the pressure off the Ethiopian government, which eased visa restrictions for journalists in part because it was also celebrating its tenth anniversary in power (de Waal 1998, 121–122). Further, when seasonal rains failed to materialize, the famine worsened, and thousands of citizens left their homes for feeding centers. Interested journalists swarmed to Ethiopia, and the now-famous BBC video by Michael Buerk and Mohammed Amin (describing a famine of "biblical proportions") galvanized audiences in both western Europe and North America to act (Harrison and Palmer 1986). In his overview of the case, Barnett writes that news outlets previously uninterested in the issue "rushed to the refugee camps to chronicle what starvation did to the body and soul. Caught in the media's web, as well, were the images of heroic aid workers persevering against the odds, representing the conscience of the West" (2011, 156). Oxfam pounced on the opportunity, helping to arrange visas for interested reporters and carting them to camps around the country when they arrived. The organization's role was key, as one involved journalist would later recall: "When Ethiopia's famine hit the headlines, it did so because of the relationship between private relief agencies [NGOs] and the television companies. Michael Buerk's visit in July was accomplished through Oxfam. In news coverage in October and beyond, the relief agencies provided most of the reference points—up-to-date information, places to visit, interviewees in the field and at home, and a means of response for concerned viewers" (Gill 1986, 93). The famine would go on to be remembered by Western audiences largely for the celebrity activism that it helped generate. The singer Bob Geldof would report being so moved by the BBC coverage that he went on to organize Live Aid, a star-studded charity concert. An estimated two billion people watched the concert, and it raised more than $150 million, which at the time was the largest amount of money ever raised in a humanitarian appeal (Richey and Ponte 2011, 32). For its part, Oxfam would take credit for helping the famine to become "the story and the cause" of 1984 (Barnett 2011, 156).[28]

Although the drive to produce information in accordance with journalistic logics is relatively old, the effort to produce information for journalists is relatively new. Beginning in the early 2000s and continuing to the present, advocacy groups have placed a growing emphasis on producing visual images that can accompany their press releases. Several organizations have audio-visual departments, and even those that do not have such a department pay freelance videographers and editors to produce visual materials. These videos are used for both fund-raising and awareness-raising purposes. Some argue that having visual materials is sometimes "the difference between getting a story on [television] or not" (Bristol and Donnelly 2011, 18). NGO staffers report an effort over time to ensure that the videos are produced in a way that appeals to journalists. As one person at Médecins Sans Frontières put it,

> We used to do b-roll with the MSF car, cut to the MSF house, cut to the MSF sign, MSF interview with the MSF person with the MSF logo on it. And obviously people wouldn't take that. So we've had to up our game and provide, roughly, what a news journalist or news cameraman would have shot. Obviously, MSF is still the main interview and we're trying to frame things from our point of view. But we also try to find what they would actually want to shoot.[29]

In addition to video, NGOs have begun to work with photojournalists to illustrate their research reports, publicize their findings, and promote their organizational brands. This work can take the form of contracting prominent photographers. For several years, Human Rights

Watch has regularly worked with leading photojournalists as well as free-lancers. As Kate Wright (2016b) has argued, these efforts are the product of a number of intersecting forces. Photojournalists are able to report on stories that news organizations typically are unable to fund, and advocacy groups gain access not only to high-quality images but also to the social networks that freelancers have. The result, she convincingly argues, is a blurring of the lines separating journalism from advocacy.

As news outlets reduce their commitments to international coverage, NGOs report seeing themselves as "responding a little bit to a resource gap probably in the news-gathering budget."[30] One trend among leading NGOs is to have what is called a "roving correspondent"—someone who goes from crisis to crisis working as the primary publicity person for the organization. This person is often a former journalist, and his or her utility is twofold. First, this person helps ensure that the organization receives publicity on the ground. The people who work these types of disasters tend to have contacts in the news media, and they work to convince journalists of possible story angles that will benefit their NGOs. One roving correspondent relayed a story she had written for her organization's website about an Iraqi woman who had donated goats to a relief project. An NBC television producer got in touch with her, saying, "I just love this piece, you know, dying to do it," and asked, "Can you take us there?" NBC did a piece on it. "It was like a commercial for [our organization]!" she exclaimed.[31] A second utility of roving correspondents is that they take publicity pressure off of other organizational personnel in the field, including researchers and aid workers. They provide a way for the organization to insulate staff from media demands while also drawing out the organization's "success" stories as they see fit.

NGOs experiment with a variety of other organizational and communication forms in addition to roving correspondents. All organizations have websites and social media accounts, and on them they post a variety of news and information related to their work (see chapter 4). Amnesty International has a dedicated team of "news writers" who are charged with making the organization's website the online portal for human rights news. Human Rights Watch hires photographers and increasingly produces multimedia content in its reports. In all of these approaches, advocacy groups produce more and more types of information than ever before. These types of information are increasingly meant to "look and read and feel and smell like journalism."[32] The need to diversify information formats was a key theme in my interviews with NGO professionals. One person conceptualized NGOs' work as being like "a seedpod: it has to sprout in all directions. You can't just be one thing. You can't just be one format."[33]

This growth of the seedpod results in various media products. In recent years, many organizations have begun producing irregular podcasts. For these podcasts, publicity professionals conduct interviews with researchers either in advance of an upcoming report or in response to breaking news events. The basic idea is to cut down on unnecessary duplication that occurs when researchers repeat their findings to journalists from different publications. This approach has the added bonus of saving researchers' time and letting them explain their findings in a friendly interview setting where the interviewer is sympathetic—and familiar—with their area of research. These podcasts receive small audiences, typically composed of journalists. "They can cut it [the interview] up and use it. You also have media outlets like CNN take the whole thing, or the *Washington Post*, take and run the whole thing, which is great."[34]

One example shows how this works. When a stadium massacre occurred in Guinea in 2009, International Crisis Group had a researcher in the field who was "bombarded" with media requests.[35] The publicity team quickly decided that the only way to satisfy journalist demand while also enabling the researcher to continue doing his job was to interview him and make the interview available on the organization's website. The interview was more or less indistinguishable from a journalist-source interview: it discussed the background to the event, what happened, who was involved, and what developments might come in the event's wake. The publicity person tasked with doing this podcast remarked that much of her work "is producing your own quote/unquote news to push out into the news atmosphere."[36]

Changes in technology not only alter advocacy groups' publicity strategies but also influence the production of research. Information technologies are increasingly used to supplement the information-gathering process. Because it is impossible for researchers to be on the ground all the time, such technologies allow them to stay abreast of developments from afar. Researchers use online videos posted by local activists to estimate the extent and amount of violence in particular areas. Amnesty International culls eyewitness videos that they verify as truthful into stand-alone websites, such as the one called Eyes on Syria. Teleconferencing tools and satellite phones allow researchers to stay in touch with local activists on the ground. This capacity has given birth to a lively discussion among NGO professionals about how to exploit these technologies securely—that is, without giving up vital information about who their informants are and where they are reporting from (Faris 2012; McPherson 2015).

More advanced technologies, such as satellite imagery, make it possible not only for researchers to witness events at a distance but also for a different sort of witnessing to occur (Aday and Livingston 2009). Unlike eyewitness reports, these images provide literally a bird's-eye view of events on the ground—allowing researchers to detail the overall amount of destruction wrought upon a specific locale. In cases where access is difficult and reports are conflicting, such imagery is increasingly used as a monitoring device. Both Amnesty International and Human Rights Watch have made use of such imagery (obtained by commercial providers) in Syria—at times to demonstrate the severity of military destruction on civilian residences, at times to alert the international community of movements by the Syrian military, and at times to point out that opposition forces themselves are guilty of human rights violations (Amnesty International 2012; Herscher 2011, 128–129; Human Rights Watch 2012).

The availability of these novel technologies is both a boon to and a source of tension for researchers. The technologies help yield exponentially more data, but they also muddy the process of verification. Sometimes the existence of a video can be useful in proving or disproving violations—several NGO professionals told me that a reliable video lessens the burden to gather additional eyewitness accounts[37]—but the sheer number of videos produced means that a number of fraudulent claims are also circulated. Researchers struggle to differentiate between the two and acknowledge that the benefits of these new technologies come with additional responsibilities to verify that they struggle to meet.

In the fall of 2011, both Amnesty International and Human Rights Watch drew attention to the case of an eighteen-year-old Syrian woman who, they claimed, had been beheaded by the Syrian government. A video uploaded to YouTube by a local group of Syrian activists appeared to support the claim. Both Amnesty International and Human Rights Watch interviewed the young woman's surviving family—all of whom confirmed the identity of the woman in the video as that of their daughter. Several media outlets—CNN, the Associated Press, and others—in turn broadcast or published the story. Weeks later, however, the young woman appeared on television, identification card in hand, claiming that she had fled her home to escape abuse from her brothers. Both Amnesty International and Human Rights Watch issued retractions, calling the error, not unreasonably but also not altogether comfortably, "an honest mistake" (Mawad 2012).

NGOs produce a broader array of information materials than ever before, and the values that guide the production of such materials overlap with key journalistic norms such as accuracy and pluralism. The historical perspective provided in this chapter situates these changes within several longer-term processes. The professionalization of advocacy led NGOs to focus on credible reporting as a way to pursue their advocacy aims, while growth and competition in the advocacy sector intensified these groups' use of communication to secure donations and promote organizational brands. These longer-term processes intersect with changes in journalism and technology, which make advocacy groups more aware of the types of information that will interest journalists, even as new technologies allow NGOs to experiment with new digital formats. The result is that NGOs are increasingly seen as "boots on the ground" producing information that in many ways overlaps with—even though it is not equivalent to—the work of journalists.

This view complicates extant perspectives on NGO communication work. Rather than see the development of NGO communication efforts as a response to changes in journalism and technology, I situate these developments as part of a broader dynamic involving changes both within and beyond the advocacy sector. Moreover, rather than viewing NGO efforts as wholly good or bad for journalism, I suggest that they can be seen as a double-edged sword. On the one hand, the drive to professionalize boosts the extent to which such groups are able to provide reliable reporting from around the world, including places where the news media have few resources and in which they have limited interest. On the other hand, competitive tendencies and organizational demands also lead advocacy groups to see publicity as a way to boost their brands and raise funds. Although understandable, these efforts raise concerns about the extent to which the news media may become a platform for advocacy aims.

On the whole, the preceding narrative thus leads to two empirical questions. First, given the extent to which NGOs have ramped up their publicity efforts, to what extent does this effort make news organizations—which are dedicating fewer resources to international news coverage—more likely to include advocacy groups in the news? Second, given the wide range of digital tools available to advocacy organizations, how and in what ways do they use such tools to complement and expand their extant publicity efforts? It is to answering the first question that I now turn.

CHAPTER THREE

The Partially Opening News Gates

Research has long found that NGOs struggle to make the news (Jacobs and Glass 2002; Lang 2013; Sobieraj 2011; Thrall 2006; Trenz 2004). To what extent do changes in journalism, politics, and advocacy alter this established wisdom?[1] Extant scholarship offers contrasting answers to this question. To some, diminished newsroom resources make journalists increasingly likely to accept third-party materials, so that leading NGOs, which have ramped up their publicity efforts, are seemingly well positioned to garner news coverage (Cooper 2011; Fenton 2010). Others, however, argue that current shifts do not alter key barriers of access to the news media. Specifically, the news media's bias toward government officials minimizes both the amount and types of coverage advocacy groups receive; accordingly, NGOs receive news coverage only when speaking on topics legitimated by government officials (Lang 2013).

This chapter, a longitudinal examination of the amount and types of news access NGOs garner in the news media, puts these perspectives to the test.[2] It presents the results of analysis of human rights coverage in a strategic twenty-year sample of leading US news outlets. For each outlet, it identifies four dimensions—prevalence, prominence, geographic location, and story frame—along which news access can be measured so that it not only documents whether news access has changed but also adjudicates competing claims about NGOs' discursive effects on mediated human rights discourses. These claims revolve around the extent to which advocacy groups draw the media spotlight to new issues and countries as well as the extent to which these groups displace other sources—government officials according to some or less-well-resourced activists according to others—from news coverage.

On the whole, the findings reveal what I term a *partial opening* of the news gates for humanitarian and human rights groups. On the one hand, NGOs are more likely to appear in the news today than they were in the past, and they are increasingly able to insert human rights frames into news articles that are already circulating in the news media (and that initially contain no human rights dimension). On the other hand, how these groups appear in the news continues to follow well-established theories of news access: leading advocacy groups tend to be referred to late in news stories and after other news sources, especially government officials, are cited. Moreover, efforts to drive news coverage to new issues or topics are seldom successful. Finally, despite efforts by humanitarian and human rights groups to expand their advocacy efforts to include economic, cultural, and social rights, news coverage continues to privilege political and civic violations. Taken together, the data suggest that although NGOs enjoy greater news access today than they did in the past, the power to shape—or challenge—the rules of news access continues to exceed their grasp.

RECONSIDERING NEWS ACCESS

Scholars have long stressed that news access is shaped by a combination of professional and economic factors (Gandy 1982; Hall et al. 1978). Professionally, journalists see themselves as keepers of a public record that details the actions of public officials. Economically, news organizations often lack the time and resources to produce news without the help of sources. Together, these factors lead reporters to favor government officials, who provide the "information subsidies" (Gandy 1982) necessary to fulfill both professional and economic considerations. Although the resulting news coverage is not homogeneous, scholarship suggests that it is typically "indexed" to journalistic perceptions of the concentration and balance of power in government circles (Bennett 1990) and, more broadly, that it is "coproduced" by news media and government officials (T. Cook 1998).

For NGOs, this official bias has long made for an uphill battle in their struggle for visibility in the media. Studies have repeatedly found that such groups are only rarely included in news coverage (Lang 2013; Thrall 2006; Trenz 2004). To improve their chances at garnering publicity, NGOs adapt their messages to acceptable journalistic formats and newsworthy topics (Cottle and Nolan 2007; Fenton 2010; Waisbord 2011). Yet even when they adapt to news media demands, achieving news coverage remains difficult for them. Sabine Lang, for example, notes that NGOs are likely to receive coverage "only if there is valorized input from government representatives" (2013, 127). Because NGOs infrequently align with media demands and government opinions, they have historically struggled to receive news coverage.

As detailed in chapter 1, today the constituent elements of a perfect storm appear to be taking shape, which some suggest will result in increased news access for NGOs. Three elements are especially relevant in this chapter. First, changing economic conditions at news outlets—specifically, diminished revenues coupled with intensified profitability expectations at US news organizations (McChesney and Nichols 2010)—have reduced the resources most news organizations commit to international news gathering. Since the end of the Cold War, US news outlets have cut back on the number of foreign-news bureaus and full-time correspondents (Kumar 2011). In their place, freelance reporters and parachute journalists have become increasingly common (Hannerz 2004). As a result, news organizations find it increasingly difficult to adequately monitor international news with their own network of correspondents (Sambrook 2010).

Second, NGOs in general—and humanitarian and human rights NGOs in particular—enjoy relatively high levels of both public and official acceptance. In a climate of public skepticism toward governments, many people view NGOs as both trusted sources of information and potential organizers for political action (Castells 2009; Lang 2013). Humanitarian and human rights groups benefit from a political climate in which their shared discourse—human rights[3]—enjoys widespread public acceptance (if uneven application). Historical scholarship shows that government use of human rights discourses exploded in the early 1990s (amid the collapse of the Cold War and the emergence of the so-called humanitarian wars), peaked in the mid-2000s (with both pro–Iraq War and anti–Iraq War sides using human rights language), and decreased slightly in the United States during Barack Obama's presidency (Keys 2014). This usage has led both humanitarian and human rights groups to interact more regularly with government officials, whether in the provision of humanitarian services or in the reporting of human rights violations. Taken together, these developments appear simultaneously to give official legitimation to NGOs (i.e., include them within the range of official viewpoints) and to decenter government officials as the primary authority on certain news topics.

Third, as described in the preceding chapter, NGOs have professionalized their information offerings in order to improve their chances of making the news. Leading organizations now dedicate substantial resources to producing reports about topics of importance (Hopgood 2006). Large NGOs also sustain substantial communication staffs—many with journalism backgrounds (Cooper 2011)—that seek to communicate issues to broader publics by issuing press releases, staging media events, producing multimedia content, and enlisting celebrities as spokespeople. Taken together, professionalization processes at NGOs mean that these organizations have more—and more types of—information that they can use in their quest to garner news coverage.

These three elements—economic constraints for news outlets, acceptance of NGOs in official circles, and professionalized publicity efforts by leading advocacy groups—point to seemingly favorable conditions for increased news access for NGOs. What type of news access these elements might lead to is less clear. Some researchers envision growing opportunities for advocacy groups to drive news coverage across a wider range of countries. Others argue that these groups are likely to continue being subordinated to the demands and preferences of the news media and government officials upon whom journalists rely for information. Parsing these competing arguments requires explicating the various dimensions along which news access can be measured. Such a conceptualization can help ascertain both the nature and some of the effects of NGOs' news access over time.

MEASURING NEWS ACCESS

The study of news access examines who gets to be a news source and what sort of news source they get to be (Cottle 2000). Undoubtedly, this vast topic spans a wide range of actors and influences. Previous research suggests that access varies depending on news outlet, political context, topical focus, and a variety of other factors (see the overview in Bennett 1996). Thus, to avoid the risk of overgeneralizing, this chapter draws on the existing literature examining NGO–media relations in order to develop a parsimonious conceptualization of news access. From this literature, it identifies four dimensions of access: prevalence, prominence, story location, and human rights frame—each of which captures different facets of how NGOs appear in the news. Although not exhaustive of news access in all forms, this four-part conceptualization documents aspects of news access that can adjudicate specific claims about the effects of NGO news access on norms of news construction.

The term *prevalence* refers to the frequency with which NGOs appear in the news. Several studies suggest that NGOs receive more overall coverage today than they did in the past, though historical evidence to support this claim is scant (Beckett 2008; Sambrook 2010). Moreover, discussions of prevalence remain underspecified in two ways. First, it is unclear whether claims of growing access reflect an uptake in the usage of NGO materials by news organizations or simply an expansion in the population of NGOs and news outlets. By limiting my analysis to a fixed number of leading groups and news organizations, however, I am able to control for this concern. Second, it is uncertain whether growing prevalence is a general phenomenon among all NGOs or an unevenly distributed one across NGOs. Previous research suggests that a few organizations are especially "media savvy" and thus drive the majority of the growth in NGO prevalence in the news. In particular, scholars have argued that both Human Rights Watch and Médecins Sans Frontières are especially well adapted to the current media environment. Unlike their competitors, these two groups are posited to invest more resources in maintaining a nimble media profile that can respond to journalists' needs and demands (Hopgood 2006; Van Leuven and Joye 2014).

Third, it is uncertain whether prevalence varies by advocacy organization and news outlet. Humanitarian and human rights groups maintain distinctive relations to the political field, and these relations presumably shape the amount of news coverage each desires and receives. In order to do their work (e.g., provide medical care, relief, or something else), humanitarian groups need access to disaster zones. As a general rule, such groups do not speak out publicly against host governments for fear of losing that access.[4] Human rights groups, by contrast, need not concern themselves with maintaining a working relationship with host governments, nor must they worry excessively about losing operational access. In principle, fewer limitations on human rights groups' communication efforts suggests that such groups ought to enjoy greater prevalence in the news. Prevalence of advocacy groups may also vary among media outlets. Research suggests that general print and broadcast media have cut back the most on their international news staff, whereas prestige outlets like the *New York Times* have retained a fairly stable international staff (Keller 2013; Kumar 2011). If NGO access increases in relation to decreases in newsroom staff, we should expect the greatest increases of access in general print and broadcast media. Beyond this point, broadcast media also provide advocacy groups with access to large general audiences, and previous research suggests that humanitarian groups target broadcast media in order to boost donations (Powers 2014). The prestige media, although also exposing advocacy groups to large audiences, are important in that they provide advocacy groups access to elite political debate.[5] Because advocacy groups vary in their reasons for seeking media attention, we can expect further differences in prevalence along these dimensions, too—with those groups that are interested primarily in mass fund-raising preferring broadcast media and those groups that are interested primarily in shaping elite debate targeting the prestige press.[6]

The term *prominence* refers to the position and placement of NGOs within news articles (in relation to other news sources). According to some, NGOs may in some ways be changing the construction of news not only by appearing in more news articles than in the past but also by being cited more prominently within them. Natalie Fenton suggests that time- and cash-strapped journalists frequently copy NGO press releases— which prominently feature the organizations themselves—"verbatim"

(2010, 162). Relatedly, some argue that NGOs increasingly decenter the prominence of government sources and perhaps increase the position of civic voices in news coverage (Beck 2006; Castells 2009; Silverstone 2007). Others, however, suggest that claims of "verbatim" reportage and the displacement of government sources by NGO sources are overstated. In keeping with theoretical premises of indexing, Silvio Waisbord argues that the "organization of news work is lopsided against NGOs" in favor of government officials (2011, 146). Several studies of the European press find that NGOs are used to "counterbalance" the messages put forward by officials (Van Leuven, Deprez, and Raeymaeckers 2013, 430). Together, these studies suggest that the number of NGO-driven press releases are quite low and that NGOs still typically appear later in stories, after government officials are cited.

The term *story location* refers to the geographic location (by country) of a story. International news coverage in general—and human rights coverage in particular—is known to be highly concentrated and focused on a handful of countries (Ramos, Rom, and Thoms 2007; Zuckerman 2004). Some suggest that professionalization has given organizations both the skills and the resources to bring news coverage to a wider range of countries than they did in the past (e.g., Ron, Ramos, and Rodgers 2005). Others argue that NGOs appear most often in news articles that focus on the small number of countries in which the news media already have an interest. This leads some scholars to express concern that NGO news access will reinforce rather than challenge norms regarding the construction of international news (Cottle and Nolan 2007; Fenton 2010; Waisbord 2011).

Finally, the term *human rights frame* refers to the type of human rights issue an article describes. Scholars have long noted that human rights news focuses primarily on political or civil violations (Moyn 2010). Such violations typically pertain to issues of government repression, military abuses, illegal detentions, curtailment to free expression, and related topics, and their presence in the news is sponsored by leading advocacy groups. In response to criticisms that because such an emphasis on political or civil violations elides the root causes of the social problems they describe, leading NGOs have in the past several decades broadened their remit to examine social, cultural, and economic rights, which explore issues related to the causes and consequences of the deprivation of basic needs as well as of rights to self-determination. Many leading advocacy groups have created new programs or departments that focus specifically on issues related to gender, corporate malfeasance, minority rights, and health concerns (Roth 2007), which creates the possibility that the number of human rights frames will expand alongside these changes.

In conceptualizing news access along these four dimensions, this chapter seeks to examine both (*a*) how and in what ways NGO news access has (or has not) changed over time and (*b*) what effects, if any, these changes have on the construction of international news. It is possible, for instance, that NGOs' prevalence has increased but that their prominence has decreased and that government sources remain dominant in news articles. Such a finding would suggest that news-construction norms have changed little because NGO access is still mediated primarily in relation to more established news sources. Alternatively, it is possible that both prevalence and prominence of NGOs have increased and that NGOs are cited in connection with a wider range of countries over time. Such a finding would support claims of both increased news access and the idea that NGOs may partially alter extant norms of news construction. To be sure, the range of potential permutations is wide. This chapter simply seeks to test common claims and assumptions regarding changes to NGO news access.

DATA AND METHODS

This chapter examines human rights coverage in a strategic sample of leading US news outlets from 1990 to 2010. My focus on the US case supplements extant scholarship that examines the prevalence of NGOs in European news media coverage (Trenz 2004; Van Leuven, Deprez, and Raeymaeckers 2013; Van Leuven and Joye 2014). More broadly, two factors informed my decision to investigate legacy news media as opposed to satellite or online-only providers. First, NGO professionals themselves care a great deal about appearing in these legacy outlets, and they dedicate time and resources to these efforts. Whether these attempts translate to greater news access is thus an important empirical question. Second, analyzing legacy outlets enables me to examine news access over time. This type of longitudinal analysis is not possible with pan-national satellite channels and online sites, the latter of which did not exist in 1990. Of course, the findings for legacy media in the United States cannot automatically be assumed to hold for legacy news media in other parts of the world or for satellite and online-only news providers.

The news outlets I included in the analysis are the *New York Times*, *NBC Nightly News*, and *USA Today*. I selected these outlets both to provide a broad picture of NGO visibility in the legacy news media as well as to test whether patterns of news access vary by outlet. Elite newspapers such as the *New York Times* still retain ample foreign-reporting staffs. As of 2013, the "newspaper of record" reported having thirty-one full-time bureaus in operation around the world (Keller 2013). General-audience newspapers and broadcast network news have cut back on foreign reporting far more substantially. A survey in 2011 found *USA Today* to have just five full-time bureaus in operation and NBC to have fourteen (Kumar 2011). With the selection of these three outlets, the research design can test specific claims about whether diminished editorial resources may or may not offer increased access to NGOs.

In order to create the sample, I entered the phrase *human rights* into the LexisNexis search database. For the *New York Times* and *USA Today*, I began the search with the year 1990 and repeated the search at five-year intervals up to and including 2010. This time period enables a lengthy longitudinal analysis, and its selection coincides with decreased editorial resources, increased NGO professionalization, and rising acceptance of human rights discourses. Because full-text archives of *NBC Nightly News* begin in 2000 (and because the Vanderbilt archives—the most comprehensive source of television news content—provide only news summaries, which precludes systematic textual comparison), analysis of that outlet begins in 2000. For all three news outlets, the unit of analysis is the news article. This procedure yielded 10,310 news articles that include the search phrase *human rights*, which are referenced here as the *total sample*. Each of the articles is coded for year (e.g., 1990, 1995) and primary country of focus (e.g., Afghanistan, Turkey).

Within the total sample, I searched for the names of the leading humanitarian and human rights groups included in this study: Amnesty International, Human Rights Watch, International Crisis Group, Médecins Sans Frontières, Oxfam, Save the Children, and World Vision. In selecting these organizations, the study can be reasonably sure that any changes in NGO prevalence over time reflect actual changes in news access rather than resulting from other confounding factors (e.g., the introduction of new NGOs in the sample). Moreover, by including several NGOs that previous scholarship has identified as being especially media savvy (Barnett 2011; Hopgood 2006)—namely, Human Rights Watch and Médecins Sans Frontières—this research design is able to test claims about whether the leading NGOs' media strategies allow some organizations more access to the news than others. Finally, by including a mixture of humanitarian and human rights groups, I was able to investigate the extent to which news access varies according to NGO type. The number of articles in the total sample in which NGOs are mentioned is 2,077.

In order to compare citation patterns of articles in which NGOs are mentioned to those in which they are not, I also drew a random subset of news articles in which leading NGOs are not mentioned. This subset included 100 articles for each news outlet in each time period (1990, 1995, etc.). For any news outlet with fewer than 100 articles in a given year, I coded all items. This segment of the total sample included 1,034 news articles. This subset and the sample of articles mentioning leading NGOs are referenced here as the *core sample*. It contains 3,111 news articles.

All articles in the core sample were coded in relation to specific claims about how NGO news access has changed and what effects, if any, such changes have had on the construction of human rights news. (See the methods appendix for specific codes.) To capture the prevalence of NGOs in the news over time, I coded by number each article for the specific organization mentioned, assigning a zero to those that don't mention any organization. This method allows for a simple measure of total NGO mentions over time and analysis of how many mentions each NGO garnered. I compared the number of NGO mentions to the total population of human rights articles (i.e., the total sample) to examine the prevalence of articles in which leading NGOs are mentioned as a percentage of all human rights news coverage.

To further contextualize prevalence data, this study utilizes an independent measure of human rights discourse by government officials. Scholars working under the theoretical premises of indexing call for independent measures of political discourse in order to trace more carefully the degree to which media coverage of an issue departs from political debates (Zaller and Chiu 1996). I entered the search term *human rights* into the *Congressional Record* online database to create a general measure of human rights discussions in US policy circles. Then I entered the name of each leading NGO alongside the search term (e.g., "Amnesty International" and *human rights*) to capture the prevalence of NGOs within congressional debates.

Several measures coded for prominence. To assess claims that NGOs decenter government officials within news articles, I coded each article in the core sample for its first five sources. I deemed any individual or group receiving direct attribution a source. I categorized each source as a government official, civil society group, academic, businessperson, legal or medical professional, celebrity, United Nations official, or unaffiliated individual (see the methods appendix for the full coding protocol). I coded each source for its position within the news article (first source, second source, etc.). After coding, I averaged each source's position codes. I also did a simple word count of each news article to ascertain whether the NGO was mentioned in the first or second half of the news article. Finally, I coded each article for whether the NGO was the clear initiator of the news or not, tagging an article as "NGO driven" when it clearly signaled that an NGO was the source for the article (see Livingston and Bennett 2003 for a similar measure). Such articles report statements made by an NGO in the first paragraph (e.g. "According to Human Rights Watch, seventeen people were killed in bombings today"). This is a conservative estimate because NGOs may "drive" news articles in less-visible ways; however, the indicator allows for the testing of claims about whether NGOs find their work increasingly used "verbatim."

To assess claims about how changes in news access affect what locations are covered in articles that mention NGOs, I coded all articles—that is, the total sample—for country focus. Following research by Howard Ramos, James Ron, and Oskar Thoms (2007), I coded each article for the first country mentioned. This measure likely undercounts the total number of countries because some articles about human rights issues include multiple countries. However, it allows for longitudinal analysis of whether the number of countries in which NGOs are mentioned has expanded over time, while also retaining high levels of code reliability. To test claims that NGO mentions cluster around a small number of countries, the study reports what percentage of all NGO mentions is connected to the five most frequently mentioned countries for each collection period.

Finally, to test whether the framing of human rights stories has changed over time, I coded each story in relation to the primary frame in which the NGO is cited. At its most basic, a frame defines the *type* of human rights issue at stake (Entman 1993).[7] After reading a combination of news articles and academic studies about human rights news, I arrived at a list of seven human rights frames: political rights (i.e., some form of government repression, including but not limited to torture, military abuse, and capital punishment), free expression (i.e., some curtailment of speech rights, often by restricting public assemblies or by impeding the conduct of free elections), gender and family (i.e., exclusion or violence committed on the basis of gender), humanitarian issues (i.e., deprivation of basic needs such as access to shelter as well as basic goods and services, but with no reference to the culpable party), economic issues (i.e., deprivation of basic needs, with reference to a specific culprit, usually a corporation or government), cultural issues (i.e., right to self-determination, often focused on issues related to indigenous persons), and health and environment issues (i.e., right to sanitary living conditions).

The research design aims to test competing claims in the extant scholarly literature regarding the role of NGOs in the legacy news media. I report these results in three parts: first, by describing the extent to which NGO prevalence in the news has increased over time; second, by detailing how and in what ways NGO prominence in the news has and has not changed over time; and third, by analyzing the types of human rights frames that NGOs tend to propagate.

INCREASED ACCESS FOR NGOS?

NGO prevalence in the news has risen sharply over time, both in absolute terms and as a percentage of all human rights coverage. The growing prevalence of leading humanitarian and human rights NGOs in the news far outpaces their presence in congressional debates, which remains largely constant during the same time period. News access does vary by NGO type in that most humanitarian groups tend to appear more frequently in broadcast media, whereas human rights groups cluster in the prestige press. Across all time periods, the news outlets that dedicate the fewest resources to international news coverage are also the most likely to mention NGOs in their reporting. On the whole, the data suggest that the two primary factors responsible for driving the increase in news access are (*a*) the growing professionalism of NGO publicity efforts and (*b*) the decreased resources of news organizations. By contrast, validation from political elites seems to play a less-direct role in shaping the prevalence of advocacy groups in the news. (See figures 3.1 and 3.2 as well as table 3.1.)

In 1990 and 1995, the presence of humanitarian and human rights NGOs in the news tracks with their prevalence in the *Congressional Record* (see figure 3.1). In 1990, 13.5 percent of all congressional discussions of human rights include the mention of a leading NGO; 8.5 percent of all news articles do. These figures rise about 5 percentage points for 1995: that year, 18.3 percent of all human rights discussions in Congress include mention of a leading NGO, and 12.2 percent of news articles do. Beginning in 2000, the two diverge: whereas congressional mentions of humanitarian and human rights groups decrease slightly, the portion of human rights news stories that mention a leading NGO rises to 18.4 percent. This pattern intensifies throughout the first decade of

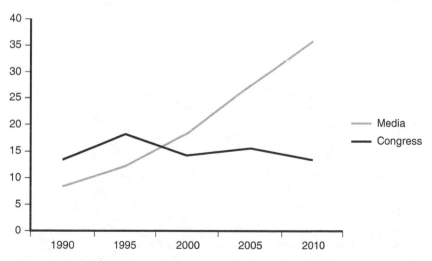

FIGURE 3.1 NGO Prevalence in the News as a Percentage of Total Human Rights Coverage

the twenty-first century: whereas the mention of humanitarian and human rights groups in Congress remains roughly constant, their inclusion in human rights news coverage continues to rise. By 2010, nearly 36 percent of all human rights news articles include the mention of at least one NGO in them.

The growing prevalence of leading NGOs in the news cannot be attributed simply to a general "explosion" in the use of human rights discourses by political elites. If that were the case, one would at least expect the usage of human rights discourses to rise among various government officials. Yet total mentions of human rights in the *Congressional Record* actually decrease from a high of 970 in 1990 to a low of 428 in 2010. Similarly, invocations of the term *human rights* by sitting American presidents (as measured by the copresence of a president's name and the phrase *human rights*) rise steadily in the 1990s, peak in 2005, and drop off thereafter. Finally, the news media's own use of the term follows a pattern similar to presidents' use, rising until 2005 and dropping sharply thereafter. Clearly, something more than government validation is at work in boosting the prevalence of NGOs in the news.

The professionalization of NGO publicity seems to be responsible for some of the growth in news access (see figure 3.2). In 1990, the two most media-savvy organizations in the sample—Human Rights Watch and Médecins Sans Frontières—account for just 16.5 percent of all NGO

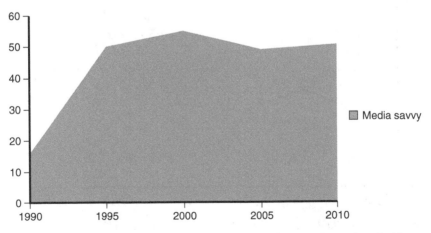

FIGURE 3.2 Media-Savvy NGOs as a Percentage of NGOs Mentioned in the News

mentions in the core sample. By 2010, however, these two groups garner half (50.8 percent) of all mentions. This gain boosts the overall prevalence of leading NGOs in the news because most other groups see their presence either undulate moderately across time periods or rise slightly. Both Amnesty International and Save the Children see their number of mentions rise modestly in absolute terms even as their share of total mentions diminishes considerably, from 75.6 percent in 1990 to just 25.1 percent in 2010. Oxfam and World Vision see their prevalence grow over time in absolute terms (from 6 and 8 mentions in 1990, respectively, to 46 and 33 mentions in 2010; figures not displayed in table 3.1), but this remains a small proportion of all NGO mentions. For no group does the number of mentions decline over time. Taken together, the data support the proposition that media-savvy groups help boost the overall prevalence of leading NGOs in the news above and beyond levels that correlate with government validation.

At the same time, news access does vary according to NGO type. Leading human rights groups are twice as likely to appear in the news than humanitarian groups (1,378 versus 699 citations, respectively; see table 3.1). They are also more likely to appear in the prestige press than their humanitarian group counterparts: more than 85 percent of citations of them appear in the *New York Times*, compared to 78 percent of those for humanitarian groups. The figure for humanitarian groups in the prestige press is driven almost exclusively by Médecins Sans Frontières and Oxfam, two groups that strongly embrace human rights principles and have long histories of public-oriented advocacy. Without those two

TABLE 3.1

Prevalence of Humanitarian Versus Human Rights Groups in Prestige and Broadcast Media

NGO Type	Prestige Press N (%)	General/ Broadcast Media N (%)	Total
Human rights groups	1,183 (85.8)	195 (14.2)	1,378
Humanitarian groups	545 (78)	154 (22)	699

groups, the percentage of citations of remaining humanitarian groups found in either the broadcast media or in *USA Today* is 38.5 percent (data not shown in table 3.1). These differences are stable across all time periods. Taken together, the data support the proposition that different types of organizations seek and receive coverage in different types of news media.

NGOs' publicity efforts coincide with the news media's increasing openness to third-party messages (presumably as a result of staffing cutbacks). In all news outlets, the prevalence of humanitarian and human rights groups rises over time. Moreover, the news outlets that have cut back on international news gathering the most are also most likely to mention NGOs in their human rights coverage. The outlet that has cut back the most on international news gathering—*NBC Nightly News*—references a leading NGO on average in 42.5 percent of its human rights coverage, and this percentage grows over time. By 2010, nearly 60.0 percent of its human rights pieces reference a leading NGO. *USA Today's* coverage of human rights issues declines each year from 1990 on, but the shrinking coverage coincides with increased mentions of NGOs. By 2010, 41.6 percent of all human rights stories in *USA Today* include mention of a leading humanitarian or human rights organization (up from just 11.7 percent in 1990). Prevalence of NGOs in the news as a percentage of total human rights coverage is lowest in the *New York Times* (19.7 percent on average), in part because the *Times* produces a much larger number of human rights articles in absolute terms than either of the other two news outlets.

Could real-world events be responsible for the growing prevalence of NGOs in the news? In 2005 and 2010, a number of human rights situations—as well as NGO responses to them—seem tailor made for increased news access. In 2005, ongoing concerns about human rights abuses in the American-led "war on terror" gave rise to widespread allegations, covered in the news, about abuse and torture by the US government or its proxies (Bennett, Lawrence, and Livingston 2007). In that same year, Amnesty International released a report calling the American detention camp in Guantánamo Bay "the gulag of our times" (Amnesty International 2005, i). In 2010, human rights concerns in the aftermath of the Haiti earthquake generated a wave of news articles detailing the human suffering resulting from that disaster, many of which featured humanitarian groups prominently. In contrast to human rights news in the 1990s (which mostly covered Europe with the dissolution of the former Yugoslavia), these events occurred in places where many news outlets had cut news staff (Iraq, Afghanistan) or where they had never established foreign correspondents (Haiti).

At the same time, it is important not to overstate the degree to which real-world events drive patterns of news access. For starters, the percentage increase for the 2000–2005 collection period is actually smaller than the growth in the preceding period (a 79.2 percent increase versus a 50.8 percent increase, respectively). Yet the year 2000 lacks a major human rights situation that could account for the growth. When looked at over time, the general pattern is instead one of growing news access with fluctuations across different outlets and time periods. For the most part, NGOs' publicity efforts and news organizations' decreasing resources seem to drive this growth in news access. Indexing, thus, does not dictate how often humanitarian and human rights groups show up in the news, but it does shape how these groups appear when they are cited in news coverage.

THE PERSISTENCE OF INDEXING

Although NGOs have appeared in the news more frequently over time, how they appear has continued to follow the basic precepts of indexing. Leading organizations are mentioned fairly late in news articles and almost always after government officials are mentioned. To the extent that the growing prevalence of NGOs in the news displaces any source type, that source type tends to be smaller civic groups, not political elites. Moreover, leading humanitarian and human rights groups typically show up in news stories that cover topics that are already in the media spotlight: although efforts to alter that spotlight are occasionally successful, those efforts prove to be narrow in time and limited in scope. On the whole, the growing inclusion of NGOs in the news seems to derive from NGOs' acceptance of the news media's basic rules and norms.

In all human rights news and across all news outlets, government officials are by far the most prominent source (see table 3.2). They are slightly more prevalent in articles where leading NGOs are not mentioned (32.4 percent versus 28.0 percent of all mentions, respectively).

TABLE 3.2

Average Distribution of News Sources in Human Rights Articles

Source	Human Rights News % (*N*)	Articles with NGO Citation % (*N*)	Difference % points
Government officials	32.4 (1,261)	28.0 (2,128)	−4.4
Media	6.1 (238)	4.8 (367)	−1.3
Leading NGO	—	31.3 (2,377)	+31.3
Civil society	23.9 (931)	9.5 (722)	−14.4
Business	2.3 (89)	2.5 (193)	+0.2
Arts/Education	7.4 (288)	4.8 (366)	−2.6
United Nations	12.6 (489)	6.5 (496)	−6.1
Individual	10.6 (414)	9.6 (730)	−1.0
Other	4.6 (180)	2.8 (214)	−1.8

Note: Core sample, $N = 3,111$ articles. For human rights news, $N = 3,890$ sources. For articles citing NGOs, $N = 7,593$ sources. Due to rounding, percentages and figures may not add up exactly to total.

Nowhere, though, are government officials decentered from the news coverage. In fact, government officials are most likely to be the first source mentioned in any human rights news article (34.2 percent of all first mentions, figure not shown in table 3.2). By contrast, humanitarian and human rights groups tend to be mentioned later in news stories and after other news sources. In fact, whereas NGOs' prevalence increases over time, their prominence actually decreases. In 1990, 50.0 percent of NGO mentions occur in the first half of articles in the core sample. By 2010, only 40.9 percent do. In addition to being mentioned later in news articles, they are also increasingly mentioned after other news sources (see table 3.3). In 1990, the NGO position in the order of sources mentioned averaged 2.12. This figure drops gradually over each time period; by 2010, their average position in the order of sources mentioned is 3.19.[8]

An example illustrates the extent to which government officials

TABLE 3.3

Indicators of NGO Prominence, 1990–2010

	1990 % (*N*)	1995 % (*N*)	2000 % (*N*)	2005 % (*N*)	2010 % (*N*)
NGO-driven article	17.0 (30)	12.7 (30)	13.5 (57)	15.2 (97)	13.6 (82)
Citations in first half of news article	50.0 (67)	49.7 (93)	41.4 (153)	40.5 (214)	40.9 (208)
Average position in order of citations	2.12	2.71	3.26	3.09	3.19

Note: All figures based on average of the three news outlets studied. Total sample of articles in which NGOs are mentioned, $N = 2,077$.

continue to drive news coverage. On September 2, 2005, the *New York Times* published an article titled "European Commission Seeks Faster Repatriation of Some Migrants" (Bowley 2005). The article detailed efforts by the European Commission to convince member countries to agree to a common set of policies on the return of illegal immigrants and failed asylum seekers to their home countries. The head of the commission is the first source in the article; further sourcing is drawn from public statements by British prime minister Tony Blair and a spokeswoman for the British government, which opposed the effort. In the final paragraph of the article, a legal adviser for Amnesty International is quoted criticizing specific components of the measure. As a source, the adviser thus brings a different perspective to the news article, though this perspective is included at the very end of the news item.

To the extent that the growing prevalence of NGOs displaces any source, they tend to replace smaller-size civic groups or United Nations officials. The latter two are more commonly mentioned in human rights articles where NGOs are not included as sources: civil society groups (i.e., any civic group that is not one of the leading humanitarian or human rights organizations) garner 23.9 percent of mentions in human rights articles but only 9.5 percent of mentions in those articles where leading NGOs are mentioned; United Nations officials are twice as likely to appear in articles that don't mention leading NGOs. This finding dovetails with qualitative speculation that a few elite NGOs might crowd out smaller civic groups (Bob 2006) as well as with more recent quantitative research highlighting similar dynamics (Thrall, Stecula, and Sweet 2014). It also raises important questions about whether and how larger NGOs interact with their smaller counterparts (i.e., to what degree do the concerns of smaller civic groups filter up to and influence the platforms of larger groups).[9]

Despite claims that NGOs find their publicity attempts increasingly used "verbatim" by the news media, NGO-driven articles constitute only a small portion of total NGO mentions. The number of such articles rises in absolute terms (30 in 1990, 82 in 2010) but declines as a proportion of the core sample (17.0 percent in 1990, 13.6 percent in 2010; see table 3.3). More media-savvy NGOs are the most successful in placing such articles: Human Rights Watch and Médecins Sans Frontières generate 58.0 percent of all NGO-driven articles. Amnesty International accounts for another quarter (25.6 percent) of all such articles. The remaining mentions are split fairly even among the remaining groups.

For the most part, NGOs show up in stories that are already in the media spotlight. News coverage of human rights issues (the total sample) typically occurs in roughly 100 countries (see table 3.4). This figure remains largely constant, even as media coverage of human rights issues decline in absolute terms. In all time periods, the *New York Times* far exceeds all other news outlets in the number of countries it reports on (143 versus 73 in *USA Today* and 32 in *NBC Nightly News*). It is also more geographically diverse in its coverage of human rights issues. On average, the top-five countries most frequently cited are mentioned in between 47.1 and 61.1 percent of *Times* articles in the total sample, as compared to 59.2 and 89.2 in *USA Today* and 80 and 100 percent in *NBC Nightly News* (figures not shown in table 3.4). Thus, although the degree of concentration varies, all news outlets generally concentrate on a few countries. Excluding the five most frequently cited countries, the average number of citations per country across all outlets is 10.12 annually.

Growing NGO prevalence does little to change this equation. Although leading advocacy groups are mentioned in connection to a growing number of countries (40 in 1990, 74 in 2010), the bulk of their mentions comes in connection to the countries that the news media are already reporting on. Like news media coverage of human rights issues

TABLE 3.4

Patterns of Human Rights Coverage in the US News, 1990–2010

Outlet		1990	1995	2000	2005	2010
Articles citing an NGO	(a) Total number of countries	40	52	56	72	74
	(b) Percentage of mentions in connection with top-five countries covered	57.4	46.6	57.2	63.8	53.6
Total human rights coverage	(a) Total number of countries	100	87	109	100	110
	(b) Percentage of mentions in top-five countries covered	56.0	57.3	52.1	57.6	56.7

Note: Total sample, $N = 10,310$ articles.

more generally, NGOs tend to be mentioned in connection to just a few countries. In any given year, between 46.6 and 63.8 percent of all NGO mentions occur in connection to the five countries that garner the most media coverage for human rights issues. Patterns over time—either toward greater or lesser concentration of NGO citations—are unclear. The percentage of NGO mentions occurring in connection to the top five countries drops 10 percentage points from 1990 to 1995, only to rise in both 2000 and 2005 and then to drop slightly (to 53.6 percent) in 2010.

Interestingly, although the number of NGO-driven stories is small, NGOs do appear more likely to drive news coverage when reporting is done on issues in a country not already in the media spotlight. Of the 237 NGO-driven articles in the core sample, 61.2 percent mention countries outside the media spotlight (as indicated by a country's exclusion from the top-five countries mentioned in any given year). Typically, these citations are one-off mentions of a country that otherwise receives very little coverage. A single organization occasionally appears able to bring sustained media attention to a country otherwise unlikely to receive news coverage. In 2005, for example, Human Rights Watch was cited twelve times in connection with Uzbekistan, a country with otherwise very low prevalence across the core sample (across all outlets and time periods, it gathers only twenty total mentions). This suggests that although NGOs are generally mentioned in news articles about countries within the media spotlight, they may be most likely to succeed in driving news coverage when the news focuses on countries outside the media spotlight.[10]

THE PRIMACY OF POLITICAL AND CIVIL VIOLATIONS

Across all time periods, political and civil violations constitute the dominant framing of human rights stories. NGOs also become an important source for issues pertaining to violations of political or civil rights. As sources, leading humanitarian and human rights groups perform a dual role: on the one hand, they provide the news media with factual reporting regarding events on the ground; on the other hand, they circulate advocacy statements about how best to address the human rights abuses in those situations. Over time, these groups are also able to introduce human rights frames (particularly around political and civil rights) to stories that are not primarily about human rights (e.g., trade pacts between governments). At the same time, NGO efforts to diversify the definition of human rights to encompass cultural, social, and economic issues find only marginal success. Across all time periods, such frames constitute a small proportion of all human rights news coverage (see figure 3.3).

Human rights news focuses primarily on violations of political and civil rights. Across all time periods, approximately two-thirds of all human rights stories focus primarily on government repression, torture, illegal detentions, curtailment of freedom of expression, and the need for free and fair elections. The use of humanitarian frames, which emphasize the deprivation of basic human needs, seems to rise and fall in line with real-world disasters. Their use peaks in 2005 and 2010, for example, as a result of human rights issues related to the effects of the tsunami in Southeast Asia and the earthquake in Haiti, respectively. On average, humanitarian frames constitute 15.4 percent of all human rights stories. The remaining frames are split more or less evenly among issues that relate to economic rights (6.4 percent), gender and family (5.4 percent),

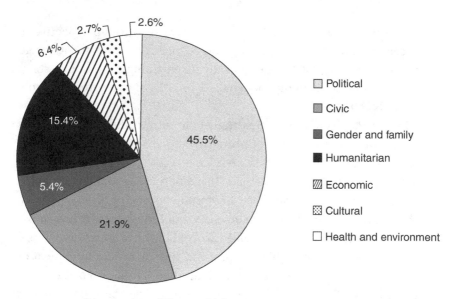

FIGURE 3.3 Distribution of Human Rights Frames, 1990–2010

culture (2.7 percent), and health and the environment (2.6 percent). The use of each of these latter frames grows modestly over time, while constituting a very small portion of all human rights news coverage.

On stories that focus on political and civil rights, leading humanitarian and human rights groups provide journalists with a mixture of factual reporting and advocacy claims. NGOs sometimes provide the eyewitness reporting (or expert analysis) of political violations as a result of their presence on the ground. For example, a story about the killing of sixty-two people in a Liberian port city in the midst of that country's civil war relied on staffers from Médecins Sans Frontières for details about the events: "Officials of Doctors Without Borders, the French relief agency, said the wounded included a badly slashed infant, a pregnant woman who had been repeatedly raped . . . and a young girl whose head was partially split open by a machete blow" (French 1995). At other times, NGOs are quoted for their views on the appropriate course of action to remedy a human rights violation. For example, a *USA Today* article chronicled human rights groups' reaction to a failed resolution intended to criticize China's human rights record: "Abuse of this loophole in the commission's procedures should be an embarrassment to the world's top human-rights body. . . . How much longer will the world play this game with China?" (Nichols 2000). Ideally, at least from the perspective of advocacy groups, factual reporting and advocacy recommendations go together. In reality, NGOs are typically given a single quote in a story. As one person put it to me, "Journalists only have space for one quote from an NGO."[11]

Over time, NGOs are increasingly able to introduce human rights frames into stories that are not primarily about human rights. In these cases, human rights groups take an issue already in the news and find a way to insert a human rights angle. Trade or aid negotiations or global sporting events, for example, are a common source of these efforts. In such instances, human rights groups are quoted—typically late in the article—calling on the governments involved in the negotiations to stipulate improved human rights as a precondition of a trade agreement or the awarding of a sporting event such as the Olympics. For example, Human Rights Watch was quoted in a news article about negotiations between the United States and Mexico to fight drug trafficking. In the quote, the researcher for Human Rights Watch argued that the United States should withhold funding to Mexico until the country took steps to improve its human rights record. "Any withholding of funds would be a step in the right direction, but given the total impunity for military abuses and widespread cases of torture, none of the funds tied to human rights should be released" (quoted in Malkin and Archibold 2010). In these and related instances, human rights groups take the news media's coverage as given and try to find a way to make their policy positions fit within it rather than to challenge it.

The news media thus pay the most attention to human rights issues that are political or civil in nature, especially those issues that pertain to countries already on the media's radar. They infrequently discuss economic issues. In 2000, a report by Amnesty International that was profiled in several news outlets sought to define concerns about the social impacts (e.g., low wages, worker abuses) of developed countries' investments in the Global South. Summarizing the report, one article noted that one company needed to take human rights seriously "not just for the company's operations but [for] its global reputation, retention of quality employees and ultimately its shareholders" (Cowell 2000). In 2005, Human Rights Watch published and publicized a string of reports about labor violations in the American meatpacking industry. The reports led to an editorial by the *New York Times* that compared the findings to Upton Sinclair's novel *The Jungle* (1906). According to the editorial, the reports "[found] that jobs in many beef, pork and poultry plants are sufficiently dangerous to breach international agreements promising a safe workplace" (*New York Times* 2000). Médecins Sans Frontières runs campaigns criticizing multinational drug companies for using patents to enhance their profits while denying lifesaving medical treatments to those in need (Sternberg 2000). Moreover, NGOs wage campaigns that loosely knit together multiple groups in order to raise awareness of a particular problem. In 2005, for example, two leading NGOs—Oxfam and Save the Children—joined the Make Poverty History campaign, which generated widespread discussion in the news media about substandard living conditions on much of the African continent.[12]

Yet such cases are the exception, not the rule. In the course of a twenty-year period, economic frames constitute a small fraction of all the public statements NGOs make in the news media. When journalists draw from the economic reporting that NGOs provide, they tend to focus on the political or civil rights violations in these stories while minimizing discussions of other human rights angles—especially those that touch on issues of economic justice.

SIDELINING ECONOMIC ISSUES

It is sometimes claimed that because economic angles are structural, they are more difficult to convey in the news, especially vis-à-vis more personalized narrative forms (Benson 2013). There is an element of truth in this claim for NGOs, which follow a reporting strategy that seeks to link human rights claims together in a causal chain of violation, violator, and remedy.[13] At the same time, the difficulty in getting economic issues on the news agenda is not simply owing to difficult indicators. It is also part of a selection bias on the part of the news media as well as an adaptive tendency by NGOs to give journalists the types of information they want. When journalists draw from the economic reporting that NGOs provide, they tend to focus on the political violations while downplaying discussions of the economic issues. This selection bias reshapes coverage of the issue itself, so that the economic issues tend to assume political frames. As a result, NGO reporting that begins with a focus on violations of economic rights sometimes sutures that focus to frames that emphasize the political violations that stem from such economic violations.

Consider a story from Uzbekistan in 2005. In May of that year, a series of protests broke out in the city of Andijan in response to growing poverty in the region and ongoing government repression. These protests were triggered by the arrest of twenty-three businesspeople on charges of religious extremism. Within the city, the charges were seen as a ploy by the Uzbek government to control the growing power of those businesspeople, who were the primary employers in the city, generally maintained good reputations by providing wages that exceeded the government-mandated minimum, paid employees' medical expenses, and provided free meals to staff (International Crisis Group 2005). Through these businesspeople's trials, citizens protested peacefully outside the courts. At the time, the trials forced many of these businesspeople to lay off their employees, a result that was described at the time as "devastating" (Human Rights Watch 2005).

Shortly before the verdict was expected, long-simmering tensions boiled over into open violence. A group of friends and family of the businesspeople stormed the prison to release them and at least five hundred other prisoners. Upon the prisoners' release, they and the protestors went into the city's main square, where they were joined by thousands of other protestors. The people involved in the jailbreak spoke first, but then individuals with no involvement in it took the microphone. As the day wore on, the protest grew in size. Observers noted that the majority were unarmed. At its highest point, the protest was reported to have included more than ten thousand people. For most of the day, the protestors were subject to periodic attacks by security officers. In interviews with local journalists, protestors made clear that they were staying in the square to make their demands known (a rumor also had it that the president would be coming, and protestors reportedly cheered at the opportunity to speak to him). Around 4:00 p.m., the military blocked off the streets leading into the square. Shortly after 5:00 p.m., the soldiers started shooting directly into the crowd.

The government accused the protestors of inciting religious rebellion, but observers countered the claim. As one Western journalist put it, "This rebellion has nothing to do with religion" (Institute for War and

Peace Reporting 2005). At the heart of the protestors' demands were improved economic conditions and freedom from government repression. It was calculated that 31.8 percent of the population in the Andijan region experienced poverty; 9.1 percent experienced extreme poverty (per the World Bank Living Standards Assessment). As a result, many Uzbeks came to rely on bazaar trading to support themselves. In the bazaars, people sold inexpensive clothing, often from China. Traditionally, such bazaars had taken place informally. However, in 2002 the government became concerned about hard currency leaving the country, so it began to place new tariffs and regulations on the bazaars, which made it increasingly difficult for these informal forms of trade to occur. It was these conditions of poverty and government repression that formed the primary background to the protests.

News coverage of the events in Andijan by US news outlets was minimal at best. Neither *USA Today* nor *NBC Nightly News* carried a single story about these events. The *New York Times* initially carried a wire story repeating the basic facts, while emphasizing the religious angle: protestors, the story said, were demanding "the release of 23 Muslims charged with religious extremism" (*New York Times* 2005b). Days later, the *Times* published its own story of events, which characterized the region as a place where "Islamic and antigovernment sentiment has long simmered" (Meyers 2005). Only at the end of the story was an economic frame suggested, when the reporter quoted an American lawyer living in Uzbekistan as saying, "This is more about them [the government] acquiring economic clout, and perhaps refusing to pay off the local authorities, than about any religious beliefs."

For about a week, the *Times* ran stories about the protests and the crackdown. It framed these events primarily through the lens of political repression, political conflict, and civil society demands. Factual accounts centered on the crackdown itself, and subsequent reporting typically focused on what response, if any, the US government had to the events. (At the time, the US government had a military base in Uzbekistan that was an important point of entry for its operations in Afghanistan). The discourse was dominated by official sources (Uzbek and US government officials). To the extent that Uzbeks (either as individuals or as groups) were included, they were often seen through the prism of religion. On May 21, for example, the *Times* carried a photograph showing people praying in a mosque on the Kyrgyz side of the border. The picture carried a caption attributing the events to "an Islamic-inspired revolt against the Uzbek authorities."[14]

Leading NGOs were included as sources in this news coverage. Human Rights Watch, for example, was quoted multiple times conveying its worry that all dissidents would be labeled religious extremists. It was credited for providing the "most thorough description of the crackdown" (Chivers 2005). In the aftermath of events, leading NGOs played an important role in calling on governments in the region not to deport activists back to Uzbekistan. They called for an international inquiry into the events (no small feat, given that the US government initially waivered on this point), and they publicized the use of psychiatric drugs on activists as a form of punishment.

What NGOs did not do was contribute an economic frame to the news coverage. This is somewhat surprising because their research reports *did* emphasize the economic background. Human Rights Watch noted that interviews "with numerous people present at the demonstrations consistently revealed that the protesters spoke about economic conditions in Andijan, government repression, and unfair trials—and not [about] the creation of an Islamic state" (2005, 11–12). International Crisis Group began its reporting by noting that the protest "was not a one-off affair. It was the climax of six months in which especially ruinous economic policies produced demonstrations across the country" (2005, 1). Amnesty International reported that during the protests "the vast majority of the speakers spoke about the economic hardship in the region and gave examples of their own economic problems" (2005, 9).

In their press releases, however, NGOs downplayed this economic angle and focused instead on political violations and civil society demands. Human Rights Watch put out twenty-six press releases between May and December; none emphasized the economic dimension of the problem. Amnesty International put out fewer press releases but called for an international investigation into the events. In nearly all the press releases, human rights groups focused on political violations, government actions, and civil society demands.

The case of Andijan and Uzbekistan provides an example of a key dilemma for humanitarian and human rights groups. Although NGOs have dedicated growing resources to covering issues of economic rights, they are often unsuccessful in getting such frames into the news. Yet this issue seems at least partially self-induced. NGOs include economic frames in their reporting, but they tend to downplay such frames in their media work, focusing instead on political violations. The latter framing fits comfortably within established indexing norms: human rights groups are sought out for their views on what political violations have occurred.[15] They garner publicity when they can find a way to "shame" governments on issues in which they are already invested, but in the process they leave their economic analyses by the wayside. News access thus may help to make some frames visible while actively marginalizing other frames.

This chapter describes a partial opening in the news gates for leading humanitarian and human rights organizations. These groups are more likely to appear in the news today than they were in the past, and they are increasingly able to insert human rights frames into news stories. Yet how these groups are cited continues to follow the already established precepts of indexing. NGOs are typically cited late in news stories and after official news sources. They also tend to appear in stories that are already in the media spotlight. Efforts to alter these patterns of coverage, although occasionally successful, are typically short-lived. Moreover, despite their efforts to address economic, social, and cultural rights, NGOs tend to be associated primarily with their work on political and civic violations.

Extant theories of news access correctly predict the types of coverage that NGOs receive. However, they do not predict the amount of coverage they receive. For example, indexing theories suggest that nonofficial sources tend to receive coverage only when they "express opinions already emerging in official circles" (Bennett 1990, 106). Thus, logically, NGO prevalence ought to rise and fall alongside the inclusion of leading NGOs within official circles (as measured via the *Congressional Record*). Yet the findings indicate that NGO prevalence in the *Congressional Record* is largely constant over time. It may be that additional measures of government valorization of NGOs are needed. Nonetheless, something more than government indexing appears responsible for the growing prevalence of leading NGOs in the news.

In this vein, scholars have suggested that NGOs boost their chances of breaking into the news by professionalizing their publicity strategies (Bob 2006; Hopgood 2006). The findings here offer support for such claims. In particular, media-savvy NGOs, especially Human Rights Watch and Médecins Sans Frontières, are responsible for much of the growth in NGO prevalence over time. This finding connects with findings by scholars who note that the chances for news access are distributed unevenly across NGOs. Although other research has noted that resource-poor organizations face much higher barriers to news access (Thrall, Stecula, and Sweet 2014), this study shows that even among well-resourced NGOs, an organization's chance of making the news is moderated by media skills that are themselves unevenly distributed across leading NGOs. It also seems to vary according to organizational type, with humanitarian groups more likely to appear in broadcast news media and human rights groups in the prestige press.

Diminished editorial resources do seem to make some outlets more likely to feature NGOs in their news coverage. Both *NBC Nightly News* and *USA Today* have less human rights news overall but include leading NGOs in a greater proportion of it. At the same time, in no outlet does increased NGO prevalence appear to alter or modify the general patterns of human rights news coverage. The one countertendency to this finding is that NGO-driven articles tend to focus on countries not already in the media spotlight, which could be the result of a number of factors. On stories already in the news media's zone of interest, NGOs may be more likely to be used as an accompanying rather than driving voice in news coverage. In contrast, when publicizing issues outside the media spotlight, leading organizations may compete with fewer voices for attention. I explore these issues—specifically, the roles played both by NGOs and newsrooms in shaping this state of affairs—in greater detail in chapters 5 and 6.

A number of factors may have influenced the findings. With the five-year sampling increments, the data are subject to world events that may drive leading NGOs—and human rights topics more generally—into and out of the news cycle. It may be, for example, that the moderate drop in human rights coverage from 2005 to 2010 reflects a heavy focus on Iraq at the beginning of that period and on the financial crisis at the end of it. By calculating NGO prevalence as a percentage of all human rights articles, the findings can claim with some confidence that prevalence has increased. Whether the overall prevalence of human rights discourses is on the decline—as some have suggested (e.g., Keys 2014)—requires further research.

Prominence data find that NGOs tend to be mentioned later in news articles over time. In their place, unaffiliated individuals increasingly occupy prominent positions. Theoretically, this finding is in keeping with scholarship that notes the rise of narrative forms of journalism that emphasize unique individual experiences as a way to tell complex stories (Benson 2013). This trend seems especially likely in human rights coverage, which centers to a large degree on the suffering of individuals—and increasingly on the individuals in the Global North who donate to these causes (Chouliaraki 2013; Dogra 2012; Orgad and Seu 2014). Some scholarship suggests, however, that NGOs play a key role in connecting reporters with individuals on the ground who can dramatize events (Cottle and Nolan 2007; Powers 2013; Reese 2015). If this is the case, data on the growing prominence of unaffiliated individuals in the news might partially obscure the role NGOs have in their being there. Furthermore, scholarship also suggests that advocacy groups are more successful in framing their messages visually than textually, where sourcing remains "strongly statist" in orientation (Wozniak, Wessler, and Lück 2016). By restricting the analysis to textual frames, these data possibly overstate the extent to which NGO messages are subordinated to indexing dynamics.

Making the news is itself no small feat for NGOs. Mainstream news access allows humanitarian and human rights groups to push civil society demands that often stand at odds with the wishes of the powerful. Moreover, governments are themselves often divided; NGOs can amplify these divisions and in doing so introduce their advocacy aims. Yet these actions occur within the standard norms of news construction; they do not alter them in any significant manner.

In sum, this chapter shows how long-held news norms shape the reception of NGO news-making efforts. Yet what happens when these groups shift to online tools that, at least in principle, provide them with an opportunity to bypass legacy news outlets and to target audiences directly?

CHAPTER FOUR

The Strategic Advocate
in the Digital Storm

For the latter part of the twentieth century, NGOs interested in publicity had one primary forum in which to pursue that aim: the mass media. As I showed in the preceding chapter, coverage in that medium, although increasing over time, remains elusive. More importantly, how humanitarian and human rights groups appear in the news continues to reflect journalistic norms of indexing, which tend to subordinate advocacy groups to the statements of political officials. Today, digital tools provide these organizations with alternative points of entry into the public sphere. Websites, for example, allow them to push information out to diverse audiences, and social media platforms provide new formats in which they can interact with various stakeholders. How and in what ways do these groups use digital technologies in their publicity efforts?[1] That is the core question I pursue in this chapter.

To date, scholars have offered opposing answers to this question. Some see digital tools as ushering in a new era of direct-to-public communication: no longer strictly dependent on the mass media for publicity, NGOs are imagined to use digital tools in ways that creatively engage stakeholders and potentially constitute new forms of global citizenship (Bennett and Mannheim 2006; Chadwick 2013; Russell 2016; Smith 2010). Others take the opposite view. According to them, NGOs' online efforts mostly replicate mainstream news norms (Cottle and

Nolan 2007; Fenton 2010; Sommerfeldt, Kent, and Taylor 2012). Rather than use digital tools to bypass the news media, such groups take on the function of journalists. In providing information that more or less mimics the materials mainstream reporters would produce, this development threatens to dilute advocacy agendas and turn NGOs into a proxy for—rather than a genuine source of—public engagement (Lang 2013; Naudé, Froneman, and Atwood 2004).

Drawing on observations and interviews at leading NGOs, this chapter complicates both of these claims and in doing so contributes to a growing literature that analyzes the organizational imperatives shaping technological adoption (Briones et al. 2011; Dogra 2012; Orgad 2013; Waisbord 2011). In contrast to arguments about a new era of direct-to-public global communication, it finds that NGOs use digital tools primarily to capture the attention of journalists and only secondarily to communicate with their supporters. Moreover, the very visibility afforded to advocacy groups in the online environment also enables politically motivated critics to launch public criticisms that aim to delegitimize NGOs as credible sources of information. This criticism leads humanitarian and human rights groups in turn to be cautious about utilizing some of the web's more interactive features. The result is that leading humanitarian and human rights groups minimize public engagement and instead utilize highly strategic forms of information management.

Yet although NGO publicity strategies frustrate the expectations of a new era of public communication, they also complicate the view that online efforts dilute their advocacy aims. These groups see online news as chaotic and thus to a certain degree permeable: they monitor the news with the hopes of grafting their advocacy reporting and action recommendations onto news flows. Their overall rate of success in getting these messages picked up is relatively low, but they are sometimes able to insert their advocacy agenda into the mainstream news. The result is that their highly strategic efforts help to diversify the news agenda by adding advocacy frames to extant news coverage.

On the whole, this chapter suggests that the online efforts made by humanitarian and human rights groups are neither as transformative as some hope nor as regressive as others worry. Their publicity strategies instead primarily reflect their pragmatic calculation about how best to maximize positive publicity while minimizing the potential for negative coverage. The chapter's title signals this pragmatism. At times, this pragmatic orientation helps to expand news coverage of issues to include humanitarian and human rights angles. At other times, it makes organizations cautious—sometimes overly so—about protecting their brand. In both instances, technological opportunities and the changing media environment create the context that shapes NGO actions, even as these groups seek to exert influence on the larger news environment in which they are embedded. The result is an online effort that in some ways diversifies news even while in other ways it reinforces the status quo.

NGO PUBLICITY ONLINE: BRINGING THE ORGANIZATION BACK IN

To date, scholarship examining the online publicity efforts of NGOs has largely advanced a set of opposing views. One school of thought holds that new information technologies make possible a new era of advocacy-driven communication. No longer bound by the conventions of the mainstream news media, advocacy groups can utilize digital tools to directly target relevant stakeholders (see, e.g., Bennett and Mannheim 2006; Dean, Anderson, and Lovink 2004; Hiebert 2005; Russell 2016). In this model, NGOs no longer wait for journalists to pick up their press releases. They instead use email lists, online websites, and social media feeds to target their information to stakeholders directly. Lance Bennett's influential statement on this development nicely captures the way in which digital tools help to reorient the relationship between advocates and the news media: according to him, digital technologies "offer activists an important degree of information and communication independence from the mass media" (2003, 151).

Several studies lend empirical support to the view that NGOs are enjoying a new era of advocacy-driven communication. Adrienne Russell, for example, finds that such groups are "becoming more interested in and better at making media and producing news outlets of their own, serving up do-it-yourself news to supporters and millions of potential followers" (2016, 35–36; see also Greenberg, Knight, and Westersund 2011). In fact, and in a twist that reverses the traditional dependence of NGOs on the news media, the coverage provided by advocacy groups is so exhaustive that many news organizations simply direct readers to it techniques to garner attention—using, for instance, dramatic stunts involving media actions—they also sought to reshape the debate once they received attention (e.g., by stressing the more conventional aspects of their organizations, including their affiliation with other advocacy groups) (1992, 702). A comparable dynamic is at work with humanitarian and human rights groups. NGOs do adapt their online publicity efforts to the mainstream media's requirements and preferences. However, they do so with the aim of inserting advocacy reporting into news flows. This adaptation reflects a pragmatic orientation: NGOs see mainstream media attention as necessary for the fulfillment of their organizational objectives, and they use digital tools to maximize their positive publicity while minimizing negative effects. This approach downplays the potentially interactive aspects of digital technologies even as it seeks to diversify the news agenda.

These concepts—legitimacy and strategic action—help to situate the findings about humanitarian and human rights groups' online publicity efforts. By providing organizational and institutional context, they shed light on how advocacy groups utilize digital technologies. These concepts do not, however, explain why NGOs pursue the types of news-making strategies they do. That is a task that I take up in the following chapter. In this chapter, I contribute to scholarly discussions about the way advocacy groups are and are not using digital technologies. Such an analysis, I suggest, can complicate the claims offered by both sides in the current debate and in doing so provide the groundwork for a more finely tuned analysis of the different ways that international NGOs' communication strategies are evolving in the digital world today.

THE STRATEGIC ADVOCATE IN THE DIGITAL STORM

In principle, as detailed earlier in this chapter, the online environment offers humanitarian and human rights groups a range of ways to pursue publicity. In practice, these groups' online efforts rely heavily on both the news agenda and the organizing values of the mainstream media. Communication professionals, including those working exclusively in the online domain, structure their days in large part around monitoring the flow of popular stories in the hopes of getting their messages into the news. Moreover, because of their need to promote and protect

for more complete coverage of the events. Ella McPherson (2015) has explored how human rights groups use social media tools to verify information circulating in the midst of human rights crises. In these and related examples, scholars argue that NGOs use new technologies to put issues on the public agenda that the mainstream media otherwise ignore (see, e.g., Aday and Livingston 2009; Reese 2015; Smith 2010).

Scholars in this vein also suggest that digital tools, in addition to affording NGOs with increased independence from the media, may help deepen the engagement between advocacy organizations and citizens. In contrast to a previous era of "checkbook activism," today's advocacy groups can use information technologies to interact with—and potentially learn from—their constituencies. Dave Karpf (2016), for example, calls attention to the way advocacy groups routinely test their messaging strategies to find the issues and frames that appeal to the broadest swath of citizens. Lance Bennett and Alexandra Segerberg (2013) highlight a number of ways in which advocacy groups can deploy "personalized action frames" in order to boost public interest on a specific issue. NGOs are imagined to be key actors in these efforts because they provide the organizational backbone by combining problem definitions with flexible modes of civic action. Finally, a host of studies points to instances where advocacy groups utilize blogs, websites, and social media feeds to interact with citizens on issues of public importance (Castells 2009; Chadwick 2013; Wells 2015).[2] Scholarship along these lines suggests that digital tools enhance public engagement and to varying degrees enable NGOs to be less dependent on the news media.

A second school of thought is far less optimistic about the capacity of information technologies to usher in a new era of advocacy-driven communication. Although the scholars in this school agree that new technologies create the potential for new patterns of NGO communication, they argue that actual patterns of use tell a different tale: advocacy groups are in fact becoming *more* reliant on the mainstream media rather than bypassing them. The dizzying amount of information available online makes it difficult for users to locate the messages of advocacy groups (Seo, Kim, and Yang 2009; Thrall, Stecula, and Sweet 2014). Therefore, such groups seek to attract the attention of mainstream media outlets (Cottle and Nolan 2007; Fenton 2010; Waisbord 2008a, 2011). To garner media interest, NGOs are said to adapt to the norms of the news media: personalizing and sensationalizing news coverage, overhyping and distorting the issues they care about, and engaging in celebrity-driven publicity strategies (Chouliaraki 2007). The adoption of these "media logics" (Cottle and Nolan 2007) threatens to dilute advocacy agendas by making NGOs "no different to [other] elite sources of information" (Fenton 2010, 167). Simon Cottle and David Nolan put the case even more starkly: how NGOs pursue online media coverage, they write, "practically detract[s] from their principal remit . . . and symbolically fragment[s] the historically founded ethic of universal humanitarianism" (2007, 863–864).

Scholars in this second vein of thought also worry that NGOs' online efforts, in addition to adapting to news norms, do little to boost public engagement. Because advocacy groups rely on media and political elites for legitimacy, they exhibit a tendency to orient their communication practices toward these entities. In Sabine Lang's evocative phrase, this tendency leads organizations to function as "proxy publics" that stand in for rather than discursively engage with diverse constituencies (2013, 8; see Bob 2006 for a related criticism). To the extent that NGOs harness the affordances of online tools, scholars suggest that these affordances will be directed primarily toward enhancing this legitimacy. Accordingly, researchers have documented a range of highly targeted campaigns that seek primarily to engage political elites (Bob 2006; Lang 2013; Powers 2014). This second school of thought expresses doubt about the capacity of digital tools to advance NGOs' advocacy aims, whether the NGOs are adapting to mainstream media norms or targeting political elites directly.

Clearly, NGOs' digital publicity strategies to varying degrees follow both transformative and conservative logics. Yet these divergent perspectives, despite their substantial differences, share a tendency to see external factors as the primary source of continuity or change. In the first school of thought, changes in society (e.g., changing citizenship styles) and technology (e.g., low-cost digital tools) constitute the primary drivers of change. In the second, the demands made by the news media and political elites act as forces of continuity. These perspectives thus offer a rich portrayal of the context in which advocacy groups find themselves operating. However, they are generally less attentive to the specific ways

that organizations seek to balance these varying forces as they pursue publicity online.

In recent years, scholars working across a range of disciplines, often under the banner of new institutionalism, have sought to make organizational analysis a central locus of inquiry. A central tenet of this scholarship is that external changes—whether technological, social, or journalistic—need to be processed by organizations and the institutional fields in which they are embedded (Benson 2013; J. Campbell 2004; Moon 2017; R. Scott 2014; Waisbord 2008b; Wright 2016b). Two key insights from this scholarship are especially useful in exploring the online publicity strategies of humanitarian and human rights groups. The first has to do with the preservation of legitimacy: that is, the perception that an organization's actions are "desirable, proper or appropriate within some socially constructed systems of norms, values, beliefs and definitions" (Suchman 1995, 574). On this view, organizations respond to new developments in part by asking what opportunities and threats these developments present to their reputation. NGOs perceive the digital environment to some degree as a threat. The same tools that allow them to bypass the news media also enable their opponents to attack and challenge their reporting in real time. Thus, NGOs work to preserve their organizational reputation by falling back on some of the strategies that secured their legitimacy in the predigital era (e.g., on-the-ground reporting, often based on months of research). Because these strategies require time and resources, they are often out of sync with the news cycle. I suggest that this seemingly irrational behavior—that is, an organization's apparent failure to utilize digital tools to engage with the public—is better understood as an effort to preserve and protect the organization's reputation.

A second insight from the literature on organizations has to do with strategic action. Even though reputational concerns constrain behavior, organizations respond to constraints strategically in order to turn them to their advantage. For example, advocacy groups may find it necessary to adapt their publicity materials to journalists' expectations, but they may also seek to manipulate the news in their favor. In their work on the media strategies of Earth First! and ACT UP, Kimberly Elsbach and Robert Sutton found that although both groups employed media-friendly their organizational brands, these groups are cautious about embracing some of the web's more interactive features. And yet, as I show, these efforts have a reflexive character: NGOs have clear advocacy aims in mind as they pragmatically use digital tools—to graft advocacy angles onto news coverage so as to diversify news coverage. At least sometimes, these efforts are successful.

Humanitarian and human rights groups use digital tools to pursue publicity in three interrelated ways: first, to monitor news and mimic news norms; second, to promote and protect their organizational brands; and third, to graft humanitarian and human rights frames onto existing news coverage. Each way reflects the strategic and pragmatic calculations of organizations seeking to maximize their positive publicity while minimizing the potential for negative coverage of their work. Together, these ways depict the double-edged sword of NGO communication as it pertains to digital communication by showing, as noted earlier, that NGOs' efforts are neither as transformative as some would hope nor as regressive as others contend.

Monitoring News, Mimicking News Norms

"We're constantly following tweets, trying to see what reporters are thinking, where they're going, what stories they're covering, what they're planning, if they're planning any specials where we might be able to get in ahead of time."[3] This was how a media officer at the International Crisis Group responded to a question about how her group utilizes digital tools. Her response was typical: at most NGOs, professionals described using digital tools to follow news coverage and to create online materials that can be linked up with and integrated into the day's news. In none of these efforts is the mainstream media bypassed or neglected; in fact, news in the mainstream media is actively monitored so that an organization's coverage in the media can be more effectively pursued. Although NGOs do sometimes use digital tools to directly target relevant stakeholders, they often tie those efforts to issues or themes already circulating in the mainstream news.

The importance of the mainstream news agenda was made clear to me during my attendance of organizational meetings. In those daily encounters, communication professionals—including those working exclusively in online units—gather to discuss their strategies for publicizing their organization's efforts. At Amnesty International's UK section, for example, these meetings are typically structured in five parts:[4] the first details whether there were any overnight calls or emergencies (one staff person is on call throughout the night); the second part reviews any mentions of Amnesty International in print or broadcast media, which blends into the third part of the meeting, a conversation about hot or trending news topics; the fourth part identifies what the organization's blog post for the day should be and what else the organization should do online; and in the fifth part, the meeting concludes with everyone providing an overview of his or her activities for the day. In short, public communication is still structured primarily around the news media's agenda, and garnering coverage in the mainstream media is still seen as a primary aim, even for those working exclusively in the online domain.

The news meeting is one instance of a larger effort by NGOs to orient their practices and information products in accordance with the needs and requirements of the news media.[5] Stories that are published online are often made to mimic the style of wire-service agencies. As one person put it, "We consciously ape the styles of media in our communication in order that what we produce looks like journalism. . . . [Our news releases] are meant to look like a wire story, so that when it appears in the inbox of a journalist . . . it moves seamlessly through the media" (Bogert 2012). Another person cautioned against seeing the use of digital tools as anything other than traditional public-relations work. "Sometimes journalists may pick it [our press release] up through a blog or through Twitter and not our traditional press office. But that doesn't mean that it's not really just a press release. It just means it's a really well-written press release with lots of cool multimedia stuff attached to it."[6] A third described tracking keywords and select news organizations so that she could craft messages that would increase her organization's chances of garnering favorable news coverage. "My goal was not necessarily knowing every little thing going on in the world, but I wanted CARE to be a resource for journalists."[7]

In order to adapt their materials to mainstream media norms, advocacy groups turn to journalists for assistance in at least three basic ways. First, many advocacy groups hire journalists to help them develop their digital content in ways that will satisfy news media norms. Nearly for more complete coverage of the events. Ella McPherson (2015) has explored how human rights groups use social media tools to verify information circulating in the midst of human rights crises. In these and related examples, scholars argue that NGOs use new technologies to put issues on the public agenda that the mainstream media otherwise ignore (see, e.g., Aday and Livingston 2009; Reese 2015; Smith 2010).

Scholars in this vein also suggest that digital tools, in addition to affording NGOs with increased independence from the media, may help deepen the engagement between advocacy organizations and citizens. In contrast to a previous era of "checkbook activism," today's advocacy groups can use information technologies to interact with—and potentially learn from—their constituencies. Dave Karpf (2016), for example, calls attention to the way advocacy groups routinely test their messaging strategies to find the issues and frames that appeal to the broadest swath of citizens. Lance Bennett and Alexandra Segerberg (2013) highlight a number of ways in which advocacy groups can deploy "personalized action frames" in order to boost public interest on a specific issue. NGOs are imagined to be key actors in these efforts because they provide the organizational backbone by combining problem definitions with flexible modes of civic action. Finally, a host of studies points to instances where advocacy groups utilize blogs, websites, and social media feeds to interact with citizens on issues of public importance (Castells 2009; Chadwick 2013; Wells 2015).[2] Scholarship along these lines suggests that digital tools enhance public engagement and to varying degrees enable NGOs to be less dependent on the news media.

A second school of thought is far less optimistic about the capacity of information technologies to usher in a new era of advocacy-driven communication. Although the scholars in this school agree that new technologies create the potential for new patterns of NGO communication, they argue that actual patterns of use tell a different tale: advocacy groups are in fact becoming *more* reliant on the mainstream media rather than bypassing them. The dizzying amount of information available online makes it difficult for users to locate the messages of advocacy groups (Seo, Kim, and Yang 2009; Thrall, Stecula, and Sweet 2014). Therefore, such groups seek to attract the attention of mainstream media outlets (Cottle and Nolan 2007; Fenton 2010; Waisbord 2008a, 2011). To garner media interest, NGOs are said to adapt to the norms of the news media: personalizing and sensationalizing news coverage, overhyping and distorting the issues they care about, and engaging in celebrity-driven publicity strategies (Chouliaraki 2007). The adoption of these "media logics" (Cottle and Nolan 2007) threatens to dilute advocacy agendas by making NGOs "no different to [other] elite sources of information" (Fenton 2010, 167). Simon Cottle and David Nolan put the case even more starkly: how NGOs pursue online media coverage, they write, "practically detract[s] from their principal remit . . . and symbolically fragment[s] the historically founded ethic of universal humanitarianism" (2007, 863–864).

Scholars in this second vein of thought also worry that NGOs' online efforts, in addition to adapting to news norms, do little to boost public engagement. Because advocacy groups rely on media and political elites for legitimacy, they exhibit a tendency to orient their communication practices toward these entities. In Sabine Lang's evocative phrase, this tendency leads organizations to function as "proxy publics" that stand in for rather than discursively engage with diverse constituencies (2013, 8; see Bob 2006 for a related criticism). To the extent that NGOs harness the affordances of online tools, scholars suggest that these affordances will be directed primarily toward enhancing this legitimacy. Accordingly, researchers have documented a range of highly targeted campaigns that seek primarily to engage political elites (Bob 2006; Lang 2013; Powers 2014). This second school of thought expresses doubt about the capacity of digital tools to advance NGOs' advocacy aims, whether the NGOs are adapting to mainstream media norms or targeting political elites directly.

Clearly, NGOs' digital publicity strategies to varying degrees follow both transformative and conservative logics. Yet these divergent perspectives, despite their substantial differences, share a tendency to see external factors as the primary source of continuity or change. In the first school of thought, changes in society (e.g., changing citizenship styles) and technology (e.g., low-cost digital tools) constitute the primary drivers of change. In the second, the demands made by the news media and political elites act as forces of continuity. These perspectives thus offer a rich portrayal of the context in which advocacy groups find themselves operating. However, they are generally less attentive to the specific ways that organizations seek to balance these varying forces as they pursue publicity online.

In recent years, scholars working across a range of disciplines, often under the banner of new institutionalism, have sought to make organizational analysis a central locus of inquiry. A central tenet of this scholarship is that external changes—whether technological, social, or journalistic—need to be processed by organizations and the institutional fields in which they are embedded (Benson 2013; J. Campbell 2004; Moon 2017; R. Scott 2014; Waisbord 2008b; Wright 2016b). Two key insights from this scholarship are especially useful in exploring the online publicity strategies of humanitarian and human rights groups. The first has to do with the preservation of legitimacy: that is, the perception that an organization's actions are "desirable, proper or appropriate within some socially constructed systems of norms, values, beliefs and definitions" (Suchman 1995, 574). On this view, organizations respond to new developments in part by asking what opportunities and threats these developments present to their reputation. NGOs perceive the digital environment to some degree as a threat. The same tools that allow them to bypass the news media also enable their opponents to attack and challenge their reporting in real time. Thus, NGOs work to preserve their organizational reputation by falling back on some of the strategies that secured their legitimacy in the predigital era (e.g., on-the-ground reporting, often based on months of research). Because these strategies require time and resources, they are often out of sync with the news cycle. I suggest that this seemingly irrational behavior—that is, an organization's apparent failure to utilize digital tools to engage with the public—is better understood as an effort to preserve and protect the organization's reputation.

A second insight from the literature on organizations has to do with strategic action. Even though reputational concerns constrain behavior, organizations respond to constraints strategically in order to turn them to their advantage. For example, advocacy groups may find it necessary to adapt their publicity materials to journalists' expectations, but they may also seek to manipulate the news in their favor. In their work on the media strategies of Earth First! and ACT UP, Kimberly Elsbach and Robert Sutton found that although both groups employed media-friendly techniques to garner attention—using, for instance, dramatic stunts involving media actions—they also sought to reshape the debate once they received attention (e.g., by stressing the more conventional aspects of their organizations, including their affiliation with other advocacy groups) (1992, 702). A comparable dynamic is at work with humanitarian and human rights groups. NGOs do adapt their online publicity efforts to the mainstream media's requirements and preferences. However, they do so with the aim of inserting advocacy reporting into news flows. This adaptation reflects a pragmatic orientation: NGOs see mainstream media attention as necessary for the fulfillment of their organizational objectives, and they use digital tools to maximize their positive publicity while minimizing negative effects. This approach downplays the potentially interactive aspects of digital technologies even as it seeks to diversify the news agenda.

These concepts—legitimacy and strategic action—help to situate the findings about humanitarian and human rights groups' online publicity efforts. By providing organizational and institutional context, they shed light on how advocacy groups utilize digital technologies. These concepts do not, however, explain why NGOs pursue the types of news-making strategies they do. That is a task that I take up in the following chapter. In this chapter, I contribute to scholarly discussions about the way advocacy groups are and are not using digital technologies. Such an analysis, I suggest, can complicate the claims offered by both sides in the current debate and in doing so provide the groundwork for a more finely tuned analysis of the different ways that international NGOs' communication strategies are evolving in the digital world today.

THE STRATEGIC ADVOCATE IN THE DIGITAL STORM

In principle, as detailed earlier in this chapter, the online environment offers humanitarian and human rights groups a range of ways to pursue publicity. In practice, these groups' online efforts rely heavily on both the news agenda and the organizing values of the mainstream media. Communication professionals, including those working exclusively in the online domain, structure their days in large part around monitoring the flow of popular stories in the hopes of getting their messages into the news. Moreover, because of their need to promote and protect their organizational brands, these groups are cautious about embracing some of the web's more interactive features. And yet, as I show, these efforts have a reflexive character: NGOs have clear advocacy aims in mind as they pragmatically use digital tools—to graft advocacy angles onto news coverage so as to diversify news coverage. At least sometimes, these efforts are successful.

Humanitarian and human rights groups use digital tools to pursue publicity in three interrelated ways: first, to monitor news and mimic news norms; second, to promote and protect their organizational brands; and third, to graft humanitarian and human rights frames onto existing news coverage. Each way reflects the strategic and pragmatic calculations of organizations seeking to maximize their positive publicity while minimizing the potential for negative coverage of their work. Together, these ways depict the double-edged sword of NGO communication as it pertains to digital communication by showing, as noted earlier, that NGOs' efforts are neither as transformative as some would hope nor as regressive as others contend.

Monitoring News, Mimicking News Norms

"We're constantly following tweets, trying to see what reporters are thinking, where they're going, what stories they're covering, what they're planning, if they're planning any specials where we might be able to get in ahead of time."[3] This was how a media officer at the International Crisis Group responded to a question about how her group utilizes digital tools. Her response was typical: at most NGOs, professionals described using digital tools to follow news coverage and to create online materials that can be linked up with and integrated into the day's news. In none of these efforts is the mainstream media bypassed or neglected; in fact, news in the mainstream media is actively monitored so that an organization's coverage in the media can be more effectively pursued. Although NGOs do sometimes use digital tools to directly target relevant stakeholders, they often tie those efforts to issues or themes already circulating in the mainstream news.

The importance of the mainstream news agenda was made clear to me during my attendance of organizational meetings. In those daily encounters, communication professionals—including those working exclusively in online units—gather to discuss their strategies for publicizing their organization's efforts. At Amnesty International's UK section, for example, these meetings are typically structured in five parts:[4] the first details whether there were any overnight calls or emergencies (one staff person is on call throughout the night); the second part reviews any mentions of Amnesty International in print or broadcast media, which blends into the third part of the meeting, a conversation about hot or trending news topics; the fourth part identifies what the organization's blog post for the day should be and what else the organization should do online; and in the fifth part, the meeting concludes with everyone providing an overview of his or her activities for the day. In short, public communication is still structured primarily around the news media's agenda, and garnering coverage in the mainstream media is still seen as a primary aim, even for those working exclusively in the online domain.

The news meeting is one instance of a larger effort by NGOs to orient their practices and information products in accordance with the needs and requirements of the news media.[5] Stories that are published online are often made to mimic the style of wire-service agencies. As one person put it, "We consciously ape the styles of media in our communication in order that what we produce looks like journalism. . . . [Our news releases] are meant to look like a wire story, so that when it appears in the inbox of a journalist . . . it moves seamlessly through the media" (Bogert 2012). Another person cautioned against seeing the use of digital tools as anything other than traditional public-relations work. "Sometimes journalists may pick it [our press release] up through a blog or through Twitter and not our traditional press office. But that doesn't mean that it's not really just a press release. It just means it's a really well-written press release with lots of cool multimedia stuff attached to it."[6] A third described tracking keywords and select news organizations so that she could craft messages that would increase her organization's chances of garnering favorable news coverage. "My goal was not necessarily knowing every little thing going on in the world, but I wanted CARE to be a resource for journalists."[7]

In order to adapt their materials to mainstream media norms, advocacy groups turn to journalists for assistance in at least three basic ways. First, many advocacy groups hire journalists to help them develop their digital content in ways that will satisfy news media norms. Nearly every organization discussed in this study has in the past several years hired a person with a recent background in journalism—that is, who has worked for a legacy news organization—to help with the development of its digital-content efforts. Second, advocacy groups hire journalists on a freelance basis. Sometimes these interactions are with prominent photojournalists, who provide the symbolic capital that NGOs hope will boost the visibility of their efforts. The efforts by Human Rights Watch detailed in chapter 1 highlight one important manifestation of this development. At other times, these interactions are with less-well-known freelance journalists, who provide the know-how and the social networks necessary to boost the advocacy group's digital news-making chances (Wright 2016b).

Third, NGOs learn to adapt their messages through regular online interactions between NGO professionals and journalists. A longtime professional at Human Rights Watch, for example, moderates a closed Facebook group, the Vulture Club (Murrell 2014). The group comprises several thousand journalists and human rights professionals, and they interact in order to arrange ground transportation, translation, and related reporting needs. As the founder of the Vulture Club writes, "We're in contact . . . with each other" (quoted in Murrell 2014, 18). Such groups have been criticized as fostering overly cozy relationships between NGO professionals and journalists,[8] but, regardless of one's evaluation of such relationships, it is clear that this type of semiregular contact helps to make NGOs aware of the types of things that journalists are interested in.

Although digital tools—podcasts, email lists, multimedia slideshows, interactive maps, and so forth—can theoretically be used to bypass the mainstream news media, in practice I found them utilized mostly in efforts to garner those media's attention. At several organizations, NGO professionals described their use of podcasts as an effective way to provide news outlets with background to the issues on which the outlets are working. Others noted that news outlets can readily pick up NGOs' online products such as interactive maps, thus boosting an advocacy group's chances of garnering media attention.[9]

All organizations have an active social media presence, which fulfills a variety of organizational needs. Those working in the marketing department stress the importance of such tools for donor cultivation. "I'm a fund-raiser," said one person at CARE. "Everything I do around social media is [geared] toward the goal of turning people into donors."[10] Others described this social media presence as a tool to communicate with supporters: "It is the best way for CARE to engage our audience regularly. I want people to see what we're doing, what the success stories are, what the challenges are, outside the context of fund-raising."[11] Researchers and advocacy officers explained how they use social media to produce a partial public record of their efforts. One person working in South Africa on intellectual property and AIDS drugs remarked that she posts the comments made by officials at meetings she attends. "It's a way to keep a record and hold people accountable later on."[12] Still others described using social media to interact with other NGO professionals and journalists.

Most NGO professionals stressed the underlying importance of being part of the public discussion. Social media, they informed me, is useful as a way to get the pulse of the news, to try out new angles, and to see what sticks. Mostly, though, it is another way to seek out news coverage. As one person put it, "We tweet several times a day. We should probably be doing it more. Other organizations are doing the same. And what remains to be seen is how much of an impact it is having. It's a great dissemination tool, but whether or not it leads to what we wish to see— which is coverage of Amnesty in traditional and new media—that remains to be seen."[13]

Promoting and Protecting the Organizational Brand

NGOs are not just in the business of providing information; they are also selling a product—their organizational brands (Benthall 1993). The extraordinary growth of the humanitarian and human rights sector has helped to create what Clifford Bob terms a "market for loyalties" (2006, 14–53). In this market, organizations compete intensely to secure funds and other forms of public support (Cottle and Nolan 2007). In interviews, many professionals noted that the need to promote and protect the organization's brand shapes—and in important ways limits—their organizations' use of digital tools. In particular, respondents suggested that the need to promote and protect the organizational brand makes them cautious about embracing some of the web's more interactive features. They reported that rather than use digital tools to boost public engagement, they use them primarily to disseminate information that promotes their organizational agendas. Moreover, the very way in which NGOs seek to protect their organization relies on earlier "predigital" patterns of image management (e.g., lengthy fact-checking processes that make it difficult to respond in real time to the need for human rights information). Rather than adapt to the speed and nature of online visibility, many organizations dedicate time and resources to conserving their organizational reputation. Both processes lead to online strategies that frustrate optimistic expectations about deeper forms of public engagement.

In their everyday work, communication staffers spend a great deal of time communicating *to* the public but proportionally less time communicating *with* that public. Advocacy groups' online websites mostly provide informational accounts about the work the organization is doing.[14] A longtime media officer at Oxfam, for example, explained that most issues of his online newsletter simply seek to tell donors about what the organization is doing. He wants supporters to read, "Hey, I'm sure you've heard of what's going on in Colombia or Pakistan or Haiti, and here is what we're doing about it. And thanks again for supporting [what we're doing]."[15] This informational orientation is prevalent even in social media tools that allow for direct interaction with the public. At CARE, one person described the organization's aim in using social media in the following terms: "I want audiences to see CARE post about child marriage and some of the programs we have to address it. And with the same frequency that they're only getting news updates from their local newspapers."[16] In other words, these organizations see their social media as functioning more or less like a news organization by pushing out information to supporters.

NGOs pursue this informational strategy for multiple reasons.[17] As several people explained to me, "getting the message out" is a top priority. One person stated, "There are lots of organizations people can support, and we recognize that. . . . [So] we try to make sure people know who we are and what we do."[18] Moreover, journalists encourage organizations to constantly provide information to the news outlets. "If we don't put a press release out," one Amnesty press officer explained to me, "then people think there are some politics behind [that decision]. And they will not buy it if we say that the press office did not think [the event in question] was newsworthy."[19] The press officer noted that this claim intensifies in an online environment, where journalists expect the organization's website to constantly include press releases pertaining to the latest news.

Conversely, there is much less urgency in finding ways to engage with people online. For example, one day in conversation with a press officer at Médecins Sans Frontières, I learned about the various ways the group uses social media to pursue journalists and to push out information about some of the group's advocacy work. After pointing out that many of the people who follow the organization are not journalists, I asked what the organization wants from those people. She hesitated and then responded: "We should probably do something with those people, but I'm not sure what."[20] This response was fairly common across all organizations: beyond branding their organization to audiences, groups were often unclear about what other potential ways public engagement by means of digital tools could be used to further their advocacy agendas.

In contrast, nearly everyone had stories about ways that public interactions could potentially be harmful to NGOs. In a world where anyone can monitor their work, advocacy groups not only circulate their information quickly but also find that information called into question by opponents and detractors. Perhaps the starkest example comes from a situation Human Rights Watch found itself in during the war between Israel and Lebanon in 2006. Although this event occurred prior to my research, multiple respondents—from several organizations—discussed it in interviews to describe some of the problems advocacy groups have in adapting their publicity strategies to the online environment. It thus illustrates a larger dynamic that NGOs face online as they seek to promote their brand while protecting their credibility.

On July 23, 2006, Israeli drones struck two clearly marked Red Cross ambulances. When the strike hit, the ambulance crews were carrying wounded civilians from one ambulance to the other. The Red Cross workers were injured during the attack, and three of the civilians suffered additional injuries. One man lost his leg as a result of the strike on the ambulances, and his elderly mother was left partially paralyzed (Human Rights Watch 2006a). Researchers from Human Rights Watch immediately launched an investigation into the events.

The ambulance attack formed one piece of a report Human Rights

Watch released on August 3, 2006. Titled *Fatal Strikes*, it documented violations of international humanitarian law by the Israeli Defense Forces. According to the report, the Israeli military had killed an estimated four hundred people during the war, the vast majority of them civilians. Drawing on interviews and on-the-ground research, the report concluded: "Israeli forces have consistently launched targeted artillery and air attacks with dubious military gain but excessive civilian cost" (Human Rights Watch 2006a, 3). The attack on the ambulances was one of twenty-three documented incidents in the forty-nine-page report. With respect to the ambulance attack, the report noted: "Making medical or religious personnel, medical units or medical transports the object of attack is a war crime" (41).

Upon the report's publication, a small but vocal group of unnamed online commentators questioned its veracity. Specifically, they claimed that the ambulance attack could not have happened as described. One person argued that it could not have happened on July 23 because photographs showed evidence of rust on an ambulance roof where shrapnel had scraped away the paint—rust that should have taken months to develop "in dry climates such as Lebanon in the summer." Another suggested that the missile could not have left a man without a leg because the photographs showed the gurney inside the ambulance to be undamaged.[21] In relatively short order, the accusations made their way into the mainstream media, where government officials saw it. Within weeks of the report being published, Australia's foreign minister was quoted as saying that "it is beyond serious dispute that this episode has all the makings of a hoax" (Schubert 2006).

Human Rights Watch had to take these accusations seriously because its legitimacy is premised upon an assumption that the information it circulates is accurate. As John Thompson (2000) has shown with respect to political scandals, credibility is a symbolic resource at stake in struggles over an individual's or organization's reputation and in the trust the public can maintain in that individual or organization.[22] To protect its credibility, Human Rights Watch sent its research team back to the scene to reexamine the events. The team conducted interviews with the ambulance workers and Red Cross supervisors involved in responding to the incident as well as eyewitnesses; they visited the ambulances to find physical evidence that could confirm or negate claims of what happened;

and they reviewed the records of local Red Cross offices to track the movement of the ambulances prior to the evening of July 23. The research and writing required to respond to the accusations took months.

In December 2006, Human Rights Watch published its findings, entitled *The "Hoax" That Wasn't: The July 23 Qana Ambulance Attack* (Human Rights Watch 2006b). The report provided detailed evidence refuting the critical claims against its prior reporting. In response to the assertion that someone had removed the ambulance's air vent, the researchers "recovered the air vent, which showed it to have been penetrated by a missile" (21). They also located the exit point of the missile from the ambulance floor. They debunked claims that the attack could not have occurred on July 23 because rust does not form that quickly by pointing out that coastal Lebanon is an extremely humid place, not a dry climate. Finally, they showed that claims of an undamaged gurney were false: the bloggers had looked at photographs of the wrong ambulance. "In conclusion," the report stated, "there was no hoax. All of the available evidence shows that the Israeli attack . . . took place as reported" (24).

Although it was crucial for Human Rights Watch to respond to these allegations, it was also costly and time-consuming. Moreover, the allegations were made possible only because of digital media, such as blogs, yet the method of responding to the criticisms was, as one person put it, "predigital": the response was accurate, but it took months to report. How could the organization maintain its credibility more quickly in the face of such attacks in the future?

Complicating matters is the fact that NGOs have in recent years unintentionally circulated inaccurate information as a result of using digital technologies to augment their reporting. This problem is not a wholly new one. The need for publicity (to raise funds, to boost the organizational profile) sometimes creates "dueling incentives" between accurate reporting and organizational objectives (Cohen and Green 2012). Digital tools intensify this mix: in chapter 2, for example, I described a case in which Amnesty International and Human Rights Watch incorrectly claimed that an eighteen-year-old Syrian woman was beheaded by the Syrian government. NGO professionals discussed this case as a cautionary tale about how digital tools and a constant media cycle create incentives for publishing items that may threaten the organizational brand in the long run.

Cases like this reinforce the idea that NGOs should protect their organizational credibility by using predigital modes of information management (e.g., eyewitness verification and on-the-ground reporting). This predigital approach is seen as both necessary and time-consuming: necessary because negative publicity can threaten an organization's political standing and reduce its capacity to attract donors and time-consuming because an organization has no easy way to rapidly refute allegations. As several people stressed, digital technologies intensify the number of allegations such groups receive, and their preexisting need to promote and protect their organizational brands shapes how they respond to such claims.[23]

In sum, although digital tools make it in principle possible to bypass the news media, in practice advocacy groups utilize them primarily to capture the attention of journalists. The possibility of politically motivated "scandal" often makes these groups conservative in their usage of interactive aspects of these technologies. And yet NGO online publicity strategies are not wholly defensive. They are also characterized by a reflexive effort to insert advocacy recommendations into news coverage.

Grafting the News: Inserting Advocacy Reporting Into News Flows

Although NGO professionals discussed the impediments to utilizing digital technologies, they were also quick to point out that they use these tools with a clear advocacy aim in mind: to graft humanitarian and human rights angles onto news coverage.[24] By "graft," I mean to add advocacy frames onto news stories that nominally—at least in the news media's initial telling—have nothing to do with humanitarian or human rights issues. For example, when Hillary Clinton announced her bid for the presidency in June 2015, the director of Human Rights Watch took to Twitter with a question: "Will Hillary Clinton stop treating Burma as her big victory & start speaking out for Rohingya?" In raising this question about the treatment of ethnic minorities in a country that Clinton traveled to as secretary of state, Human Rights Watch sought to take the hottest issue in the news media that day (Clinton's campaign kickoff) and introduce a new angle to it: namely, human rights violations in Myanmar.

Put simply, a major reason why NGOs dedicate time and resources to monitoring news and mimicking news norms is that they want, as one person pithily put it, "to inject the human rights aspect of a story."[25] Communication professionals at numerous organizations discussed these efforts routinely.[26] At Christian Aid, the head of the news unit told me: "We try where possible to spot stories that we think we can use to promote our message."[27] At Save the Children, a press officer described her use of social media as "my way of following the news . . . so that later we can find ways to get our messages into it."[28] Finally, someone at Oxfam described efforts to graft a human rights angle onto stories about piracy in East Africa, which were trending at the time: "I push my guys to say, like, hey, Somalia, there's this piracy, it's in the news everyday—everyone is talking about these bloody pirates—how can we serve that wave? Because it's page 3 [in the newspaper] everyday now."[29]

Human Rights Watch's use of Clinton's announcement is in many ways exemplary of the broader efforts by NGOs. News organizations did not suddenly cease reporting on Clinton's campaign announcement and refocus their reporting on human rights issues in Myanmar, but the organization's efforts highlight the extent to which news grafting shapes advocacy groups' quotidian publicity strategies—even when such grafting is not successful, as is the case much of the time. In this way, news grafting is somewhat akin to a home run in baseball. Although the overall percentage of hitting a home run is quite low, the overall impact of success stories is large. (It is also worth noting that the cost of failure in grafting is also quite low and that even failures can be accounted for as practice on the part of NGOs that are seeking to develop a sensibility for what does and does not fit into the news agenda.[30])

Sometimes, though, this strategy does work, and it is those successes that reinforce the idea that the overall strategy itself is worth pursuing. An example of successful news grafting can be found in the multipronged campaign launched by several NGOs to draw attention to human rights issues in China in the lead-up to the 2008 Olympics. Opponents criticized the choice of China as the Olympics venue given the Chinese government's human rights record, especially in places such as Tibet, where the government had long subjected thousands of Tibetans to arrest and detention. The lengthy lead-up to the games gave activists an array of opportunities to make the news. As one organizer put it, "Our job was to take the Olympic spotlight and turn it to Tibet" (quoted in Becker 2013, 251). To do this, NGOs developed dramatic media visuals that they hoped would call attention to the issues. In 2007, the Olympic torch began its journey around the world in Greece. At many stops along the way, advocacy groups sought to interrupt the events by drawing attention to human rights issues. As Jo Becker of Human Rights Watch summarizes its work, "Protests were organized by various organizations at many locations, highlighting not only China's occupation of Tibet but also human rights abuses related to Darfur, China's relationship to Myanmar and Zimbabwe, repression against Falun Gong members, and other issues" (2013, 185). In London, activists rappelled down the Westminster Bridge to hang a large banner reading "One World, One Dream: Free Tibet 2008." In Paris, activists hung the same sign over a bridge on the Seine.

Digital tools were important in coordinating and publicizing these efforts. Text-messaging systems and social media platforms made it possible for NGO organizers to track the route of the Olympic torch and therefore to know when to unfurl their banners to achieve maximum visual impact. In San Francisco, so many people signed up for the messages that organizers shut down the torch ceremony for fear of disruption, which led the president of the International Olympic Committee to deem the situation a "crisis" for the games. The activists responsible for hanging the banners brought phones with them during their actions; several gave live interviews while hanging from bridges. Technical support allowed these groups to post their visual feeds directly to news organizations, which in turn displayed them with surprising prominence. The *New York Times* carried a front-page story, and CNN broadcast the story live to its American audience.

Digital tools also helped NGOs sustain and rejuvenate their public efforts. As the Olympic torch journey wound down, activists launched a website, www.AtheleteWanted.org, which offered athletes ways to support the cause (such as shaving one's head as a gesture of solidarity with Tibetan monks or displaying Tibetan flags or symbols). This turned the media spotlight to questions about whether athletes would or even could become part of the protest (the Olympic Charter prohibits demonstrations and propaganda from Olympic venues). The campaign's broader effect was to layer human rights issues onto the news media's coverage of the upcoming games.

As multiple respondents noted, however, tracking the news to insert advocacy reporting into it is a double-edged sword. On the one hand, the strategy represents an attempt to diversify the news: the Olympics, for example, are not intuitively about human rights issues, and no journalist was initially calling Human Rights Watch, Amnesty International, or other groups for comments about the games. But actively following the news allows humanitarian and human rights groups to pluralize the total number of news frames and in doing so to more closely approximate normative ideals of "multiperspectivalism" (Gans 1979). On the other hand, as several respondents noted, the grafting strategy takes the news agenda and its norms largely as given and minimizes the use of digital tools to explore alternative forms of public engagement (Wells 2015). Because humanitarian and human rights groups work on a range of topics that are not popular in the press, focusing on what the press does cover effectively shuns the large number of stories it does not cover. Moreover, any effort to insert advocacy views into news coverage must rely on news norms of timeliness and conflict. Stories that lack those dimensions face a far steeper barrier to publicity.

NGO professionals face these barriers constantly. Press officers described humanitarian issues that were important but lacked novelty and thus were hard to draw attention to. For example, a press officer at Oxfam told me about his frustration with trying to get journalists interested in human rights issues transpiring in the aftermath of an earthquake in Pakistan. "We couldn't bloody well sell anything," he said. "We had great VNR [video news releases], we had great pictures, we had great material—and it was very difficult to get journalists interested." When I asked about the possibility of grafting that issue onto something else in the news, he replied: "Of course I would like to see more stories about humanitarian issues. . . . But at the same time you need to think about the appetite in the American market, in the French market for people reading about misery every day."[31] On this view, the appetite for humanitarian and human rights issues is limited: not every story about a human rights issue can be grafted onto other news topics.[32]

At the same time, there are instances where advocacy groups do find these barriers surmountable. An example comes from Human Rights Watch. In 2014, it sent a research team to investigate political violence in the Central African Republic, a country with both long-standing human rights violations and relatively minimal coverage in the American news media. Human Rights Watch hired the well-known photojournalist Marcus Bleasdale to accompany the research team on its trip. At one point during their trip, the research team attended a ceremony held by the government for the National Army. At the end of the event, soldiers found a Muslim man who they claimed was an opposition fighter and proceeded to lynch him and light his body on fire. The research team rushed to the scene to capture it on camera. As they started recording, a group of soldiers came forward to pose with the body, giving the research team a thumbs-up signal.[33]

The research team posted the video to its YouTube account. One of the researchers also posted images and descriptions of the event to his Twitter account. The images and the posts quickly circulated online. The video quickly garnered three million views, which constituted a third of all views for the entire corpus of videos the organization had posted to the video-sharing site. The researcher's Twitter feed attracted increased attention as well. Before embarking on the research trip, he had approximately three thousand followers. At the end of the trip, that number had risen to twelve thousand (Bogert 2014). In subsequent trips, the research team developed a hashtag to use in its social media posts about the events.

Human Rights Watch's digital efforts caught the news media's attention. Journalists began using the hashtag. As one person involved in the campaign put it, "If you work for the [United Nations], if you work for the French government, if you work for the African Union, if you are a journalist, if you are a humanitarian aid worker, this is the guy that you are following in order to get the news" (Bogert 2014). Christiane Amanpour showed the video on her CNN program and had the researcher as a guest to discuss the events.[34] The *New York Times* embedded many of Human Right Watch's posts in its breaking-news blog, the *Lede*. A Dutch print newspaper, *NRC Handelsblad*, took the researcher's social media posts and republished them verbatim.

As its social media efforts drove mainstream media coverage, Human Rights Watch not only found success in getting a neglected topic discussed but also gained an ability to insert its specific action recommendations into the news. Its posts called for a larger peacekeeping mission from the United Nations; it cautioned about the negative economic effects of ethnic cleansing (the Muslim population have historically been the key traders in the country, especially of livestock); and it called for Western governments to make good on their promise following the Rwandan genocide to "never again" let targeted ethnic killing occur while they stand idly by. Human Rights Watch relied on a mixture of contingency and media savvy to arrive at this place. From a news angle, the research team was "lucky" to happen upon the gruesome killings (in the sense that the team did not plan on it), which made for attractive news copy. At the same time, the group had to have many elements in place in order to cover that event. Most obviously, they had to be there, in the Central African Republic, and with enough knowledge on the ground to know where to go. As one person at Human Rights Watch said, "Christiane Amanpour is not going to send a camera person to the Central African Republic. Just yesterday her producer was in our offices, and she said, 'There is no way we [CNN] can afford to do that.'" It also mattered, the producer went on, who the Human Rights Watch team was there with: "We [CNN] took this video because you had it and because it was shot by this guy named Marcus Bleasdale, who is a very highly regarded photographer and videographer, who CNN knows they can trust" (Bogert 2014).

Grafting the news thus represents a key way in which NGOs seek to insert their advocacy agenda into the news. This way relies primarily on the extant news agenda for cues regarding salient themes, styles, and topics and then seeks to reframe those issues around the ideas in which the advocacy groups are interested. At times, this method enables advocacy groups to get their action recommendations picked up in the news, as Human Rights Watch did in its reporting on the Central African Republic. At other times, these messages are lost in the "noise" that surrounds any media issue. As one person with Oxfam put it, "Our success rate isn't that high, but winning one issue once in a while goes a long way."[35]

Despite expectations of a new era of public communication, this chapter finds that NGOs use digital tools primarily to supplement rather than to challenge the relationship between themselves and legacy news organizations. Communication professionals spend much of their time monitoring the news and mimicking news norms and spend comparatively less time cultivating relationships with real or potential supporters. Drawing on new-institutional theories of legitimacy and strategic action, I suggest that this state of affairs reflects a pragmatic orientation on the part of humanitarian and human rights groups, who see digital tools as both an opportunity and a threat: an opportunity because these tools give them new ways to insert advocacy recommendations into the news and a threat because the very visibility of the Internet exposes these organizations to a growing number of potential media scandals.

In many ways, these findings resonate with those described in chapter 3. Both indicate that NGOs play a growing role in shaping—and in some cases directly producing—news coverage of humanitarian and human rights issues. Both online and off, they are more active and more visible in news coverage today than they were in the past. Yet both chapters also find that these roles continue to be deeply imbricated in the norms and practices of the mainstream news media. Rather than challenge news norms, advocacy groups accept them as given and adapt their efforts accordingly. As most respondents noted, this work is difficult, tenuous, and ongoing. This fact shapes the types of messages that advocacy groups think they can publicize as well as the methods they utilize to raise awareness of those messages.[36] Taken together, the findings of these two chapters portray a growing, if constrained, role for NGOs in the provision of news about humanitarian and human rights issues, one that is neither as transformative as some hope nor as regressive as others worry.

It is possible—perhaps even likely—that NGOs' online strategies will evolve over time and become less focused on mainstream media. Indeed, recent examples suggest that some groups may indeed be experimenting more and more with such strategies. Human Rights Watch's work with well-known photojournalists to report on countries outside the media spotlight suggests that groups may be using some media norms (e.g., professional visuals) to call attention to issues not otherwise on the news agenda. To what extent advocacy groups are capable of using this strategy thus remains an important concern for future inquiry in this research domain. At the same time, the pragmatic and strategic concerns that shape the behavior identified in this chapter are not likely to disappear entirely. Indeed, research by Kate Wright (2016a, 2016b) finds that although human rights organizations are increasingly using freelancers to produce news about underrepresented issues in various African countries, their aim in doing so has as much to do with using freelancers to make the organizations' content appear more newsworthy to news outlets than it might otherwise. In these and related instances, advocacy groups tinker with their online strategies even as the principles guiding their behavior remain largely unchanged.

The data for this chapter are drawn from leading humanitarian and human rights groups. To what extent should patterns seen there apply to "digitally born" advocacy groups, such as Avaaz in the human rights sector, which aim to conduct most of their work online? Extant scholarship points to competing possibilities. On the one hand, newer groups also seek legitimacy vis-à-vis journalists and public officials. Arguably, this need for legitimacy might minimize the extent to which they engage with their supporters, thus suggesting similarities between the technology-adoption practices of both established groups and digital-first groups. On the other hand, digital-first groups evince different organizational structures from those typically found in established NGOs. Unlike leading established organizations, digital groups do not have preexisting public-relations departments oriented toward generating mainstream media coverage. As a result, they can create departments tasked expressly with exploiting the unique affordances of digital media, unencumbered by preexisting organizational structures (Karpf 2016; Kavada 2012). Further research is needed to better understand similarities and differences in the online strategies of established NGOs and newer digital-first NGOs.

These findings leave us with at least two puzzles. First, what accounts for NGOs' news-making strategies? We have seen that humanitarian and human rights groups still care a great deal about publicity in the mainstream media and that they utilize digital tools to achieve those ends while minimizing alternative forms of public engagement. I have detailed advocacy groups' pragmatic orientation, so in the next chapter I explore the broader institutional forces—the role of donors, political elites, and journalists—that help to shape these media strategies. Second, how do new norms endure amid journalism's economic, social, and technological upheavals? Given the massive downsizing of mainstream American news outlets, the very persistence of news norms requires explanation.

CHAPTER FIVE

Publicity's Ends

Thus far, we have seen that NGOs continue to prioritize coverage in the mainstream media. This preference persists despite the explosive growth of digital technologies and staffing resources that make it possible for such groups to bypass the news media and target relevant stakeholders directly. Although such tools are indeed important, we have seen that advocacy groups typically use them to pursue the attention of journalists and political officials, not to communicate directly with supporters. Moreover, this emphasis on media coverage endures even though such groups are aware of the trade-offs endemic in media-driven activism: advocacy groups are more likely to appear in the news today, but they remain subject to journalistic norms that require them to adapt their materials to the news media's needs for drama and timeliness, which potentially distract from their advocacy goals. These findings raise an important analytical question: Why should NGOs continue to pursue mainstream media coverage?

This chapter draws from and contributes to new institutional theories of path dependence (J. Campbell 2004; R. Scott 2014) to answer this question.[1] Specifically, I argue that humanitarian and human rights groups are incentivized in three ways to pursue the publicity strategies they do. First, donors continue to value media coverage as a platform to learn about NGOs and as a mechanism for measuring these

NGOs' impact on political discourse. They are also hesitant to fund new areas such as analytics and content management that would allow advocacy groups to further develop their online strategies. Second, political officials continue to value mainstream media coverage as a way to learn about advocacy demands. Although digital technologies create new avenues for interactions with government officials, the perception among many activists is that most examples of successful advocacy include mainstream coverage. Third, NGOs occupy a position that is socially proximate to journalism, which leads the former to see the latter as an ally in the pursuit of publicity. Together, these factors lead NGO media strategies to remain intensely interested in garnering mainstream media coverage, despite the possibilities offered by digital media to bypass conventional intermediaries.

Theories of path dependence typically focus on institutions' internal capacity to reproduce themselves. On this view, institutions—once started—put in motion processes that make continuity more likely than change (Pierson 2000; Thelen 2002). Large initial investments in staff and resources make it costly to alter existing routines and strategies. Over time, an organization accumulates knowledge that helps it refine its practices, and individual actors in the organization develop interests in perpetuating the status quo. Finally, feedback loops within and beyond a single organization ensure that actors adapt their strategies in accordance with the larger political environments in which they operate. As a result, organizational actors tend to "lean heavily" on existing frameworks, "adjusting only at the margins to accommodate distinctive features of new situations" (Pierson 1994, 42). New institutional theorists characterize this tendency toward durability as "path dependence."

The empirical data presented in this chapter both confirm and extend this theory. On the one hand, sizable public-relations departments, staffed by former journalists who maintain semiregular contact with current journalists, are evidence of precisely these types of path-dependent effects. Communication professionals lean heavily on a framework that sees mainstream media coverage as the primary aim of their work. Although they do not shun digital tools, they see these tools as opportunities to extend preexisting strategies. This aspect of the empirical data confirms extant theories of path dependence. On the other hand, NGOs maintain their publicity strategies in part because other institutional actors incentivize them to do so. In different ways and for different reasons, both donors and political officials indicate that mainstream media coverage is important for NGOs. This is evidence of a different but complementary way in which institutional strategies are reproduced, which I term *reinforcing path dependencies*. In using this concept, I call attention to the way that path dependencies in one field (politics, philanthropy) interact with and reinforce path dependencies in another field (NGOs).

I begin here by reviewing current explanations for NGO publicity strategies and suggest that new-institutional theories of path dependence may help explain these continuities while also extending theories of path dependence. I then draw on my interviews with advocacy professionals to identify the specific factors incentivizing humanitarian and human rights groups to persist in their mainstream-media-centered publicity strategies. Finally, I conclude by considering what types of conditions would be necessary to incentivize NGOs to move beyond their present bias toward mainstream news coverage, while also reflecting on the implications for an extended understanding of path dependence.

EXPLAINING THE PERSISTENCE OF MEDIA CENTRIC PUBLICITY STRATEGIES

NGOs have long relied on the news media to raise public awareness, attract donations, and influence political debates (Benthall 1993; Pollock 2014; Powers 2015a). As we have seen, this struggle for publicity has been fought mostly as an uphill battle: researchers find that professional norms make journalists far more likely to utilize government and business officials rather than NGOs or other civic actors as news sources (Lang 2013; Sobieraj 2011; Waisbord 2011). Moreover, in their quest for publicity NGOs typically engage in a series of trade-offs that threaten to dilute their messages. In order to appear in the news, for example, they focus their publicity efforts on issues occurring in countries already in the news media's spotlight (Thrall, Stecula, and Sweet 2014). Less-covered or "forgotten" crises are seldom discussed in the news media, and therefore humanitarian and human rights groups do less work to get those issues covered in the news (Powers 2016d; Ramos, Ron, and Thoms 2007). Similarly, research finds that NGO messages often become sensationalized and distorted when the news media pick them up (Benthall 1993; Cottle and Nolan 2007; Sobieraj 2011). In short, reliance on the news media has long been recognized as both a necessary and a problematic strategy for humanitarian and human rights groups.

Despite suggestions of NGOs' decreasing media dependence, NGO publicity strategies continue to be media centered. Communication staffers dedicate much of their work day to following the mainstream news agenda and to brainstorming ideas for garnering media attention. They use online tools to extend preexisting publicity efforts, not to radically reinvent them, even though they continue to face enduring tensions in their relationship with the news media: the issues they care about are often distorted by journalists (Powers 2014); organizations must spend a great deal of their time fighting off negative publicity (Cottle and Nolan 2007; Orgad 2013); and only rarely are these groups able to broaden the media spotlight to include other countries and issues (Van Leuven and Joye 2014). Despite these tensions, extant research documents an enduring NGO interest in attracting mainstream media coverage (Fenton 2010; Lang 2013; Nolan and Mikami 2013; Waisbord 2008a; Wright 2016b).[2]

Why should advocacy groups persist in these media-centric strategies? For the most part, the available literature has focused on whether (and, if so, how) their publicity strategies have changed (see, e.g., Sobieraj 2011), but questions about why these groups continue to focus on the news media tend not to receive sustained attention. Simon Cottle and David Nolan discuss the increasingly competitive landscape in which NGOs operate and suggest that the need for funding leads many organizations to intensively pursue media coverage (2007, 864–866). Yet why media coverage should remain an effective fund-raising tool relative to online donation formats remains unexplained.[3] Similarly, Natalie Fenton suggests that online environments create a "tyranny of technology" in that advocacy groups always feel the need to produce content (2010, 156). This explanation similarly neglects to explain why technologies are being used primarily to pursue mainstream media coverage and not alternative forms of publicity. As a result, scholars today know that NGOs continue to be media centered, but they lack an account of why this should be the case.

New institutional theorists have long explored the reasons why institutions persist in old practices despite new contexts. Within this school of thought, one major vein of theorizing suggests that institutional developments tend toward "path dependence" (Campbell 2004; R. Scott 2014). This view holds that previous decisions shape future possibilities. In this view, sequencing—that is, *when* something happens—matters. Early choices foreclose some options while opening up others. Because institutions tend generally to reproduce themselves, path dependence is typically seen as a constraint on any sort of radical change. Critical junctures—that is, major moments of disruption when the status quo is thrown into question (Starr 2004)—may produce dramatic changes, but those changes tend to be incremental (if they happen at all) more often than not. The empirical challenge for the researcher is thus to locate the factors that incentivize an institution to follow a path-dependent trajectory.[4]

The theory of path dependence provides an account of stasis that is rooted in history and social processes rather than in organizational irrationality. From such a perspective, it is not the case that organizations are unwilling to change; rather, it is that they find themselves "locked in" to arrangements that are difficult to alter. Scholars have used this concept to describe things as varied as the commercial bias in American media policy making (Pickard 2014), enduring cross-national differences in journalism (Benson 2013), and the difficulties that political parties have had in making use of online technologies (Kreiss 2012; Nielsen 2012). In the previous chapter, this concept was used to explain how the desire for legitimacy influences humanitarian and human rights groups' online publicity efforts.

Arguments about path dependence typically focus on a single field or institutional space. On this view, institutions incentivize and promote stability in a number of ways: they may develop routines and practices that persist despite new possibilities; they may prescribe the appropriate goals and forms of action as well as the acceptable ways in which those activities and goals should be pursued; and they may create taken-for-granted assumptions about the nature of reality (R. Scott 2014). In each of these scenarios, institutions are motivated primarily by factors *within* the fields in which they operate. For example, once a particular routine or practice has been adopted, actors accumulate knowledge about how those practices work. As they grow more comfortable with these practices, they generally become less likely to deviate from them (Pierson 2000). The development of any new practice or arrangement typically involves large start-up costs, which on the whole serves as a disincentive for the institution and the actors within it to change their behavior.

Theories of path dependence have generally paid less attention to external pressures—that is, pressures emanating from beyond the primary institutional domain—in reinforcing routines and behaviors. When institutions do not change, theories of path dependence ascribe this resilience mostly to the power of institutions. It is when institutions do change that institutional theories focus on external pressures (Thelen 2002). Yet these external pressures are usually discussed in broad terms, as can be seen in concepts such as "exogenous shocks" and "critical junctures."[5] This broad discussion has the unintended effect of leaving undertheorized the degree to which related institutional fields shape the behaviors of a single field. In the case of NGOs, these pressures mean that publicity strategies sometimes follow in step with the strategies of those located in more powerful fields (politics, philanthropy, and journalism).

I call this tendency *reinforcing path dependencies*. In using this term, I call attention to the way in which path dependencies in one set of fields (e.g., politics, philanthropy) constrain and reinforce the path-dependent actions in a related field (e.g., NGOs). This notion takes seriously the relative stability of institutional practices over time but more precisely identifies the various interinstitutional incentives that enable such stability. It builds on recent theoretical work—usually falling under the banner of field theory (Bourdieu 1993)—that situates institutional activity within a wider constellation of interinstitutional relations (Benson 2013; Fligstein and McAdam 2012). On this view, path dependence is not simply self-reinforcing but also the product of a constellation of strategies, actions, and relations across institutional fields.

To be sure, this path dependence must be "translated" into the relevant terms and ideals of a specific field—for instance, neither donors nor political officials are able to dictate advocacy groups' publicity strategies. However, this translation often assumes many of the path-dependent tendencies already identified in the literature (e.g., start-up costs, feedback effects, knowledge accumulation). What the notion of reinforcing path dependencies accounts for is the way that proximate fields incentivize the reproduction of extant strategies, despite new developments that make it possible to imagine the introduction of new strategies. This incentivizing can occur at the practical level (e.g., when donors rely on media citations as an indicator of NGO efficacy). Alternatively, it can occur primarily in terms of perception (e.g., when advocacy groups assume that political officials pay attention to mainstream news coverage). In both cases, what matters is the appearance, real or perceived, of the impacts of other institutional fields in reinforcing a publicity strategy that is driven primarily by a desire to show up in the mainstream news media.

In sum, NGOs have long faced an uphill trajectory in their efforts to achieve publicity. Doing so has required seeking out coverage in the news media, which in turn has required a number of trade-offs. Although NGO professionalization and technological developments create the possibility of altering this relationship, research suggests that NGOs continue to place a premium on mainstream media coverage. This raises questions about what factors incentivize humanitarian and human rights groups to continue following a path-dependent strategy. Identifying those strategies requires greater attention to be paid to cognate institutional fields that affect NGOs. A greater focus on the various ways that NGOs are incentivized to continue pursuing media coverage can clarify why these organizations continue to place such a high emphasis on garnering mainstream media attention.

INCENTIVIZING MEDIA-CENTRISM

As we have already seen in the preceding chapters, NGO professionals care a great deal about mainstream media coverage. Different organizations value different types of coverage for different reasons (e.g., some prefer coverage in the elite press as a way to influence policy debates, whereas others target television news media to raise public awareness or boost funds). Moreover, there are tensions between most advocacy groups and the news media (e.g., over negative publicity or poor understanding of a particular human rights issues). Finally, the publicity strategies of all advocacy organizations are marked by a reflexive and strategic character, wherein advocates seek to make the best of sometimes seemingly unfavorable publicity conditions. Yet the enduring desire for positive publicity in the legacy news media was a constant theme across all interviews. To many interviewees, coverage in the news media remains the leading aim of publicity efforts. As a media officer at Oxfam put it,

"A page 5 in the *New York Times* will always be a page 5 in the *New York Times*. Nothing is ever going to change that."[6]

As many interviewees were quick to point out, the ongoing interest in cultivating mainstream media coverage does not mean that digital tools are shunned. In fact, most respondents discussed the possibilities (as well as the emergent drawbacks) of using digital tools to explore new forms of publicity. Nearly all organizations studied have built up their digital-media staff, and these individuals help to conduct publicity campaigns that make innovative use of online tools (e.g., websites, social media feeds, and so on) to raise awareness of issues not covered by the news media. Interestingly, though, many of the examples of successful digital-media use were campaigns that ultimately made their way into the mainstream news media. Thus, as we have already seen, digital-media tools are being used mostly to interact with—rather than to directly bypass—the mainstream media in potentially new ways.

When asked why their organizations continue to emphasize coverage in the mainstream news media, interviewees described three factors that incentivize their publicity strategies. The first two—donor demands and government officials' media-consumption habits—have little to do with what new institutional theorists describe as path dependencies (e.g., start-up costs, feedback effects, knowledge accumulation). These two factors instead detail ways in which path dependence in the fields of philanthropy and politics incentivize NGOs to continue in their "media-centric" publicity strategies. These reinforcing path dependencies are sustained via the more standard forms of path dependence. In particular, respondents described a social proximity between NGOs and journalists that have led the former to see the latter as a potential ally in the struggle for publicity.

Table 5.1 provides a brief summary of the argument. Each of the institutional actors—donors, NGOs, political officials—has distinct reasons for wanting to see NGOs in the news. NGOs are placed in the middle of the table because their actions are constrained not only by their own institutional path dependencies but also by donors' and government officials' path dependencies. The cumulative effect of all of these path dependencies is that it is difficult for advocacy groups to maneuver outside the path on which they find themselves (because doing so inevitably pushes them up against the pathways of more powerful institutional

TABLE 5.1

Reinforcing Path Dependencies

Institutional Actor	Reason for Valuing Media Coverage
Donors	Media coverage seen as a platform to learn about NGOs and as a mechanism to measure their impact on political discourse.
NGOs	Sizeable public-relations departments and regular interactions with journalists lead NGOs to view news media as an essential, if problematic, ally in the pursuit of publicity.
Political officials	Media coverage seen as a way to learn about demands made by advocacy groups.

actors). These three factors collectively help incentivize NGOs' publicity strategies to focus primarily on generating mainstream media coverage.

THE NEED FOR FUNDING: "OUR FUND-RAISERS DO BETTER WHEN WE'RE IN THE MEDIA"

NGOs need money to survive, and media serve as an important platform for raising and maintaining those necessary funds. In order to raise funds, organizations must achieve a degree of brand recognition so that potential donors can identify the appropriate organization with which they might provide funds (Bob 2006). These donors can be individuals (e.g., people who donate money to an organization) or institutions (e.g., philanthropic organizations or governments that provide humanitarian and human rights groups with funding). In either case, donors must be aware of the organization and its efforts: media publicity continues to be one important way by which this awareness occurs. Moreover, in order to maintain these funds NGOs need to prove themselves as having done their work effectively. Donors identify effectiveness in different ways (e.g., projects completed, policy outcomes, and so on). But in most cases and in part because of the murky nature of "effectiveness" in humanitarian and human rights work, media coverage functions as an important proxy for effectiveness. Despite the advent of online technologies, most organizations in this study suggested that donors often continue to privilege coverage in the mainstream mass media both because these media provide larger audiences and because of uncertainty within the donor community about how best to gauge effective publicity online. In part as a result of this donor path dependence, NGOs continue to place a high value on media-centered publicity strategies.

"Our fund-raisers do better when we're in the media," one longtime communication professional explained to me. "So there is an objective in just keeping Amnesty out there."[7] This sentiment was echoed at most every organization I visited. At Médecins Sans Frontières, the communication director told me about a number of strategic objectives in his organization's recent publicity work (e.g., seeking policy change on a specific issue, pressuring other stakeholders to act, and so on). Then, he paused and said, "Sometimes it could simply be that we want people to know [about Médecins Sans Frontières]. . . . Fund-raising is an objective."[8] At Human Rights Watch, someone told me about a blog that many United Nations officials were reading. Would it sometimes be better, I asked, for the group to pursue publicity through that blog rather than an outlet such as the *New York Times*, which has so many groups clamoring to get into it? She replied: "[The *New York Times* is] never negligible because it's the newspaper of our donor base or the largest chunk of our donor base, which is still about 70 percent American."[9]

Once the funding comes in, NGOs need to highlight the effectiveness of their work. One interviewee discussed media coverage as a way of "making sure the Oxfam name is out there . . . so supporters can see it."[10] At Amnesty's US branch, publicity professionals have consumer data on the types of publications their supporters read. "We did some research a few years ago that showed . . . that people who support human rights and are contributors to Amnesty and other groups read the *Economist* in huge numbers. . . . So we try to get into the *Economist* a lot."[11] Professionals at other organizations noted that institutional donors often want to see that NGOs are influencing policy debates. As one communications director put it, "Our major donors want to see that we're in the *New York Times* or the *Financial Times* and having influence on debates."[12] In still other cases, professionals acknowledged that success in human rights advocacy or humanitarian work can be hard to judge: "We work in countries for thirty or forty years. It's not easy to point to a single campaign and say, 'That worked.' "[13] In that context, media coverage demonstrates efficacy to donors looking for impact.[14] In all cases, the strategy of generating media coverage reflects donors' desire to see media coverage as a proxy for the effective stewardship of their donations.

Online technologies do not change these equations dramatically. As several fund-raising and marketing staffers stressed, donations still rely to a large extent on public recognition. One person explained the situation in a nutshell: "You can't donate to an organization you don't know about."[15] Mainstream media remain the most sizeable platform for reaching those large audiences. "Our own website gets around thirty thousand visitors a day," another person told me. "It's respectable for an NGO, but it's miniscule compared to the traffic on mainstream media sites."[16] Online tools are used to boost the chances for NGOs to get into the news or to make donating easier.

A second reason why NGOs continue in their media-centered efforts is that donors are unsure how to measure impact in the online environment. At one organization, I asked someone whether the organization's donors care about its online efforts: "In our annual reports, we put how many downloads [of reports] a month or something, but we really don't care. If it's 150,000 . . . or 100,000, that's not the issue. The issue is who is downloading [them]."[17] At another organization, someone explained that although donors want to see innovative efforts online, they continue to see media coverage as the clearest indicator of influence,[18] a view that stems in part from the nature of much human rights work. As several people suggested, it is hard for any one organization to prove that its publicity efforts have effected change. Garnering coverage in the news media thus functions as a useful proxy for effectiveness.[19]

Relatedly, several respondents suggested that although donors are willing to give short-term grants to support organizations in pioneering new digital efforts, relatively little funding is available to support the long-term establishment of such efforts. A survey of the NGO sector in 2015 provides support for these claims: it found that most large global organizations—such as those studied here—allocate just 1.0 to 2.5 percent of their annual income to digital technologies and staff (Breckenridge and Maloney 2015, 4). Donor hesitation is given as the primary reason for the underinvestment: "Funders are simply afraid to make investments in technology because it is something new for them. It's not something they've done, and they're not excited to step into a new funding focus" (Breckenridge and Maloney 2015, 4). This fear of newness creates a bias toward funding "the sexiest areas" of technology investment (e.g., social media tools) while ignoring some of the basic foundational needs for content management and analytics: "Underinvestment and [the] lack[] [of] capacity . . . are two of the main reasons organizations struggle to scale overall and rise and crash in a highly turbulent project-to-project life cycle" (Breckenridge and Maloney 2015, 5).[20]

In short, NGOs' ongoing focus on mainstream media, in spite of alternative possibilities, stems in part from the path dependence of donor demands. Individual donors value media publicity as a way to identify organizations worthy of their money. Similarly, institutional donors use media coverage as a tool for assessing the degree to which an organization is able to influence public discourse. Importantly, in NGO professionals' view, nearly all donors still continue to see mainstream media publicity as an indicator of success. This donor path dependence thus conditions humanitarian and human rights groups to pursue publicity strategies in accordance with this demand.[21]

THE QUEST FOR POLITICAL LEGITIMACY: "IF WE'RE NOT IN THE NEWS, POLITICALLY WE DON'T EXIST"

Just as NGOs need donors to survive financially, they need to be recognized as legitimate to thrive politically. According to interviewees, publicity in the news media provides an opportunity for advocacy groups to garner the attention of political elites. Media attention does not guarantee that officials will heed the NGOs' advice, but NGO professionals report that coverage is likely to make officials aware of their efforts. Although digital technologies broaden the consumption sources for government officials, internal research conducted by at least some advocacy groups finds that officials still get the majority of their news from mainstream media. This finding reinforces extant perceptions among advocacy groups that the most reliable way to capture government officials' attention is through mainstream media and that efforts to generate publicity outside the mainstream media often fail to capture that attention.

Thus, another reason why NGOs pursue a media-centered strategy is that government officials are perceived to incentivize this strategy.

"If we're not in the news," one interviewee explained, "politically we don't exist."[22] Many interviewees echoed this dramatic statement in more subdued forms. As one person put it, "They [government officials] can't ignore you when you're in the *New York Times*."[23] These statements reflect a general view that officials pay attention to media coverage even if such an assessment likely overstates the degree to which coverage in the media ensures that advocacy messages will be taken seriously (Wolfsfeld 2011). At the very least, though, media coverage makes government officials aware of their efforts. A member of Oxfam nicely captured this point while discussing efforts related to human rights issues in the Congo: "When [an advocacy officer] goes to the [United Nations] and meets some people about Congo, and there has just been a piece or a letter to the editor about the role of the [United Nations] in protecting civilians from attack and rape, . . . believe me, it has a greater impact. Because the first thing they do when they sit down is say, 'Hey, I read your letter. That was interesting.' You know, because they do read news as well."[24]

NGOs report that when they do get into the news, political elites will sometimes take the issue more seriously.[25] For example, one interviewee discussed a publicity campaign his organization (International Crisis Group) conducted in 2011 on issues of governance in Afghanistan. At the time, US government officials were focused on strategies for exiting the country as quickly as possible. By contrast, "some of the stuff we're saying is really very different from what you're hearing now in America." Efforts to engage political officials on the organization's point of view were difficult. Yet after the organization garnered several prominent op-eds and news coverage, "all of the sudden our talking points started developing some more traction."[26] Success stories like this one reinforce the view that mainstream media coverage can occasionally influence officials.

According to interviewees, political elites tend to see media coverage as a proxy for public opinion. Many NGO professionals recognize that such a viewpoint is to some degree an artificial construction: "Just because something is on the editorial pages of the *New York Times* and *Washington Post* doesn't mean that most people actually care about it."[27]

Yet advocacy professionals also believe that it is media coverage itself—not "public opinion" more broadly construed—that gets political elites to see issues as attention worthy. Along these lines, one person talked about the US intervention in Bosnia in the 1990s amid ethnic cleansing. "[President Bill] Clinton didn't do it [intervene] because of large shifts in public will. He did it because of the slow drumbeat of editorials in the *New York Times* and *Washington Post*" (Bogert 2012). Knowledge of the importance of media coverage on elite behavior thus leads advocacy groups to target mainstream media outlets.

Digital technologies provide a number of new ways for humanitarian and human rights groups to interact with political elites. And at least sometimes, these groups do make use of these affordances. When political elites are not addressing an issue in sufficient detail, NGOs can sometimes use social media campaigns to "open up the blockage," as one person put it.[28] Numerous interviewees pointed to the Kony 2012 campaign by the California-based NGO Invisible Children—targeting the regime of Lord's Resistance Army leader Joseph Kony, which was kidnapping children to fight as soldiers—as an example of such efforts. By reaching out to celebrities through social media, the group was able to build public awareness of a topic—human rights abuses in Uganda—that was otherwise capturing little media attention and in turn to get politicians talking about the issue in more detail than they otherwise would. At Human Rights Watch, someone described a multimedia feature it had made about child farmworkers in the United States. "The researcher went in to see the people at the Department of Labor. And literally they said, 'We already saw the movie.' So sometimes you can be very sure of a policy maker having seen [a feature], imbibed it."[29] In these and other cases, NGOs use digital tools to garner media coverage and political legitimacy in new ways.

Yet interviewees were quick to point out that such high-profile cases are the exception, not an emergent rule. Internal research conducted by NGOs finds that officials still get the majority of their news from mainstream media. Human Rights Watch commissioned studies of policy makers' news consumption in both the European Union and the United Nations: "And we did indeed determine that most of them read the *New York Times*, but we also [found that]—it was interesting—a lot of them are checking BBC throughout the day." Referring to the United Nations, the same interviewee stressed: "The *New York Times* is very influential at the United Nations. So if you really want the United Nations to sit up and pay attention to something, it's actually very helpful to have it in the *New York Times*."[30] This view was echoed by a communication officer at Amnesty International: "If we have an action . . . to get the Security Council to act . . . we look at which countries are the most likely to be interested in our point of view, and we go to the correspondents for those countries' newspapers."[31]

Interviewees also discussed the importance of demonstrating their awareness of the mainstream news agenda in conversations with government officials. Several NGO professionals discussed the importance of evincing knowledge of the media cycle—and, by extension, of the most important public issues at any one moment—in their meetings with government officials. When asked what issues these tended to be, they typically identified the news agenda set by the mainstream news media. As a result of government officials' dependence on media to take the public temperature, NGOs express efforts mostly to reframe issues already within the news agenda rather than to bring new issues to the table. As one person said, "We can't change the news agenda, but we can try to change the frame of any one story."[32]

Interviewees reported that because government officials are known to follow mainstream media, it is difficult to know how to target these officials online. "It's a constant question for us . . . how the people we're trying to reach actually look at pictures or watch video [online]," a member of the online news team at Amnesty International remarked. "Sometimes it's hard to know whether they [government officials] see our stuff."[33] Someone at Human Rights Watch described an effort to bring human rights violations in Uganda to the attention of elites before the Kony 2012 campaign: "We made a video in the hopes of getting people at the State Department to watch it. But we really don't know if they did. That's the difference. If we were in the *New York Times*, we'd know."[34]

In sum, NGOs' media-centrism stems in part from government officials' perceived path dependence. Like donors, government officials continue to pay attention to mainstream media coverage. Even if that coverage does not always influence actions by advocacy groups, it puts these groups on the officials' radar, thus bestowing them with a degree of political legitimacy. Although digital technologies open up new avenues for interaction between advocates and government officials, interviewees note that it is difficult to predict the efficacy of any specific online effort because of uncertainty about how best to reach target audiences. As a result, NGOs continue to favor publicity strategies that stand the greatest likelihood of capturing the attention of government officials.

THE SOCIAL PROXIMITY OF NGOS AND JOURNALISTS

The preceding two factors identify path dependencies in philanthropy and politics that incentivize NGOs' media-centric strategies. Interviewees suggested that these strategies are sustained through more standard forms of path dependence, such as start-up costs, feedback effects, and knowledge accumulation. Moreover, the social proximity between NGOs and journalists has encouraged the former to turn to the latter as an ally in the struggle for publicity. This proximity is evidenced by NGOs' creation of organizational units—such as public-relations departments, often staffed with former journalists—that provide the news media with content as well as by semiregular interactions between organization researchers and journalists in the field. It leads NGO professionals to see digital tools as a way of complementing extant efforts to garner media coverage, but it also often makes it difficult for advocacy groups to know how to engage in other forms of public engagement online. As a result, NGO publicity efforts are oriented primarily toward the pursuit of mainstream media coverage.

Because NGOs have long relied on the news media to garner publicity, they have built up institutional structures and practices to optimize their publicity chances. The amount of capital invested (what new institutionalists call "startup costs") in these structures makes any radical departure from this reliance unlikely. For example, all organizations studied have sizeable public-relations departments whose primary task historically has been to pursue media coverage. These departments have subunits—such as audio-visual production—dedicated to the production of materials that news outlets can use. Many hire former journalists to bring the sensibility and norms of news production to humanitarian and human rights organizations. "I bring a news sensibility to our efforts here" is how one former journalist now working in the NGO sector put it.[35] These sensibilities include structuring the workday around the monitoring of news flows (e.g., having daily morning meetings to discuss the news agenda). These "startup costs" represent a substantial investment that many organizations are unlikely to change dramatically.

NGO researchers also share a number of affinities with journalists. As several interviewees stressed, the two occupy similar social spaces: "They're sharing planes, they're sharing cars, and they're sharing food. They're living together in many cases."[36] Researchers also to a large degree share reporters' worldview. As one researcher put it, "We're out there, just like reporters, trying to figure out what happened."[37] Another echoed this value commitment while detailing the ways it has shaped her organization's reporting techniques:

> People go into the field, and they really are unbiased. You know, they're in war zones. They are not taking one side over the other. They're double or triple sourcing; they're interviewing multiple witnesses; they're interviewing them separately so they don't infect one another's stories. The process of research and what we do in the field is really very, very close to journalism, and we really approach it without bias, without predisposition of who's guilty and what happened.[38]

This social proximity creates ongoing feedback channels between journalists and NGOs, which help to shape the NGOs' belief in the news media as a natural ally in the pursuit for publicity.[39] "We try to meet with journalists from time to time to get a sense of what their interests are. Knowing that helps us craft our messages," one interviewee explained. He also stated that regular interactions make it difficult for NGOs to ignore journalists when they call looking for a quote. "They [reporters] are coming to us for expert comments, which they expect we ought to be able to get fairly quickly."[40]

This social proximity to journalists generally leads humanitarian and human rights groups to see digital tools as a way of complementing their media-centered publicity efforts. Interviewees discussed using social media to know what journalists are doing, where they are going, and what sort of information they might be receptive to.[41] "If a reporter says [on Twitter], 'I'm traveling to Sudan next week,' which they often do, then we can pick up the phone and say, 'If you're going to Sudan, do you want to meet with our person while you're there? And here are a couple of reports we've written on this [topic].'"[42] Even formats that could be used to directly target donors or policy makers—such as podcasts—are often produced mainly to satisfy journalistic demand.[43]

Because NGOs are socially proximate to journalists, it is often difficult for them to know how to engage in other forms of public engagement online.[44] At several organizations, I was told about ongoing problems in responding to claims about their research being wrong. Human Rights Watch, for example, has received complaints from online bloggers about the accuracy of its reporting on Israel. In chapter 4, I detailed one particularly prominent case where critics charged the group with inaccurate reporting during Israel's war with Lebanon in 2006. Amnesty International's Facebook page has been the target of similar claims with respect to its reporting on Syria. In both cases, the organizations have responded to these claims as if the claims were coming from serious journalists. In response to the criticism of its reporting in 2006, Human Rights Watch, for example, sent its research team back into the field to conduct another round of investigations (Human Rights Watch 2006b). Amnesty International writes back to each commenter individually: "We write, 'Thank you for inquiry into what we have been doing. . . . Please follow this link, and you can see [our range of reports].' We only have one guy moderating [the online comments]. Newspapers that encourage commenting have, like, a whole army patrolling this stuff. We have, like, one guy."[45]

In sum, NGOs maintain research and public-relations departments that are socially proximate to their journalistic counterparts. They travel to similar places and interact semiregularly. These interactions provide the opportunity for NGOs to learn more about what does and does not succeed in getting the news media's attention. This proximity reinforces the media-centrism that path dependencies in the fields of philanthropy and politics incentivize. This pattern is mostly reinforced online as well. Advocacy groups use digital tools primarily as a way to capture the attention of the news media, not to route around it. Moreover, the social distance that NGOs have from other information producers (bloggers, online commenters) make alternative forms of public engagement difficult. As a result, most humanitarian and human rights organizations continue to see the mainstream news media as an ally in their quest for publicity.

This chapter has investigated the various factors that incentivize humanitarian and human rights groups to continue in their media-centric strategies despite the rise of alternative forms of public engagement. Drawing on new-institutional theories of path dependence, it highlights the important role played by three particular factors: first, donors continue to value media coverage as a platform to learn about NGOs and as a mechanism for measuring NGOs impact on political discourse; second, political officials continue to utilize media coverage as a way to learn about advocacy demands; and, third, the social proximity between NGOs and journalists have led the former to see the latter as an ally in the pursuit of publicity. Together, these three factors have led NGOs to adopt publicity strategies that remain centered on garnering coverage in the mainstream media.

Not only are these publicity strategies centered on garnering news coverage, but they also take the media agenda as given. Most NGO professionals I spoke with expressed an assumption that news media coverage was not something they could successfully challenge. A communication professional at Oxfam shrugged, unsurprised when I said that it seemed his organization took media coverage as a given. "It's kind of hard for us to tell the media, 'Look, you've covered Afghanistan four times more than you've covered Somalia.' They'll say, 'Yeah, so what?' It's kind of obvious."[46]

This assumption that coverage of certain subjects is unlikely lowers expectations across the board. Researchers assume that information pertaining to countries outside of the media spotlight will have a relatively scant possibility of becoming news; press officers do their best to keep that expectation low. Communication professionals in particular see their task as introducing an element of realism into the organization with respect to what can and cannot be covered. The reverse is also true: when awareness of a story outside the media spotlight is successfully raised, communication professionals see a few portable lessons. As one person put it, "Sometimes people in our organization will ask me: 'Do you think the media will care about that?' And I have a three-word phrase, which is 'Never say "never."' I have been surprised myself many times by things that I didn't think would be of interest that did turn out to be of interest."[47]

Theories of path dependence usually focus on a single field or institutional space. This chapter presents evidence that both confirms and extends this theory. Sizable public-relations departments, staffed by former journalists that maintain semiregular contact with news organizations, nicely demonstrate core mechanisms—such as startup costs, knowledge accumulation, and feedback effects—previously identified by scholars of path dependence (Pierson 2000; Thelen 2002). At the same time, this chapter highlights a different but complementary way in which institutional strategies are reproduced by reinforcing path dependencies, calling attention to the way path dependencies in cognate fields (politics, philanthropy) reinforce and constrain the actions within another field (NGOs).

These findings contribute empirically to the study of NGOs and theoretically to studies of how institutions do—and do not—change over time. They offer an account of the incentives that shape NGO publicity strategies. This account complements extant research that shows the persistence of media-centered strategies despite seemingly new possibilities (Cottle and Nolan 2007; Sobieraj 2011; Waisbord 2011). Moreover, by exploring the incentives motivating these strategies, this research extends this scholarship from describing whether advocacy groups remain wedded to mainstream publicity to explaining why they do so. Rather than view NGO actions as irrational organizational behavior, this chapter attempts to describe what Adrienne Russell (2016) terms the "sensibility" that informs the otherwise puzzling centrality of mainstream news coverage for advocacy groups. Theoretically, the chapter shows how persistent practices result from the trajectories of dominant institutions that surround a single organization field, which stands in contrast to theories that typically see path dependence as the result of internal field effects (Pierson 2000; Thelen 2002). Taken together, the findings here show that although exogenous changes create the conditions of possibility for change, complex configurations within and across institutional fields are just as likely to refract those changes into more incremental developments.

The findings presented here explore path dependence for a single thematic sector of professional advocacy work—humanitarian and human rights work. Although it is not strictly possible to generalize beyond this sector, there are good reasons to assume that the analysis would hold for other advocacy sectors (e.g., those focusing on the environment, gender equality, poverty, and so on). Each of these fields is subject to professionalization processes that make them reliant on donors, interested in influencing policy, and aware of journalism's role in shaping their messages (Dale 1996; Lang 2013). These pressures make it likely that their publicity strategies will similarly remain centered on generating mass-media coverage. Research into these various thematic sectors is of course necessary to confirm, modify, or dispute this suggestion.

This chapter highlights the path-dependent effects of various institutional fields in reproducing NGOs' media-centrism. An open question remains as to the conditions under which change might become possible. In principle, it seems that such change could come about in two ways. First, there could be changes within NGOs: in this case, humanitarian and human rights groups would seek funds from different donors with less media-driven demands; they could pursue a more populist political strategy, thus partially eschewing political elites' demands; and they could hire more people with backgrounds in digital advocacy rather than in mainstream journalism. These changes could be driven by organizational leadership, for whom technological innovation might be a path to move the organization forward in novel ways. Given the fact that the executive leadership of most NGOs tends to come up through the organizational ranks, though, the opposite scenario is equally likely: new leadership will tend to reinforce extant ways of doing things, in part because those strategies helped them achieve their current status and in part because changing strategy is often organizationally unpopular.

A second potential pathway for change would occur outside of individual organizations. There could be changes with respect to the fields with which NGOs interact: donors could change their demands and provide sustainable funding for alternative publicity efforts; politicians' media consumption habits could change; and journalists could open up more to advocacy messages (as some online sites seem to be doing [see Russell 2013]). Changes in these areas would incentivize humanitarian and human rights groups to deviate to a larger degree from their current publicity practices. Here, too, however, the theoretical possibility of change is confronted with the equally likely reality of durability and stasis. The consumer surveys conducted by NGOs show that political officials continue to consume mainstream news. Moreover, a growing body of journalism scholarship finds that news organizations, despite recent cataclysmic changes to their business model, continue to operate in ways that are largely in keeping with past journalistic practices.

For these reasons, the types of possible changes outlined here seem relatively difficult to come by and will likely be slow to take shape. Here, as elsewhere, institutional theory's bias toward continuity is useful. Theories of path dependence—including the concept of reinforcing path dependencies outlined here—suggest that it is more likely than not that NGOs will persist in their media-driven publicity strategies.

Yet what explains the durability of norms in the news media? Given the massive downsizing of international news coverage, this phenomenon, like the enduring NGO publicity strategies, needs to be explained in further detail.

CHAPTER SIX

Explaining the Endurance
of News Norms

What explains the relative durability of news norms amid journalism's current economic, social, and technological upheavals? As legacy news outlets reduce the resources they commit to international news coverage, scholars have suggested that such norms might be challenged. On this view, advocacy groups might not only appear more frequently in the news but also reshape news norms in the process by infusing advocacy aims into news stories (Beckett 2008; Gillmor 2014; Sambrook 2010). However, the analyses in the preceding chapters suggest that news norms remain largely intact: government officials and journalists still set the news agenda, and advocacy groups play a peripheral, even if growing role, around it. Moreover, although NGOs seek to graft advocacy aims onto news stories, they do so largely by accepting dominant news norms that emphasize drama and personalization. All of these factors leave us with a final analytical puzzle: Why, despite reasonable expectations otherwise, should news norms remain relatively stable?

Solving this puzzle requires a different set of empirical data than has previously been draw upon. Where chapter 5 used interviews with NGO professionals to explore the reinforcing path dependencies that lead advocacy groups to prioritize mainstream media coverage, this chapter examines the other institutional half of the NGO–journalist relationship. To do so, I draw here on interviews with reporters and editors at leading international news outlets in regard to their reporting on humanitarian and human rights issues for Syrian refugees in Turkey in 2011. This case, although possessing a multitude of unique features, contains many typical elements of humanitarian and human rights situations: it occurred in a geographic setting where news outlets have few regular reporters and thus forced them to rely on stringers and "parachute" reporting efforts from journalists stationed elsewhere. In 2011, I visited the border region of Hatay, Turkey, a point from which journalists conducted much of their reporting on the ongoing Syrian civil war. I was able to meet with and observe in real time how journalists reported this story, including but not limited to their interactions with NGO professionals. The data I gathered allowed me to examine why journalistic norms continue to be reproduce.

Drawing on these data as well as on institutional theories of norm reproduction, I identify two processes that preserve extant news norms. The first, which I call *field inertia*, shows that journalists remain wedded to a view of NGOs primarily as advocates and look to NGO professionals to perform a prearranged set of tasks—provide on-the-ground news and analysis, respond to government statements, and offer dramatic visuals, which are then slotted into stories driven primarily by other sources. Editors, who remain hierarchically powerful vis-à-vis reporters, are responsible primarily for maintaining this inertia. The second process—which I term *field diffusion*—shows how the economic crisis in journalism has pushed journalists into fields such as the NGO sector. In their new roles, former (and sometimes still active) reporters bring the sensibility of journalism to advocacy groups' news-making efforts, which in turn allows journalism norms to diffuse into other sectors and makes it more likely than not that advocacy groups will produce information in keeping with the news media's preferences. Paradoxically, this diffusion is enabled by the NGO sector's own efforts toward professionalization, which puts a growing emphasis on publicity.

These findings complicate views of news norms as either entirely in flux or primarily static. Where views that emphasize change stress the importance of NGOs producing news on their own, I show that the people doing this production often come from and sometimes keep a foot in the journalistic field. Rather than bring advocacy values to journalism, these individuals mostly bring news values to advocacy groups. At the same time, stasis in news norms is not a given. Instead, it must actively be reproduced. In keeping with extant views of norm maintenance, I argue that this stasis occurs in part through journalists, who do keep the same views on news worthiness. To this argument I also add a sociological dimension that stresses news practices and organizational hierarchies.

NEWS NORMS: EXPLAINING CONTINUITY AMID CHANGE

News norms are value judgments about what counts as newsworthy. Faced with endless story options, journalists need to make decisions about what issues and events to cover and how to cover them. Decades of scholarly research have shown that these choices are derived from what Lance Bennett (1996) has identified as three distinct "normative orders." A first order, rooted in the world of professional journalism, sets forth news norms that emphasize objectivity and fairness in news coverage. On this view, journalists report on the actions of government officials as well as on disagreements among them because doing so allows them not to take sides while representing the range of official debate. A second order, rooted in democratic politics, stresses the need for journalists to promote accountability and to inform citizens. This viewpoint signals the importance of reporting news necessary for democratic self-governance. Finally, a third order, rooted in commercial considerations, emphasizes the need for news coverage to be efficient (i.e., relatively inexpensive to produce) and profitable (e.g., by attracting audiences). Despite variation across research traditions and empirical settings, scholarly research finds that these three orders tend to produce news that is driven by government officials and is often highly personalized and dramatic (Bennett 1996; Gans 1979; Waisbord 2013).

As we saw in chapters 3 and 4, these news norms minimize and constrain the presence of advocacy groups in the news. This means that NGOs typically appear in humanitarian and human rights news when speaking on topics that are of interest to political officials. Although advocacy groups produce reports from countries outside the media spotlight, this information rarely makes it ways into newspapers or onto television screens. In addition, the existence of these norms means that in their efforts to garner news coverage advocacy groups generally adapt to rather than challenge such norms. For example, they accept the news media's agenda as given and search for ways to get their issues covered within it. They also frame their issues in ways that are visually compelling and dramatically satisfying. These actions undoubtedly diversify news coverage in some ways (e.g., by adding human rights frames to news coverage), but they do so in large part because they satisfy some aspects of journalism's various normative orders.

These findings stand in contrast to some of the more hopeful assessments of changes in journalism norms. A number of authors, surveying reductions in foreign correspondence and the growth of NGO reporting, have posited that such norms may be changing. Some argue that international news might be more open to NGO perspectives today than it was in the past (Sambrook 2010).[1] Others suggest that NGO-driven news might be more cosmopolitan or critical of global inequalities (Chouliaraki 2012; Cottle 2009; Reese 2015). And still others suggest that the imbrication of journalism and advocacy creates a situation wherein advocacy groups are "questioning, and perhaps redefining, the boundaries of journalism in our time" (Schudson 2011, 228; see also Russell 2016). Given these expectations of change, the fact that news norms have altered so little thus requires analysis and explanation.[2]

Institutional theories, the core features of which I introduced in previous chapters, generally expect norms and practices to be reproduced over time. This reproduction results from path-dependent tendencies within organizations and institutional fields, which disincentivize dramatic alterations to extant ways of doing things. However, just as the persistence of media-centric NGO strategies required explanation, the endurance of news norms also requires analysis and explanation. Journalists do not unthinkingly reproduce news norms. Such norms need to be reproduced in practice—that is, in the routines and everyday actions that journalists take in making the news. Thus, it is necessary to understand the specific practices through which such reproduction occurs.

In the institutional literature, this effort to identify how norms and practices are reproduced is commonly referred to as a search for "mechanisms," or the specific actions that must take place in order to produce a given effect (R. Scott 2014, 152). For example, in his study of American newsrooms, David Ryfe (2011) shows how journalists' habits and investments remain wedded to predigital forms of news production. Even though many journalists (and management personnel) wish to alter their practices in order to better reflect the realities of digital publishing, in practice they have difficulty doing so. By highlighting the importance of habits and investments, Ryfe calls attention to a key set of mechanisms that reproduce established forms of journalism practice. More broadly, the search for mechanisms moves beyond descriptive questions about whether a given social practice has changed or not. It instead asks analytically why a given social practice or norm remains relatively stable (see, e.g., Boczkowski 2010).

In this chapter, I identify two mechanisms by which news norms are reproduced in humanitarian and human rights news reporting. The first—field inertia—entails a combination of structural and cognitive biases that lead journalists to minimize the amount and types of information they accept from NGOs. With respect to structural bias, reporters need to provide the types of coverage that will be of interest to their editors. They seek out NGOs for help in satisfying this need, and their interactions are premised upon norms of timeliness, drama, and government action. This structural bias is reinforced by a cognitive bias wherein journalists think of NGOs as fulfilling a specific set of roles, which can then be slotted into stories driven by other sources. Together, these processes lead the entire field of journalism to continue producing news in ways that more or less mirror past processes: government officials are privileged and advocacy groups are peripheral in the news-production process.

The second mechanism—field diffusion—is different. It shows how economic upheavals in journalism have created conditions wherein journalists have had to circulate into neighboring fields. NGOs constitute one such field. As NGOs seek to boost their information offerings, they hire journalists, whom they envision bringing a news sensibility to their advocacy efforts. The effect is that norms of news worthiness are diffused into the NGO sector, thus leading advocacy groups to produce information in ways that match the news media's preferences. This outcome is surprising and somewhat paradoxical. Although NGOs sense an opportunity to boost their capacity to make their own news, their hiring of former journalists (and sometimes still active in the sense of working for both news organizations and advocacy groups) reproduces news norms outside the newsroom settings in which they originated.

Taken together, these two mechanisms provide the basic components of an explanation for the endurance of news norms. They do not, by dint of their existence, guarantee the reproduction of these norms into the future ad infinitum. It is of course always possible that new actors will depart from these norms or that political or economic changes will incentivize some innovation away from them. However, these mechanisms do go a considerable distance in helping to explain how news norms endure, even in settings where the conditions for their alteration seem otherwise favorable.

THE CASE: HUMANITARIAN AND HUMAN RIGHTS REPORTING AT THE TURKEY–SYRIA BORDER

This chapter is based primarily on two data sources. First, I draw on my observations of humanitarian and human rights news reporting at the Turkey–Syria border. In the summer of 2011, I visited the Hatay region of southeastern Turkey, which served as the unofficial headquarters for reporting on what was initially a relatively small influx of Syrian refugees into Turkey. In the provincial capital city of Antakya, reporters assembled translators and regional guides and slept in local hotels. They visited refugee camps run by the Turkish government and located in towns outside of the main city. Finally, journalists assembled in small border towns, from which they could literally see into Syria and view citizens leaving the country amid Syrian tank movements.

My aim in these visits was to understand how journalists conducted their reporting in this type of situation. Given that the closest news bureau was more than seven hundred miles away in Istanbul,[3] I wanted to know how reporters developed story ideas and went about their reporting in an environment with which they had little familiarity. At the time, I was not aware that the data I was collecting would speak to the endurance of news norms. I simply sought to investigate the production of humanitarian and human rights news from the perspective of journalists. I initially secured access to this group of journalists by sending emails to journalists whose work on the issue in question had been published or broadcast in leading international news outlets, including but not limited to the *New York Times*, CNN, National Public Radio, the *Washington Post*, *El País*, and the *Times of London*. Initial interviews with journalists, usually at cafes in the city of Antakya, allowed me to learn of social engagements among larger sets of journalists, including freelancers whose work had yet to appear in major news outlets. These events allowed me to identify key spaces where journalists conducted their work and where I subsequently made further observations: press gatherings outside of refugee camps along the Syria–Turkey border as well as makeshift reporting spots from which television crews broadcast their reports and where print journalists gathered to conduct interviews with Syrian activists.

The opportunity to conduct research in this area also derived primarily from personal connections. My wife is Turkish, and my father-in-law is a journalist based in Istanbul. These connections mean that I spend most of the summer months each year in Turkey and was thus able to visit the southeastern part of the country with relative ease. Moreover, my father-in-law also initially put me in contact with journalists through his own contacts, which helped me speak with reporters who might not be inclined to respond to my emails.

The second data source was interviews with editors and reporters conducted several years later. Because I was initially uncertain about what to do with my observational data, I simply put them aside while delving more deeply into analyzing the role of NGOs in shaping international news coverage. Yet as I completed my analysis of when NGOs appear in the news, I recognized a crucial gap in my data: namely, how journalists perceive advocacy groups' contributions to the news. This realization led me to dig back into my field note data to see how and in what ways journalists talked about such groups at the Turkey–Syria border. Given that several discussed the important role of editors, I also sought to speak with editors. Due to the time gap between these parts of my research, the editors I eventually talked to were not always the same editors discussed by the reporters in 2011. In total, I spoke with eight editors at different news organizations. Given prior research that stresses the patterned nature of editorial work in newsrooms (Breed 1955; Gans 1979), it is unlikely that earlier interviews with different editors would have led to different conclusions.

To complement these data sources, I sometimes refer back to my interviews with NGO professionals, especially when discussing the mechanism of field diffusion, which results from interactions between

NGOs and journalists. On the whole, though, I draw primarily on my field notes from 2011 and my interviews with journalists and editors to develop a picture of how news norms endure in the case of humanitarian and human rights news reporting. In sketching this picture, this chapter aims to complete the circuit of message production by including the practices and perceptions of reporters and editors, which are generally absent from extant analyses of NGO communication efforts.

By definition, case studies are specific and can be generalized only with caution. That said, I suspect that several of the main patterns I identify in this chapter can be found in other instances of NGO–journalist interactions. That is, I think that reporters are generally likely to see NGO professionals as advocates and thus to look to them to help fulfill a prearranged set of tasks, which they then use in news stories driven primarily by other sources. I also suspect it is likely that editors reinforce news norms that favor the perspective of government officials over advocates. Both of these findings are rooted in general patterns of NGO–journalist interactions that emerge in a specific case. Of course, further research in other settings is necessary to confirm, complicate, or disprove this assumption.

That said, I do think there is an important caveat to be made about the case study presented here. My initial period of observation was marked by a general hope in the region that democratic uprisings were replacing unelected or unpopular leaders. Journalists thus descended upon Turkey's southern border to tell what they saw as another instance of the broader "Arab Spring." Although humanitarian issues and human rights were part of this story, they were not its central animating force. Over time, as the conflict descended into a multisided civil war, humanitarian and human rights frames arguably assumed a more prominent role, with numerous actors in the conflict accusing one another of human rights violations. As such, it may well be that the degree to which journalists shunned human rights perspectives in the early period of observation reflects broader public perceptions, not just journalists' professional worldview. Whether this is in fact so is beyond the scope of this current chapter, however.

FIELD INERTIA: JOURNALISM'S BIASES VIS-À-VIS ADVOCACY GROUPS

In June 2011, journalists descended for the first time onto Turkey's Hatay region. The initial reason for their presence was straightforward. In that month, somewhere between ten thousand and fifteen thousand Syrians had fled their homes and crossed in Turkey. This number, although tiny when compared to the eventual scale of the refugee inflow,[4] sparked the interest of news organizations, which wanted to know whether such movements represented the latest in a series of regional protests then referred to as the "Arab Spring" or constituted a harbinger of a more violent conflict in Syria. For the most part denied legal access into Syria, news organizations were largely unable to directly report on the conflict and were thus eager to interview firsthand—either with their own reporters or with freelancers—the Syrian citizens who had crossed the border.

Accomplishing this task was not easy. Most news organizations had little familiarity with the region. Few reporters had spent any time in southern Turkey and thus had a limited number of contacts in the area. The Turkish government, which at the time was hosting in camps the majority of those fleeing Syria, was largely unresponsive to media requests for interviews or access to the camps. Interviewing Syrian citizens also proved challenging. Many news organizations sent journalists from their Istanbul news bureaus, and these journalists were likely to speak Turkish rather than Arabic. Even those who spoke Arabic had to find ways to cover a story that was fluid and had few easily identifiable points of entry in terms of contacts and sources.[5]

NGOs quickly emerged as one solution to this problem. These groups had local contacts in both Syria and Turkey, and their researchers often had prior experiences working in similar crisis situations. They could help introduce journalists to sources, give them necessary background information on unfolding events, and bring them to places where they could "find" news. When I asked one newspaper reporter how he began his reporting on the situation, he replied, "I interviewed the Human Rights Watch guy. He helped me to interview refugees."[6] Thus, in the "tug of war" relationship (Gans 1979, 117) that governs reporters and their sources, NGOs provided an important set of information subsidies (Gandy 1982), which included access to sources, story ideas, and verification of claims.

In return, journalists would report on the issues that mattered most to the humanitarian and human rights communities.

On its face, this state of affairs suggested a favorable dynamic for NGOs. Not only did they stand a greater chance of garnering news coverage, but their background in the region also made it possible to imagine that they would steer news coverage in a direction that focused more on the humanitarian and human rights dimensions of the unfolding situation. Indeed, this redirection did sometimes occur. In June 2011, both the *New York Times* and the *Wall Street Journal* published news stories about media centers in Syria run by local activists. In both cases, NGOs had told the reporters about these stories.[7] These two outlets also brought the reporters into Syria so that they could interview the relevant activists. Although the NGOs themselves were not named in the story, the coverage clearly focused on the human rights and activist dimensions of the Syrian crisis (rather than on, say, troop movements or government policies).

Yet such stories were the exception rather than the rule. NGOs played a key role as news sources, but the specific roles they played largely conformed to extant news norms regarding advocacy groups: timeliness and drama. A prerequisite for journalistic interest was that the advocacy groups' message, whatever its content, fit into the reporters' ideas of what constitutes a story. The extent to which advocacy groups and journalists agree on whether something is a story varies, and issues that advocacy groups deem important are sometimes seen as too complex or uninteresting to appeal to journalists' editors and audiences. Moreover, reporters look to NGOs to fulfill a specific set of roles, which means NGOs are often used to add a "human dimension" to news stories. Although NGOs work on issues that do not fit into these news norms, these issues seldom make their way into the news. The question, therefore, is why this should be the case.

A first reason is structural. For reporters in the field, their primary goal is to get into the news. In order to get into the news, these reporters must provide the types of coverage that interest their editors. Journalists seek out NGOs for help in satisfying this need; however, because editors are above reporters in the news hierarchy, the reporters' capacity to get their stories in the news is predicated on their utilization of news norms that emphasize drama, timeliness, and conflict. Moreover, given the beat system's orientation toward government sources, reporters are required to justify their reliance on NGOs in ways that they are not when relying on government sources. Taken together, these factors lead reporters to minimize the extent to which they use NGOs in their reporting efforts.

For reporters in the field, the goal is to get into the news. This is neither an easy thing to do nor a guaranteed outcome. International news topics compete with one another for inclusion in newspapers, on radio and television, and even online. This was a theme discussed by a number of journalists: "It's a struggle to get space in the paper," one stated. "Most days, I call [the editors] in the morning and tell them what my story is. And then at 3:00 p.m. their time, they call back and tell me whether they are interested and how many words I get."[8] Others echoed this view, suggesting an intense competition between journalists at the same newspaper to garner coverage for their issue or topic. Moreover, although online news is potentially unlimited in the amount of news it can offer, journalists report that their editors typically use wire-service copy for webpages while preserving original reporting for the legacy editions. "They [editors] make their schedule for the print edition. They ask me whether I have something new to tell [beyond what the wires already reported]."[9]

In order to get into the news, journalists thus have to provide the types of coverage that will interest their editors. What this coverage is varies by publication but generally converges around topics and issues that correspond with well-established news norms of drama and timeliness. One person clarified: "My newspaper is interested in news that will draw readers." When asked to elaborate, he said: "It has to be a scoop or incredibly weird and quirky. In terms of deeper analysis, they're difficult stories to pitch."[10] One day in Turkey, for example, there were rumors that people had set themselves on fire in Syria to protest the regime. One person remarked: "If that were true, it would be a big headline."[11] Ultimately, the story was apocryphal; nonetheless, interest in it reflected a commitment to providing news that editors would find interesting.

In this setting, journalists seek out NGOs for help in satisfying this need. As several reporters noted, situations like the one on the Turkey–Syria border involve a substantial number of local activists, who maintain different types and levels of trust with international NGOs and the news media. Journalists stressed to me that NGO professionals are able to generate trust with potential sources because they are viewed as activists, who can keep their sources anonymous and will be sympathetic to activist claims. By contrast, journalists stressed that granting anonymity was for them difficult and required their editors' approval. Moreover, they reported that activists were often skeptical of the reporters' ultimate aims.[12] One journalist summed up sources' attitudes toward NGO workers and journalists in the following way:

> NGOs get more access. Or maybe it's a different kind of access. If you're a group of activists in a Syrian camp and [Human Rights Watch] comes in, they [Human Rights Watch] can say, "Look, we're activists, too." And that's a very different kind of relationship than me coming in saying, "I'm a journalist, and I'm here to talk to you about your story." I think there is a different kind of access that they get based on that mutual affiliation or recognition.[13]

When reporters turn to NGOs for help in covering the news, they must convince their editors of a story's importance. Here, reporters stressed tensions between what they see "on the ground" and which aspects of their reporting attract the interest of editors back home. These editors monitor the wire services, so they want their reporters to provide coverage that is different from what other outlets are already reporting and yet that is also in keeping with established norms of timeliness, drama, and conflict. Reporters are in touch with their editors—either by phone or via email—multiple times a day to talk about their story ideas. From these discussions, reporters understand quickly what types of stories will and will not attract editorial attention. "My editors want light, funny stories, maybe with some political element," said one person.[14] One reporter who is regularly based in Istanbul offered an example: "I did a story about [Turkish prime minister Recep] Erdoğan's daughter and this actor being suspended from a play because he had made a lewd gesture on stage. Erdoğan's daughter was in the audience, and it was directed at her, and she stormed out. And now this guy's under investigation. It was just kind of a silly story."[15]

Efforts to alter editors' preferences are difficult, given the lower status of reporters and especially freelancers vis-à-vis editors. The people doing the reporting at the border in 2011 tended to be relatively young, both in demographic and career terms. One person succinctly described his status: "I'm quite junior. I'm not a staffer. If I was an experienced correspondent and had been working for twenty years, and I said, 'Look, this social media thing is key to this, and we should do a story on this,' then the foreign desk would probably be more inclined to listen."[16] Others echoed the assessment. Generally speaking, the newsroom hierarchy works to reinforce extant news norms because decision-making power about what constitutes news remains centralized in the newsroom.

A second reason that news norms endure is cognitive. Journalists think of NGOs as fulfilling a specific set of roles, which can then be slotted into stories driven by other sources. When I asked journalists what events initially brought them to the border, most reported that they came after hearing reports of Syrian troops firing on their own citizens. "I went when the news broke that the Syrian army was getting closer to the border."[17] According to most traditional definitions of news, this qualified as a news story. It was highly dramatic and focused on the actions of government officials. Moreover, given its connection to the ongoing "Arab Spring" throughout the region, the story could be linked to other developments around the region, thus lending an important sense of timing to the events. But as both Syrian activists and NGO professionals stressed, this story was hardly the only one to be reported: nascent camps raised questions about the legal status of Syrians in Turkey, and civil society efforts in Syria provided different lenses through which to understand these events.[18]

In this context, reporters look to NGOs to fill a specific set of roles, and they slot them into news stories driven by other news criteria (official action, drama, timeliness). NGOs could bring refugees to journalists to "add a human dimension" to the story. These persons could also add to the drama of the unfolding news and situate it within a broader theme of democratic uprisings. "This is a story that we need people to tell effectively. . . . They [NGOs] help us do that."[19] Finally, by linking journalists with activists, NGOs also fulfilled the reporters' need for perceived authenticity. As one person put it, turning to NGOs helped to legitimate their reporting efforts to the people they wanted to interview as sources.[20]

Interestingly, reporters also looked to NGOs for help performing some of their own work, especially fact checking. In the Syrian refugee situation discussed here, because journalists had little rapport with local activists, they had a difficult time differentiating true and false rumors. One day, for example, rumors began to circulate about a bakery in Syria being bombed by government forces. This was a strong allegation and one with potential news value: if true, it would highlight the regime's increasing brutality to its own citizens. The focus on a bakery also personalized the event in a compelling way. Human Rights Watch researchers conducted phone interviews with residents in the affected city in order to confirm the claim. In another case, a reporter described a relationship with a different NGO: "He [the NGO's representative] has a clear of idea of what's happening and why it's happening. Every time I heard news in Guvecci, I would call him and say, 'Here's what I'm hearing. Is it true?' And he would tell [me]. Or if he didn't know, he would call around and check for me."[21] In cases like this, NGOs do work that is more or less indistinguishable from mainstream concepts of journalism.

At the same time, NGOs sought to tell a variety of other stories that did not make it into the news. Both humanitarian and human rights groups focused their attention on ensuring refugees would have access to the United Nations. They worried that the Turkish government was bringing Syrian officials into the camps and trying to get them to take the refugees back, which violated international law and thus drew NGO ire. Yet these stories stood outside the established news narrative: journalists were there to cover the story of Syria's uprising. They thus saw the dynamics of international humanitarian provision as outside their scope: "There are some things that are extraordinary stories but don't get a lot of play," one person explained. "But [the camp story is] a difficult pitch for the *Times*. It's too involved for them. They also say it's a story that hasn't happened yet. It's frustrating."[22] These stories failed because they did not accord with news norms. In short, reporters were happy to use NGOs when the NGOs' efforts accorded with the reporters' aims and to jettison them when they did not.

The result is thus field inertia: that is, the field's tendency to reproduce its own norms despite changing conditions of production. Reporters draw from NGOs in order to improve their chances of getting their stories in the news; however, established news norms place NGOs' newsmaking efforts within a narrow frame of possible functions that center primarily around adding color, personalizing and dramatizing information, and to some degree evaluating the accuracy of claims on the ground. Newsroom hierarchies, which place editors in a superior position to reporters, function as a mechanism for ensuring the reproduction of these norms, even when journalists are exposed to situations that might produce alternative reporting outcomes.

A conversation with an Istanbul-based freelancer nicely illustrates these dynamics. We met for coffee on the morning he was due to fly back to Istanbul. I asked him whether he would be coming back to the Syrian border. "They [my editors] said to be ready to come back if things kick up again." I asked what "kicking up" might entail. "The situation they said was if you have Syrian soldiers firing on Turkish soldiers," he replied.[23] This event was unlikely in geopolitical terms at the time, but it encapsulated all the elements that his editors wanted in a story that would be worth their resource expenditures. He said good-bye to me and to one of the NGO professionals he had worked with and departed for the airport to return to Istanbul.

FIELD DIFFUSION: EXTENDING NEWS NORMS INTO NON-NEWS SETTINGS

News norms are not only reproduced within the journalistic field but also diffused outward onto other fields, such as that of NGOs. Economic challenges within journalism have led journalists to seek employment in cognate fields. Although journalists leaving journalism is by no means new, having fields that hire journalists in order to do journalism (e.g., report news, produce multimedia) is. In these new roles, former (and sometimes still active) reporters bring the sensibility of journalism to advocacy groups' news-making efforts: they discuss the need for timely, balanced, dramatic, and personalized news reports. This sensibility allows journalistic norms to diffuse into the NGO and other sectors, which in turn makes it more likely that advocacy groups will produce information in keeping with the news media's preferences. This diffusion is enabled by the NGO sector's own efforts toward professionalization, which places a growing emphasis on publicity. It also dovetails with what Ben Jones (2017) calls the "mediatization" of NGOs.

The combination of newsroom cutbacks and NGO professionalization has helped to bring journalists into the NGO sector in at least two ways. First, former reporters take positions within the communication departments of advocacy groups. In a survey of leading groups that I conducted, more than half (57.7 percent) of the individuals working in communication departments had prior job experience in the media industry (Powers 2013). Interviews with senior officials at these organizations suggest that the proportion of former journalists switching to the humanitarian and human rights sector is growing over time.[24] This change is one of degree because former journalists have for decades switched from journalism to advocacy. Yet the frequency of the change has grown, as has the corresponding perception that such a shift is more natural today than it was in the past. A freelance journalist working for several American news organizations told me that he had interned at Human Rights Watch while in graduate school prior to embarking on a journalism career. In the course of our conversation (and unbidden by me), he mentioned several "colleagues" who had switched back and forth between the advocacy and journalism sectors.[25] The point was further brought home by a person with a journalism background who had worked at Human Rights Watch for several decades and who described the transition from journalism to advocacy as follows:

> I think in retrospect often people in the very troubled news business today credit me with some sort of clairvoyance for having made the switch to [Human Rights Watch] [laughs], but it did not appear to be such a brilliant choice at the time. It was kind of like you are the international correspondent for *Newsweek* magazine. You know, my beat was the world; I had, like, a global remit. Why would you want to go and work at [Human Rights Watch]? It sort of wasn't obvious. Whereas today many more people, journalists, have come to [Human Rights Watch], many more journalists are leaving the profession and looking for homes at NGOs. And it seems kind of a more natural thing to do. Not that it was unnatural at the time. But it was a less-trod path.[26]

A second, less-permanent form of field diffusion occurs with temporary contract work between freelance journalists and advocacy groups. Economic necessity (and, to some extent, ideological affinity) leads reporters and photographers to perform contract work for NGOs.

There are no available quantitative data regarding the extent of these interactions, but multiple qualitative studies suggest such interactions are regular and growing over time. David Conrad (2015) has explored partnerships between nonprofits and freelancers and documents contestation over how events are framed and represented as a result. In several thoughtful publications, Kate Wright (2016a, 2016b) has documented regular interactions between human rights organizations and freelance journalists working in various parts of Africa.[27] Finally, Louise Grayson (2014) reflects on her own experiences as a contracted freelance photojournalist working with an NGO.

Freelancers are motivated in part by the financial remuneration by NGOs, which typically rivals the contracts offered by news organizations to freelancers. They also are motivated by a desire to continue reporting on the stories that they find personally and professionally meaningful but that news media are either unable or unwilling to fund. In her study of freelancers who work for NGOs, Wright reports one journalist's explanation for taking up work with NGOs: "I wanted to be *freer* to do the kind of journalism that I think needs to be out there" (2016b, 1001, emphasis in the original).[28] As Wright emphasizes, such a remark points to the ambivalent nature of freelance labor. On the one hand, journalists interact with advocacy groups primarily because of structural shifts in journalism employment over which they have little agency. On the other hand, the experience of freelancing also appears to open up new possibilities for those same journalists, who often report a greater ability to tell the stories that interest them most when they work with advocacy groups.

Whether as contract workers or full-time staffers, journalists bring a news sensibility to NGOs. This sensibility aims to instruct advocacy groups about how to capture media attention. Former journalists turned communication professionals described efforts to distill news norms of timeliness, balance, personalization, and drama to their media products for NGOs. At several organizations, individuals attempted to get their organizations to produce information in accordance with news norms of timeliness. "As an organization, we take a long time to get things approved. By the time they're approved, journalists have moved on [to another story]."[29] Others echoed this point, and in at least some organizations this drive for timeliness has resulted in the creation of "emergency" units charged with providing research in real time (see chapter 2).

Journalists working at NGOs also described efforts to bring norms of balance to media products. At Médecins Sans Frontières, one person with a background in television described her organization's prior audio-visual productions as "glorified ads" that simply moved from one scene featuring the organization to another and reported that news organizations would not take up such productions. "To be honest, if we provide bad footage, Reuters just won't take it.[30] A former journalist now working at Amnesty International described similar efforts to ensure that his organization took into account "the interest of broadcasters" and did not "give too much praise" to only the groups Amnesty supports.[31] This former journalist's colleague at Amnesty, also with a background in journalism, added that he was now encouraging the organization to get the perspective of opponents so that the resulting media product "has some balance to it."[32]

Journalists working at NGOs also describe efforts to bring norms of drama and personalization to their new employers. Advocacy groups are not uninterested in these norms; however, the trajectory of their research practices has long led them to produce detailed and often policy-oriented reports. For individuals with backgrounds in news, such reports look stale and uninteresting. They view their job as drawing out the human-interest aspect of those stories. "This research is filled with human emotion, but it's often left out of the reports. I try to bring it back in."[33] At Amnesty International, the head of the news unit described his task as finding the dramatic story line that could garner the media's attention. One day, for example, research staff disclosed that they had obtained a draft copy of a Saudi Arabian antiterrorism law. The research staff's primary interest in the law was its proposal to treat domestic dissent as a crime. Everyone saw it as an important issue, and several members of the publicity team were brought in to find the best way of framing the issue for news coverage. After poring through the document for hours, they came across a passage indicating that citizens could serve jail time for criticizing the king. "You can get ten years for insulting the king—that's the lead for the *New York Times!*" one person exclaimed. In conversation later that day, the head of the news unit at Amnesty stressed to me: "That's where our skills are—finding the news hook."[34]

Of course, journalists must adapt to their new work environment, and they do not unilaterally control all the information work done in their new organizations. Former journalists describe initial forms of "culture shock" when arriving at their new workplaces. One person discussed her surprise and impatience, for example, with the amount and duration of meetings. "I don't think I ever was in a meeting in twelve years at *Newsweek* that lasted more than an hour. I mean, that would have just been unthinkable."[35] This type of organizational slowness, she suggested, cuts up against the news media's need for information presented in a timely manner. Others echoed this point while expressing their frustration with trying to get things "to move through the organization more quickly."[36] In these and related instances, one can see path dependencies within the NGO field that allows NGOs to stave off external demands for change.

Despite these frustrations, the presence of journalists within an advocacy organization does increase the journalists' control over the content and style of the group's public messaging. As public-relations officers, they get to decide how a press release should be written, which leads them to emphasize the news norms discussed earlier. As freelance contract workers, they get to narrate their stories in ways that are in keeping with their news sensibility. Although it is true that some research or advocacy aims will not be subjected to public messaging, the parts that do are subject to established norms of news worthiness. And although former journalists initially do not enjoy high status within their new organizations, they do increasingly come to exert their influence in deciding how to tell news stories. Several examples from the extant literature can illustrate these points.

Drawing on her own experiences as a freelance photographer, Grayson nicely demonstrates the extension of news norms. At the outset of her assignment, she is "required to take photographs of particular activities . . . that reflect the positive impacts of the work being done [by the NGO]" (2014, 636). Other NGO staffers make specific suggestions of what she should photograph, thus demonstrating a "preconceived idea of the kinds of photographs they want" (637). As her work continues, though, these staffers "have begun to get to know and trust me, so [they] give me greater autonomy" (638). This autonomy allows her to take photographs that focus less on the NGO's positive impacts and more on the social contrasts and the human drama that the photographer sees. She finds that the latter images ultimately more closely approximate the types of photographs that might interest news organizations.

Wright provides a related example. Through interviews with freelance journalists working for NGOs, she discovered that although they work with advocacy groups in the hopes of gaining greater autonomy to do the work they find meaningful, that autonomy is in fact circumscribed by demands that the content they produce be newsy. Because advocacy groups want to appear in the news, they hire journalists who have established relations of trust with prominent news outlets. A former journalist's article, for example, was accepted for the front page of a prominent newspaper because the editor was "so impressed with his [the former journalist's] master of in-house style, which meant that the article would require very little editing." Moreover, "the veracity of the material could be ensured" because the people involved in producing the article were former journalists (Wright 2016b, 997). Thus, what happens is that news norms diffuse into the advocacy sector as a function of the diffusion of former journalists into the NGO sector (see also Jones 2017).

Paradoxically, part of what drives the diffusion of news norms is NGO professionalization. As discussed in the previous chapter, news coverage is viewed by donors and political officials as one indicator of NGO efficacy. Humanitarian and human rights groups work on issues where success is often difficult to define. When asked whether a particular advocacy effort "worked," one person responded: "No, it wouldn't be that quick. . . . It's hard to be really direct about [whether an effort worked or not]."[37] In those settings, media coverage thus becomes an indicator of effectiveness and impact. Moreover, media coverage is a way of ensuring the relevance of both the organization in general, and the communication staff in particular. As one person at Amnesty International put it, "Our argument [i.e., the communication staff's argument] is [that] Amnesty needs to be seen in order to be relevant."[38] In order to get their organization's name out, NGO staffers see themselves as "walking into the [news] media's turf," as another person put it. "We have to play by their rules."[39]

Growing professionalization and competition within the NGO sector thus make news coverage more important, which helps propagate news norms in spite of the media's growing institutional weakness (in terms of jobs for journalists). Because editors retain their power to decide news, they continue to enforce news norms, even when the reporters producing copy at times work for advocacy organizations. Thus, the growing resources that advocacy groups acquire are converted—or attempts are made to convert them—into media coverage. Freelance and former journalists are hired explicitly in the hopes of "leveraging their social networks" in the press, as one NGO professional explained to Wright (quoted in Wright 2016b, 997). On the whole, this development points to the importance of diffusion dynamics as a way to ensure that news norms endure, even when the historical bases of international news production are transforming rapidly.

Despite expectations of changes in news norms, in reality those norms remain relatively stable. News coverage of humanitarian and human rights issues is shaped by the long-established values of timeliness, drama, and conflict. Although NGOs have developed ways of inserting their messages within this normative order, a whole range of stories they would like to tell remain absent from the news. This is the case even though advocacy groups dedicate greater resources to news production today than they did in the past. This contradiction creates a puzzle, which this chapter has sought to unravel: how to explain the relative continuity of news norms in a period of dramatic changes in journalism, politics, and advocacy.

This chapter has drawn on the concept of "mechanisms" described in institutional theory to explain this puzzle. Specifically, it has identified two distinct sets of actions that reproduce news norms. In the first, inertia is produced through the specific actions taken both by reporters in the field and their editors in newsrooms. Journalists remain wedded to a view of NGOs primarily as advocates, and they look to NGO professionals to complete tasks that fulfill that advocacy function. This view is reinforced by editors, who are farther up in the newsroom decision-making hierarchy and ensure adherence to news norms. In the second, news norms diffuse into the NGO sector due to the increasing circulation of former (and sometimes still active) reporters in advocacy groups, who bring news norms into the groups' news-making efforts. This allows journalism norms to diffuse into other sectors, which in turn makes it more likely that advocacy groups will produce information in keeping with the preferences of the news media.

Although distinct, these two mechanisms—field inertia and field diffusion—help to reproduce news norms. Their existence suggests that extant forms of news production are unlikely to change radically, even though the social bases of news production are indeed experiencing dramatic changes. In this way, the research dovetails with recent empirical and theoretical work that argues that journalism has in the past several decades extended its "unique epistemology and form of producing knowledge" into an array of social fields (Waisbord 2013, 139), even as its economic foundations have been crumbling. More generally, this research contributes to an emerging literature that identifies strong continuities in journalistic norms over time (Anderson 2013; Graves 2016; Ryfe 2011).

Although this chapter stresses the role of mechanisms in shaping continuity, it is important to note that such continuity is not automatic. It is possible that the conditions under which the mechanisms identified here occur will change and that this change could trigger a larger transformation in news norms. The mechanism of field diffusion, for example, captures NGOs at a specific moment in time—namely, a moment when the importance of media publicity to fulfilling their organizational goals is on the rise. This situation gives media professionals prominence in the organizations at which they work, if only because their skills hold the promise of fulfilling specific aims.[40] Crucially, this importance exists not simply due to some pervasive media logic that saturates all social institutions but also because of independent developments within the NGO sector related to fund-raising and philanthropy, which are then connected to the aim of generating media publicity.

Media power is not total, and countervailing tendencies within advocacy organizations can turn against the adoption of news norms. For example, as we have seen in prior chapters, advocacy strategies are premised on the idea that coverage in the mainstream media remains important. However, there are a number of reasons to be skeptical that this will always remain true. For humanitarian and human rights groups, sometimes they just need to reach a limited number of decision makers. As these groups develop their digital strategies, they might encounter (or create) ways of reaching these decision makers that have little to do with media coverage. Such a possibility can be glimpsed in efforts by human rights groups to amplify pressure on governments through social media campaigns. Similar efforts could conceivably put advocacy professionals on the ascent within these organizations and lead to a concomitant de-emphasis on individuals with journalism expertise.

At the same time, it is important not to overstate the potential for radical change. The extent to which contemporary advocacy is "mediated" is difficult to understate. Like other social groups, NGOs think about how their efforts will play in "the media" as they strategize other aspects of their work (Jones 2017). Rather than journalism and advocacy being viewed as independent and separate, it is more plausible to see them as interacting in a hybrid media system that contains both media and advocacy logics (Chadwick 2013). Moreover, there are strong institutional reasons for NGOs to persist in adapting to news norms. On the whole, then, the continuity of current news norms seems likely, though it is not guaranteed.

A more plausible way that the mechanisms discussed in this chapter may change has to do with ongoing changes in foreign correspondence. Given the central role of the editor–reporter relationship in shaping news norms, it is possible to imagine this relationship changing as fewer and fewer reporters are dispatched to cover humanitarian and human rights issues around the world. Put bluntly, editors can enforce news norms only in places where reporters are stationed. As news outlets continue to cut back on international news gathering, the possibility of a growing number of places without correspondents is likely to increase. This means that NGO professionals will lose their on-the-ground ally in getting news coverage.[41] One possible result would be a loss in coverage of humanitarian and human rights issues in places where the news media do not send reporters and in general. Given the site of my research and the fact that journalists were there, if only briefly, it is difficult to know how and in what ways this loss of coverage might affect NGOs. It might lead advocacy groups to further utilize digital platforms, as can be seen in the development of issue-specific websites that provide in-depth reporting on humanitarian or human rights problems. It might also lead advocacy groups to further intensify their efforts to recruit journalists to accompany their research teams on specific trips, in the hopes of boosting their chances of getting news coverage. Whether news norms change, mechanisms are important analytical tools for explaining their stability or evolution. The fact that norms do not change is an important finding; however, explaining precisely what needs to occur in order to ensure continuity is another. This chapter has sought to engage the latter aim and in doing so to close the circuit of cultural production that shapes the production of contemporary humanitarian and human rights news.

CHAPTER SEVEN

The Possibilities and Limitations of NGO Communication

Throughout this book, I have explored the growing role played by NGOs in shaping and in some cases directly producing news coverage about humanitarian and human rights issues. In contrast to optimistic and pessimistic views alike, I have suggested that NGOs are best viewed as a double-edged sword. On the one hand, these groups do expand news coverage. They are more likely to appear in the news today than they were in the past. Moreover, with digital tools and a growing media savvy, these groups are increasingly able to graft advocacy angles onto trending news topics. As a result, such groups play a critical role in shaping public awareness of humanitarian and human rights issues. On the other hand, these efforts also have a cost. In their quest to garner publicity, NGOs adopt news norms that leave journalists and government officials with the upper hand in defining newsworthy topics. This means NGOs tend to appear on issues and in places where the news media are already interested. Moreover, despite the potential for digital technologies to circumvent these patterns of control, NGOs use such tools primarily to interact with journalists and to protect their organizational credibility. Exploring alternative forms of public engagement is secondary.

In describing the double-edged nature of NGO communication efforts, I have sought to account for the complex mixture of continuity and change in the fields of both advocacy and journalism. NGO communication has grown and diversified in recent years, and it has done so in part due to the shifting institutional environments in which these groups are located. Donors fund these groups in part for their capacity to generate public awareness of key humanitarian and human rights issues; government officials include such groups in their deliberations because they view these groups as public representatives, and this inclusion diversifies the number of institutional voices involved in elite debates; and news organizations—confronting staff reductions—are increasingly likely to turn to these groups to help them cover humanitarian and human rights issues. At the same time, NGO communication is also marked by clear continuities with past practices. Such groups continue to rely heavily on the news media for publicity and utilize digital tools strategically and with an eye toward potentially negative outcomes. Such continuities are also institutional outcomes. Donors want to see these groups in the news; government officials pay attention to legacy news outlet coverage; and journalists—who continue to see NGOs as advocates—occupy socially proximate positions to NGO professionals in the social world. Each of these factors incentivizes continuity of NGO communication efforts.

In this final chapter, I bring these various strands together to discuss the possibilities and limitations of NGO communication. I begin by evaluating the findings presented in this book in light of normative theories of public communication. I proceed to describe ways in which NGO communication can be improved from its current status to accentuate its strengths while correcting to some degree for its weaknesses. I then situate the findings of this book within a discussion of the broader rise of what I term news-oriented practices—that is, efforts by nonjournalistic actors to directly shape public communication. Finally, I conclude with a discussion of what I see as the core analytical contribution of this book: how institutions matter.

EVALUATING NGO COMMUNICATION

NGOs are awkward symbols of the contemporary landscape of international news.[1] In their efforts to raise attention toward—and to design action recommendations for—pressing humanitarian and human rights issues, they highlight some of the highest aspirations of global communication. Individuals connected by little more than news coverage can learn and do something about human suffering half a world away (Appiah 2006; Beck 2006; Silverstone 2007). At the same time, these efforts are hampered by organizational and institutional constraints that I have detailed throughout this book. These constraints not only frustrate the cosmopolitan aspirations articulated by some NGOs and academics theorists but also can and do produce communication that misrepresents the causes and nature of humanitarian and human rights problems.

How, then, should we evaluate such efforts? My own view is that the efforts I chronicle in this book are on the whole salutary. NGOs produce information about important and often ignored events. In some cases, they are one of the only institutional actors providing credible information about humanitarian and human rights issues to Western audiences. Institutional forces amplify some aspects of this information (by encouraging mainstream media coverage of traditional human rights issues) while downplaying others (by accepting news norms as given and trying to adapt to them). Although this situation represents a double-edged sword, I would rather live in a world that has advocacy groups producing these mixed effects than one where they are less involved in the public sphere.

In saying this, I do not want to suggest that NGO communication is an unalloyed boon to the public sphere. Clearly, there are shortcomings to this development, and I have chronicled many of them in this book. Nor do I wish to imply that NGOs' efforts cannot be improved from their current state. They can and should, and my discussion in this chapter suggests some ways in which that improvement might occur. What I do want to suggest is that insofar as the choice is between NGOs communicating in the ways they do (i.e., imperfectly) or not at all, I would vote for the former. NGOs are not a blank slate onto which normative aspirations can be drawn; rather, they are historical creatures embedded in a social context. My evaluation of their efforts is based on an analysis of what they can do based on the possibilities and limitations inherent to this context.

Before further articulating my perspective, I think it useful to situate a discussion about the evaluation of NGO efforts in relation to broader normative theories of public communication.[2] Such theories prescribe the ideal roles and responsibilities for both the participants and outcomes of public communication (Benson 2009; Christians et al. 2009; Ferree et al. 2002). These broader ideals provide a measuring stick that is useful for evaluating the relationship between how public communicators perform and how they ought to perform in order to best satisfy their civic obligations. As such, these normative theories provide the background that inform my thinking about how to evaluate NGOs' communication efforts.

As I see it, normative theories of public communication suggest four distinctive roles for NGOs: first, as experts, a role rooted in representative liberalism; second, as advocates, a role tied to participatory democracy; third, as facilitators of dialogue, a role found in deliberative traditions; and, fourth, as critics, a role associated with radical theories of democracy. My reading of the literature, including the findings presented in this book, suggests that NGOs most closely approximate the aims of the representative liberal and participatory democratic traditions while downplaying deliberative and radical aims. I briefly want to highlight the four roles articulated by these traditions and suggest how and in what ways NGOs fulfill or frustrate these roles. After doing so, I then return to my own evaluation of NGOs as being, on balance, salutary for the contemporary public sphere.

NGOs as Experts

The normative tradition that NGOs in their capacity as news providers most closely approximate is representative liberalism. This tradition begins from the premise that contemporary societies are complex and differentiated; therefore, citizens are not expected to be especially knowledgeable about public affairs (Lippmann 1922). Journalists and public communicators are thus tasked with bringing informed views to their audiences. To do so, they rely on government representatives and, to a lesser degree, on experts who have the knowledge necessary to inform and enlighten (Schudson 2008). For representative liberals, news should generally aspire to a norm of impartiality: all else being equal, journalists are tasked with presenting the facts of a story and airing opposing views among government representatives and experts (Ferree et al. 2002).

Within the representative liberal tradition, the primary value of NGOs is their role as experts.[3] They can and do provide information—to journalists or to the public directly—that is factual in nature and based on evidence. This information certainly can support a particular cause; however, insofar as the information is seen as credible—that is, that a different party would collect similar information and arrive at similar conclusions (Korey 1998)—the NGO retains its authority as an expert. This authority can be damaged when a group fails to live up to this evidence-based standard, as when it allows advocacy or fund-raising aims to drive its coverage (de Waal 1998). This criterion of transparency governs the actions of NGOs and journalists alike. One example of applying this criterion in practice would be in the growing utilization of NGO materials by news organizations (Powers 2015c; Van Leuven and Joye 2014; Wright 2016b). From the representative liberal perspective, the question is whether the materials relay expert information (e.g., field reports, visual documentation of human rights violations, and so on). Despite occasional issues with accuracy, NGOs can and do seek to provide exactly this sort of information.

NGOs as Advocates

NGOs also closely approximate participatory democratic normative traditions. This theory articulates a vision of public communication that centers on the promotion of participation in civic life. Like representative liberals, participatory democrats agree that contemporary societies are complex and differentiated; however, theorists in this tradition believe that citizens have the capacity to become more deeply knowledgeable about public affairs (Dewey 1927). News media are understood to be key vehicles in achieving this aim. Unlike representative liberalism, the participatory democratic perspective encourages a wide range of communicative styles (Ferree et al. 2002): some argue that tabloid models of journalism might spur otherwise apathetic citizens to become interested in politics (McNair 2000); others suggest that mainstream news media should provide a greater array of perspectives (Gans 2003). Although participatory democrats disagree about the optimal style and form of communication, they generally agree that journalists can—and should—move beyond the dispassionate accounts of daily events that representative liberalism requires.

Within the participatory tradition, NGOs are valued primarily for their role as advocates. They are expected to help raise public awareness of key social issues (Keck and Sikkink 1998). Informing citizens may be an important aspect of the advocacy role, but it is not central; instead, participatory democrats emphasize that NGOs as newsmakers should strive to make citizens aware of—rather than just fully competent in—previously ignored issues. This initial awareness forms what is sometimes called a "ladder of engagement," wherein initial awareness spurs further discussions and civic action. Advocacy efforts that fuel this engagement may be optimal, but participatory democrats are not united on this point: in general, it would be fair to say awareness is seen as the key end in its own right. In order to achieve this goal, NGOs can and do utilize a wide range of communicative styles, including but not limited to conducting campaigns and producing arresting visuals (Ferree et al. 2002).

NGOs as Facilitators

Although NGOs approximate the representative liberal and participatory democratic ideals, the research presented here suggests that they struggle to achieve the norms required in the discursive tradition. Theorists of this tradition share with participatory democrats a belief that public communication should actively promote civic engagement. They differ, however, on how best to achieve this aim. For those in the discursive tradition, the route to civic engagement must pass through a process of reasoned debate among ordinary citizens (Friedland and Hove 2016; Habermas 1998). Journalists are tasked not only with informing their audiences but also with ensuring that news will shape an atmosphere of debate wherein the best argument can carry the day. To do this, journalists should include a wide range of perspectives drawn from a cross-section of society, including but not limited to NGOs.

Discursive theorists accord an important role to NGOs as facilitators of public communication. As the dominant organizational layer of civil society, such groups act as an intermediary between different pockets of civil society and the mainstream media (Habermas 1998; Wessler 2008). As we have seen, though, these groups tend to have relatively low levels of interaction and engagement with the public. Online tools, which in principle might be assumed to boost this interaction and cultivate novel forms of engagement, do little to alter the equation. Moreover, deliberative traditions assign a core role for NGOs to facilitate deliberation across diverse social groups. Yet we have seen that the presence of leading NGOs in the news tends to crowd out smaller civil society groups. A final way in which NGOs fall short of discursive ideals is the tendency—at least among some organizations—to use publicity as a way to raise funds or awareness rather than to facilitate debate.[4] In this book, we have seen that communication professionals view disaster situations—such as the aftermath of an earthquake or tsunami—as an opportunity to raise funds. This suggests that NGOs' news-making efforts focus less on facilitating debate and more on achieving strategic objectives.

NGOs as Critics

In their public communication efforts, NGOs appear least likely to satisfy the ideals put forth by radical democratic traditions. In radical democratic theories, NGOs are tasked primarily with the role of social critic (Curran 2005). In their communication efforts, they are valued for their capacity to question the status quo and to expose systemic injustices. Like participatory democrats, they may utilize a wide range of communicative styles in order to achieve this aim; controversial presentations are especially valued (Downing 2001). However, these styles must be used toward achieving the ideal of emancipation; they are not valued simply for their capacity to garner attention. NGOs can work successfully with journalists only insofar as these collaborations help to realize radical aims. When journalistic norms impinge upon such a capacity, NGOs are encouraged to seek alternative publicity avenues (Fenton 2010).

Throughout this book, however, we have seen that NGOs do little to alter dominant news norms. Instead, these groups package and pitch news stories in ways that mimic or "clone" (Fenton 2010, 156) the news that journalists would make on their own. Moreover, these groups use digital tools mainly to monitor news norms and mimic news codes rather than to circumvent those norms and codes. Further, although some researchers argue that the adoption of news norms helps advocacy groups compete with better-resourced competitors, such as government and business (Greenberg, Knight, and Westersund 2011), most argue that such a move makes NGOs less able to engage in radical forms of social criticism as called for in radical democratic theory (Fenton 2010). One effect is that NGOs tend to shun discussions about the root causes of the problems they describe.

Given the mixed evaluations described in the preceding material, why do I suggest that NGO communication efforts are on the whole salutary? My view is rooted in part in the idea that something is better than nothing. NGOs can and do provide important functions in contemporary public communication. The information they provide is often undercovered, and the perspective they insert is at least sometimes distinct from the perspectives of government officials and business leaders. The contemporary landscape of international news would be diminished without their presence in it, and it is important to acknowledge that contribution—even though NGOs do fail to live up to other normative functions with which they are tasked.

My view is also rooted in part in a historical understanding of what these groups set out to be. Put bluntly, none of the advocacy groups studied here intended to be deliberative or radical organizations. Human Rights Watch, to take one example, was created by liberal American political elites to combat the foreign-policy claims of a resurgent conservative elite. It did not set out to provide a radical criticism of American foreign policy. It is therefore not only unrealistic to assume that these groups can provide functions they were never intended to provide but also likely a misplaced target because other groups are set up to be more deliberative or radical in orientation. To say this is not to sanctify the role these groups play in public communication but to clarify it.

Of course, to offer this evaluation is not to suggest that there is no room for improvement among these groups. NGOs are institutions, and institutions are the product of human action, which can (with effort) be changed. In the next section, I highlight some of the ways in which these groups might be able to address some of the limitations I have discussed in this book. But my suggestions are rooted primarily in an understanding of what leading NGOs can plausibly be expected to do.

IMPROVING NGO COMMUNICATION

In the conclusion of her own study on NGO communication strategies, Sabine Lang writes that such groups "tend to act in and respond to an institutional environment that steers political action into institutionally desired forms, while, in the process, limiting public discussion and alternative action repertoires" (2013, 218). The empirical findings presented here echo this analysis. More broadly, Lang suggests that such empirical findings stem in large part from organizational arrangements and institutional environments, both of which can in principle be changed. To that end, I focus in this section on steps that might be taken among the major actors involved in shaping NGO communication to strengthen NGOs' contributions to the public sphere.

Donors play a major role in shaping NGO communication strategies. They value media publicity as a way to identify whether organizations are worth giving their money to, and they use media coverage partly as a tool to assess the degree to which a given NGO is able to influence public discourse. Although online technologies provide organizations with new ways of pursuing publicity, most donors continue to privilege coverage in the mass media both because these media provide larger audiences and because of uncertainty within the donor community about how best to gauge effective publicity online. Donors thus incentivize NGOs to pursue publicity in the mass media, but they place emphasis on organizations cultivating engagement with citizens.

Donors might take several steps to incentivize NGOs to modify their publicity efforts. For starters, there is a need to invest in alternative forms of publicity, including that which can be conducted online, and to support training for these efforts, too. Donors have good reason for wanting NGOs to appear in the mainstream media; however, those outlets are simply a few among many in a diversified "hybrid" media system (Chadwick 2013). Moreover, whereas donors evince interest in giving money to "sexy" areas such as social media, they show less excitement about funding some of the basic tools that organizations need to innovate in these areas, which makes it difficult for advocacy groups to invest heavily in them. As a result, these aspects of their work are underfunded and underexplored.

Beyond simply investing in alternative forms of publicity, there is also a need to move beyond performance-based results and to think of ways that better capture the public "voice" of an advocacy group. Scholars have long stressed that donors' language of accountability is articulated in corporate terms, with discussions revolving around "stakeholders" and "management." This language reinforces the emphasis on using communication to market the organizational brand. Such an emphasis avoids deeper discussions of what NGOs can and should be achieving through their public communication efforts. For instance, in many organizations I heard people discuss an effective publicity campaign, where effectiveness was judged primarily by the amount of attention garnered. When asked whether these campaigns achieved the results they aimed for, respondents would often express uncertainty. To be sure, there is no easy or single answer to the question of effectiveness—and public communication can be an important outcome in and of itself—but simply having the discussion can be worthwhile.

Finally, there is a need for donors to facilitate better engagement among NGOs. The field of organizations is highly crowded, which leads to a competitive orientation in which funding is often seen as a zero-sum game. Although organizations do occasionally engage in cross-organizational partnerships, such efforts continue to be difficult to achieve in practice and even harder to sustain when they are occasionally realized. This problem is larger than can be address simply by donor demands, but funders could create incentives for NGOs to collaborate together on specific issues or problems.

Beyond donors, government officials also shape NGO communication strategies. As Lang (2013) argues, NGOs are rooted in civil society and thus aim to be a voice for citizens (or for a segment of them). However, as NGOs become further integrated into governance, they are typically used as "stand-ins" for civic engagement. Rather than conduct the messy work of soliciting citizen feedback, government officials utilize organized advocacy groups as a "proxy" for public opinion. This is not always a negative development, and NGOs sometimes effectively use their proxy status to "signal" public discontent about a given issue. For instance, however one evaluates Oxfam's Make Trade Fair campaign, the effort was clearly an attempt to use public support as a way to get political leaders to take the organization's claims seriously. But when NGOs are used simply to stand in for more substantial public discussion, it is indeed a problem.

Within NGOs, there is a need to discuss frankly what does and does not work in their communication efforts. In some organizations, communication is viewed as a necessary evil, simply the cost of doing humanitarian and human rights work in the contemporary world. For others, communication is central to the organizational identity. It is even common to find these two views within the same organization. Yet in relatively few organizations is it typical for there to be a frank conversation about what communication strategies do and do not work and how these strategies can be improved or altered to better align with organizational aims. This is a conversation that management and leadership can help facilitate. In it, one discussion can and likely should focus on the emphasis of economic, cultural, and social rights. Although many groups have adopted these frames and have hired staff to address them, the publicity of such problems—as we saw in chapter 3—continue to take a back seat to the publicity of political and civil violations.

Beyond dialogue, NGOs can and probably should seek to hire people from a more diverse array of professional backgrounds. For the most part, communication staffers have backgrounds in public relations and journalism. Certainly, these fields are important, and the entrance of journalists into NGOs is only like to grow over time as the journalism job market contracts. Yet people with experience and expertise in digital advocacy remain relatively rare in the organizations studied here. Although progress in this area has been made in recent years, most organizations remain heavy in "traditional" communication staffers and possess comparatively lesser expertise in new forms of communication and advocacy.

Finally, NGO communication can be improved in part through journalists' acquiring a better understanding of what these organizations do and do not do well. As chapter 6 showed, most journalists continue to see NGO professionals primarily as advocates even though they also rely on these groups for information. But part of what is useful about the model of NGO communication is that these groups investigate problems *and* offer solutions. Of course, these solutions come from one particular perspective and should not be adopted wholesale or presented without opposing viewpoints. But the format itself—which blends credible reporting with action recommendations—is one that journalists and news organizations might consider for their own reporting on humanitarian and human rights issues.

The suggestions provided here are piecemeal, and their capacity to be implemented rely in part on changing the social conditions that I have already identified as shaping NGO communication efforts. I do not offer them in the expectation that they can be easily adopted or that adopting them will remove all the problematic aspects of NGO communication. Rather, I suggest them as a reminder that institutions are human creations and can therefore be altered.

THE BROADER RISE OF NEWS-ORIENTED PRACTICES

This book has examined the communication practices of a small number of leading humanitarian and human rights organizations. These groups are unique in a number of ways. Few other civic organizations have budgets or global remits that come anywhere near the ones boasted by these organizations, and thus their capacity to develop comparable "boots on the ground" reporting efforts is limited. At the same time, though, the activity in which these leading groups are engaged is one that cuts across many other groups and actors. This activity is part of a wider rise of what we might call "news-oriented practices"—that is, efforts by nonjournalistic actors to directly shape public communication (relatedly, see Williams and Delli Carpini 2011). Therefore, I want to specify what is particular about the case presented here and to suggest how aspects of it might be more broadly generalizable across other groups and organizations.

Although my study is limited to a small number of leading humanitarian and human rights groups, I do think it is reasonable to assume that smaller groups working on similar issues face similar struggles getting into the news. Indeed, in a content analysis of 750 civic organizations, Ronald Jacobs and Daniel Glass (2002) find that just 2 percent of all groups in the study appeared in more than one hundred news articles, and nearly 33 percent of them are never mentioned once. Relatedly, a study by Trevor Thrall, Dominik Stecula, and Diana Sweet (2014) of the prevalence of more than 250 human rights organizations in more than 600 news outlets indicates that just 10 percent of all groups capture 90 percent of media citations. Other scholarship shows that NGOs of varying sizes and with different thematic emphases are also hesitant to embrace or fully utilize digital technologies. Chris Wells, for instance, reveals a "considerable reticence" on the part of NGOs to engage with their online users. Specifically, his content analysis of the Facebook presence of 60 groups finds the majority to be "deeply hesitant to expose themselves to the considerable risks that true interactivity and openness entail" (2015, 28). Ella McPherson (2015) also highlights the degree to which social media use by human rights organizations requires substantial volumes of economic and symbolic capital and thus privileges some organizations more than others.

At the same time, a subset of groups with fewer resources might be more inclined than larger organizations to tinker with digital tools. Groups such as Avaaz and Witness, for example, are smaller in size than Amnesty International and Human Rights Watch but regularly partner with amateur activists around the world to improve their information-gathering capacities. Several years ago, for example, Witness partnered up with the Brazilian collective Papo Reto (Straight Talk), which uses mobile technologies to document political violence in favelas on the outskirts of Rio de Janeiro (Shaer 2015) and comprises mostly activists who live in the favelas and have little or no experience in either journalism or human rights activism. Witness has partnered with this group and others in places where there is limited NGO or news media presence. It holds training sessions to teach members about the types of information needed to hold human rights violators to account in a court of law. This collaboration between amateurs and professionals is relatively rare and helps to ensure that a growing number of human rights violations are documented and circulated publicly.[5] To what degree this development is specific to Witness or is enabled because of specific conditions available to smaller NGOs is an important question worthy of further investigation.

The developments described in this book are also occurring in other thematic sectors of advocacy work (i.e., those focused on the environment, gender equality, and so on). In 2015, for example, Greenpeace announced it was hiring a team of journalists and making investigative reporting a pillar of its advocacy work.[6] This team of investigative reporters has published reports on government regulations that aim to benefit the fossil-fuel industry and on the environmental records of multinational conglomerates. To what extent these efforts translate into broader media coverage for the group is uncertain, as is the extent to which these other thematic groups more fully utilize digital technologies. Some initial research suggests that these groups are more likely to utilize such tools (Reese 2015; Russell 2016), though more research is required. It would be especially useful to know how and in what ways donors, government officials, and journalists shape such groups' publicity strategies.

The case of Greenpeace also highlights some of the controversies NGOs may confront as they embrace news-oriented publicity strategies. In late 2015, for example, Greenpeace published a report showing that two American academics agreed to write papers that were in support of and covertly funded by the fossil-fuel industry.[7] In order to get the story, however, the group's reporters posed as energy company representatives and offered to compensate the academics—both prominent climate-change skeptics—for writing about the benefits of coal use and carbon emissions. The academics agreed to write the papers and not to disclose the payments. Although there is no doubt that the reporting was itself important and newsworthy, Greenpeace's embrace of deceptive tactics simply raises long-standing questions about their acceptability. To what extent might such reporting tactics diminish public trust in Greenpeace? These and related questions are likely only to increase as NGOs further boost their communication efforts.

Although the focus of this book has been on NGOs, it should be clear that the news-oriented practices I describe here can easily be used by other organizations. It is a nontrivial truism that all contemporary organizations are to some degree media organizations in the sense that they provide information and updates about their activities with the aims of steering some segment of public opinion. In recent years, for example, think tanks have dramatically increased their research and publicity operations, often in tandem (Medvetz 2012). Private businesses have also launched for-profit consultancies that aim to provide research, analysis, and insight. Much of this effort is geared toward private-paying audiences, but aspects of it are also aimed at shaping public debate (Drezner 2017). It is therefore entirely possible that the limited gains in public visibility that NGOs currently enjoy could be reversed in part by the entrance of more well-resourced actors into these debates. As Ed Walker

(2015) has shown, corporations are increasingly inserting themselves into public debate, in part through their own public-relations departments and in part via partnerships with grassroots organizers. Their presence may not exactly crowd out other civic organizations from public debate, but, as Tim Wood (2017) shows, it might lead each group to "own" its own frame on a given issue and thus to create news coverage that more closely resembles a "shouting match" than a debate.

Scholars still know relatively little about any of these organizations: their aims, their successes, their failures. This is primarily because most scholars of journalism continue primarily to study journalists. Yet as the news industry contracts, analyzing "nonjournalists" involved in producing the news will assume increasing importance. Of course, as I have discussed with respect to the case of humanitarian and human rights groups in this book, the presence of such actors in the news is not novel. It is the scale of their presence that has grown dramatically. Understanding how this works and what it means for public communication is thus a key task for scholars moving forward.

HOW INSTITUTIONS MATTER

Whichever organization is studied, it is important to keep in mind that each is part of a broader institutional environment. This seemingly anodyne statement stands in tension with much current research on the changing landscape of public communication, which focuses overwhelmingly on the possibilities brought by new technologies. There is reason for both interest and excitement in focusing on such possibilities, but doing so makes sense only when the groups studied are also situated in their social contexts. Institutions enable and constrain, and researchers need to better understand each of those effects and ultimately to bring them together into a larger account of the changing dynamics of public communication.

In this book, I have suggested that the institutionalization of humanitarian and human rights groups has helped create their capacity to produce credible information. The mere desire to produce such information was not in and of itself sufficient; rather, NGOs responded to opportunities—some in the immediate aftermath of World War II, others at the height of the Cold War. They hired people capable of producing the information they needed, and they obtained funding that supported the growth and diversification of such efforts. This means that the range of coverage that humanitarian and human rights groups provide today is an institutional outcome, not simply the result of efforts by a few individuals.

To say that institutions matter is not to imply that all their effects are positive. As I have documented throughout this book, NGOs are constrained as much as they are enabled by their institutional environments. They need to raise funds and promote their brands, and this need shapes the types of communication they do. From time to time, NGOs will undergo periods of self-reflection, where they ask whether their communication efforts undermine their stated organizational aims, yet these reflections typically produce limited long-term change. For example, in 2011 Oxfam released a report arguing that the UK public's understanding of the causes of poverty had changed little over the past several decades, despite Oxfam's numerous public-education campaigns to clarify the issue. In Oxfam's analysis, the public failed to grasp the issue because of the "transaction frame" for dealing with poverty. In this frame, "giving money to charities is understood to be the only way to engage with global poverty" (Darnton 2011, 33). NGOs operating within this frame thus turn "members" into "supporters" and "set them at arm's length" (Darnton 2011, 6). Arguably, the report (and its attendant self-reflection) has done little to alter the dynamic, in large part because the institutional conditions make dramatic change difficult.

In studying the institutional environments of "new" newsmakers, it is of course important to remember the importance of pre-existing newsmakers, too—especially journalism. For better or worse, journalism remains the core institution of contemporary public communication. Scholars occasionally talk about NGOs as if they might someday replace journalists. This is nowhere close to becoming an empirical reality. Moreover, there are good reasons to want the institution of journalism to be strong. Early in my fieldwork, one longtime NGO professional made exactly this point to me when discussing the need for journalistic oversight of NGO activities:

There's not a lot of oversight [of NGOs] in any meaningful way, minus some general sort of principles on accountability and transparency, IRS filings, and a hodgepodge of self-appointed aid charities' watchdog groups, most of which never get into the field, [and] most of which have very imprecise evaluation tools. So normally journalism would play some sort of function on that. But if you look at the reporting on the one-year anniversary of the Haiti earthquake, you can see that the ability to analyze what's going on there is [at] a very surface level.[8]

There are indeed good reasons for journalists to look beyond that surface level. In 2015, ProPublica and National Public Radio copublished a deeply reported article—relying on months of careful research and on-the-ground reporting—showing that although the Red Cross raised half a billion dollars after the Haiti earthquake, the Red Cross's own records suggest that it built just six homes with that money (Elliot and Sullivan 2015). The article documented a series of management failures that led to this state of affairs. The Red Cross contested aspects of the story,[9] but the bulk of the report has held up over time. Such reporting is relatively rare, but it remains important.

Decades ago, scholars routinely called for public communication to more closely approximate the norms of "multiperspectivalism"—that is, of bringing to the public a wider array of voices and viewpoints. Today, those aims can be realized both within and beyond the legacy news media. A key aim for scholars, therefore, is to identify where and how they are best realized: by whom, with what resources, and toward which ends.

Methods Appendix

PART 1: INTERVIEW PROTOCOL

The following questions guided my initial interviews with NGO professionals. Subsequent interviews focused on specific themes generated by earlier waves of analysis, in keeping with the general precepts of grounded theory.

Biographical Profile

1. Can you provide me with a brief biographical sketch? How did you arrive at the position you currently hold?
2. Where did you go to school, and what did you study?
3. Why did you decide to pursue this line of work?

Organizational Practice

4. Can you take me through some of the typical elements of your work day?
5. What publications do you read regularly for work?
6. How does your organization decide which issues to focus on?
7. What other NGOs do you follow closely?

8. Do you engage in direct lobbying efforts? If so, with whom?
9. How important are digital technologies in your everyday work?
10. What conferences or symposia do you attend for work?

Perceptions of the News Media

11. What are your views of the news media's coverage of issues you care about?
12. In what ways do you see your work as similar to or different from journalism?
13. How important is it for your organization to receive news coverage?
14. How do you initiate attempts to receive coverage?
15. Do you care which news outlets pick up your messaging?
16. Who do you see as your audience?

Perceptions of Change Over Time

17. How is the work you do now similar to or different from prior positions you've held?
18. In what ways has your organization changed since you joined it?

Valuations of Excellence

19. Can you tell me about something you have worked on in the past year and that you are especially proud of?
20. What other organizations are doing work that you see as especially valuable?
21. What types of work do you see as not valuable?
22. If there is one thing you could get your organization to do that it does not do already, what would that be and why?

PART 2: HUMANITARIAN AND HUMAN RIGHTS NEWS CODING PROTOCOL

Variables

v1. *Unique ID*
Write in a unique identifying number for each coded entry, starting with 1.

v2. *Year*
1 = 1990
2 = 1995
3 = 2000
4 = 2005
5 = 2010

v3. *Date*
Write in the exact date (e.g., 01/01/2000).

v4. *Sample*
1 = core sample
2 = total sample

v5. *NGO Cited*
0 = None
1 = Amnesty
2 = CARE
3 = Human Rights Watch
4 = International Crisis Group
5 = Médecins Sans Frontières
6 = Oxfam
7 = Save the Children
8 = World Vision

v6. *News Outlet*
1 = *New York Times*
2 = *USA Today*
3 = *NBC Nightly News*

v7. *Genre*
1 = news article
2 = newspaper editorial
3 = opinion (journalist authored)
4 = letter to editor (NGO affiliated)
5 = opinion (not NGO affiliated)
6 = news brief
7 = book review
8 = transcript of speech
9 = fund-raising notice

v8. *Word Length*
Record the exact number of words.

v9. *Nature of Citation*
1 = NGO driven
2 = NGO responding
3 = Neither

v10. *Story Location*
1 = top half of article
2 = bottom half of article

v11. *Order Where Cited*
1 = first
2 = second
3 = third
4 = fourth
5 = fifth

v12. *First Country Mentioned*
Write name of country.

v13. *First Source*
0 = none
1 = news outlet
2 = government official

3 = other NGO or social movement organization
4 = unaffiliated individual
5 = artist, writer, celebrity
6 = businessperson
7 = academic
8 = United Nations official
9 = public-opinion poll
10 = lawyer or legal figure
11 = other (use sparingly and keep notes)

v14. *Second Source*
0 = none
1 = news outlet
2 = government official
3 = other NGO or social movement organization
4 = unaffiliated individual
5 = artist, writer, celebrity
6 = businessperson
7 = academic
8 = United Nations official
9 = public-opinion poll
10 = lawyer or legal figure
11 = other (use sparingly and keep notes)

v15. *Third Source*
0 = none
1 = news outlet
2 = government official
3 = other NGO or social movement organization
4 = unaffiliated individual
5 = artist, writer, celebrity
6 = businessperson
7 = academic
8 = United Nations official
9 = public-opinion poll
10 = lawyer or legal figure
11 = other (use sparingly and keep notes)

v16. *Fourth Source*

0 = none

1 = news outlet

2 = government official

3 = other NGO or social movement organization

4 = unaffiliated individual

5 = artist, writer, celebrity

6 = businessperson

7 = academic

8 = United Nations official

9 = public-opinion poll

10 = lawyer or legal figure

11 = other (use sparingly and keep notes)

v17. *Fifth Source*

0 = none

1 = news outlet

2 = government official

3 = other NGO or social movement organization

4 = unaffiliated individual

5 = artist, writer, celebrity

6 = businessperson

7 = academic

8 = United Nations official

9 = public-opinion poll

10 = lawyer or legal figure

11 = other (use sparingly and keep notes)

v18. *Primary Frame*

1 = political rights

2 = free expression

3 = gender and family

4 = humanitarian

5 = economic

6 = cultural

7 = health and environment

Notes

1. A NEW ERA OF NGO-DRIVEN NEWS?

1. This story was recounted to me in an interview with one of the Human Rights Watch officials responsible for bringing Platon onto the project and involved in the subsequent negotiations with news outlets (interview with the deputy executive director for external relations, Human Rights Watch, November 29, 2010).

2. The photographs can be seen online at http://www.newyorker.com/culture/photo -booth/exiled-platons-portraits-of-burmese-refugees. The images, credited to Platon, were accompanied by a brief introduction by *New Yorker* staff writer George Packer, who noted in the text that Human Rights Watch commissioned the portraits. See Packer 2010. The online package also included video interviews with Myanmar dissidents that were conducted by Human Rights Watch staff.

3. Human Rights Watch composed a partial list of the non-US news organizations that republished the photographs. See https://www.hrw.org/sites/default/files/ related_material/Platon-BURMA-Media-Fall2010-Spring2011.pdf.

4. Initially founded as Helsinki Watch, the name of the group was changed in 1988 to its current form, Human Rights Watch. See chapter 2 for aspects of this history as well as Neier 2012, especially chapter 9, for an insider account.

5. This phrasing is one Human Rights Watch continues using in the present day. See https://www.hrw.org/our-history.

6. For a more detailed overview of these changes, see Powers 2016b and 2017.

7. In both North America and western Europe, exact figures are difficult to come by because different organizations use different definitions of the term *foreign*

correspondent. For an effort to detail some figures in the United States, see Carroll 2007. For a similar effort on parts of western Europe, see Sambrook 2010.

8. The amount of space that news outlets dedicate to international news coverage has diminished considerably, from an average of nearly 40 percent of all news content in the 1980s to about 17 percent today (Larson 1982; Pew Research Center 2009).

9. As Kenneth Cmiel has argued, to the extent that NGOs have influence, it comes from their work in making what he calls "the global flow of key bits of fact" (1999, 1232).

10. Clifford Bob (2006) makes the related point that the causes promoted by NGOs are reflections of organizational needs, not merely worthy goals, and these organizational needs in turn shape inequalities in the ecology of advocacy organizations (see also Thrall, Stecula, and Sweet 2014).

11. Natalie Fenton makes this point strongly in her call for NGOs to be "partial, occasionally illegal, and passionate about their cause—if they continue to mimic the requirements of mainstream, institutionalized news then arguably they fail in the role of advocacy" (2010, 167).

12. In drawing on the notion of institutional fields, I seek to integrate partially competing theoretical accounts within these traditions—especially field theory as articulated by Pierre Bourdieu and the concept of neoinstitutional organizational fields as developed by Paul DiMaggio and Walter Powell. For an overview of these traditions as well as a discussion of recent innovations in this more general theoretical tradition, see Klutz and Fligstein 2016.

13. Institutions and fields are not merely social constructs created by the analyst but also contexts in which actors take one another into account. Thus, for instance, journalists think about how a story will play both within their own news organizations and potentially at other news organizations.

14. A large and growing literature utilizes institutional and field perspectives to study the news media. See, for example, Benson and Neveu 2005; T. Cook 1998; Ryfe 2016; Waisbord 2013. The perspective has received less attention with respect to NGO communication efforts.

15. To be sure, the extent of variation is an empirical question. In fact, the basic premise of DiMaggio and Powell 1983 is that institutionalization leads to isomorphism across entire sectors.

16. This definition is drawn from Lang 2013. The history of the term *nongovernmental organizations* dates back to the United Nations, which first used it in 1945 to distinguish between intergovernmental agencies and groups with no government association. Any private body that was not controlled by a government, seeking public office, generating profit, or conducting criminal activity could register as an NGO. Although most scholarship, including this book, focuses on a subset of

relatively liberal organizations, the category includes business associations and religious groups of various political persuasions (see, e.g., the various organizations discussed in White 1951).

17. The process whereby NGOs become the dominant form of civil society organization is frequently labeled "NGO-ization." Evaluations of this process are typically ambivalent, with scholars noting both the potential for NGOs to serve as organizers for social action as well as their potential to harmonize the issues they cover with those that interest funders. See Lang 2013 for an overview of these debates.

18. As James Dawes has argued, the most important work these groups do entails "asking questions, evaluating answers, and pleading with those of us who observe from a distance" (2007, 2).

2. THE CHANGING FACES OF NGO COMMUNICATION WORK

1. The compensation figure comes from Hurst 2016, 152–153. See also Hopgood 2006 for a description of Amnesty International's London offices.

2. Exact salaries vary by position, educational background, and a range of other factors. For some data provided by Amnesty International, see the Amnesty International webpage "Pay at Amnesty International" at https://www.amnesty.org/en /about-us/pay-at-amnesty-international/.

3. The lack of historical scholarship necessitated reliance on a small corpus of non-scholarly texts written by either those involved with NGOs or sympathetic to them. They are thus "insider" accounts. Rather than treat them as veridical accounts of what happened, I have used them primarily to help sketch out the reasons why NGOs developed various information functions. Key texts include Black 1992 (on Oxfam); Bortolotti 2004 (on Médecins Sans Frontières); W. Campbell 1990 (on CARE); Ennals 1982 (on Amnesty International); Mulley 2009 (on Save the Children); and Neier 2003 (on Human Rights Watch). Sympathetic accounts by close observers include Harrison and Palmer 1986 (on NGOs in Africa); Kondracke 1988 (on Human Rights Watch); Korey 1998 (on NGOs generally); Larsen 1978 (on Amnesty International); Power 2001 (on Amnesty International); Rieff 2002 (on several NGOs, in particular Médecins Sans Frontières); and Terry 2002 (on Médecins Sans Frontières). The few scholarly accounts include Buchanan 2002; Clark 2001; Cmiel 1999; Dezalay and Garth 2002; Hopgood 2006; and Scoble and Wiseberg 1974. The historical portion of the argument is intended to be a synthetic account that makes sense of how NGOs came to be both capable of producing information on their own and reliant on the news media for publicity. It does not aim to be an exhaustive historical account of humanitarian

and human rights NGOs. My analysis highlights themes that are useful in explaining the developments on which I am focusing. I use source citations to provide the reader with the appropriate places to find more general information about the larger history of these organizations and the NGO sector more broadly.

4. The classic definition of professionalization comes from Weber 1947. For discussions of professionalization within the NGO sector, see Clemens 1997, Lang 2013, and Zald and McCarthy 1987. These discussions broadly fit with institutional perspectives on field formation, which highlight the extent to which professionalization is a strategy adopted by those seeking to legitimate their efforts (and existence) vis-à-vis other social actors (Bourdieu 1996; Fligstein and McAdam 2012).

5. This development parallels the shift, described by Margaret Scammell (2014), from political propaganda to political marketing. Whereas the former focuses primarily on the capacity to persuade, the latter is characterized by recurrent interactions between advocates and their various publics to cultivate a desired image.

6. The term *care package* derives from this history (Barnett 2011).

7. Francesca Wilson, the famous British humanitarian, remarked optimistically in the period after World War II that "we have at last become planning-minded." That humanitarian organizations were now conducting surveys of need in local populations, she remarked, was "an advance of incalculable importance" (1944, 269).

8. The effort to be impartial is a strong theme in the early history of Amnesty International. One of Amnesty's early leaders, Martin Ennals, wrote that the group's credibility was "always on the line" and that the organization "could not afford to make mistakes" in its reporting (1982, 73).

9. In the first decade of its existence, the International Secretariat of Amnesty International would "collect and publish important positive and negative statements about Amnesty International in order to stress its impartiality." The items in the collection included everything from newspaper editorials about the group's work in Ireland ("monstrously misguided") to comments by the US attorney general Erwin Griswold (who was "rather puzzled" by interest in the US imprisonment of a man who had refused military service) (Scoble and Wiseberg 1974, 25–26).

10. These different committees—Americas Watch, Asia Watch, Middle East Watch, Africa Watch—coalesced into Human Rights Watch in 1987. For an insider account of this history, see Neier 2003.

11. For a historical account of humanitarianism, see Barnett 2011. For a similar treatment of human rights work as well as an emphasis on its sudden explosion in the 1970s, see Moyn 2010.

12. Interview with news unit producer, Amnesty International, July 22, 2011.

13. A brief overview from the perspective of Amnesty International can be found at https://www.amnesty.org.uk/nelson-mandela-and-amnesty-international.

14. The International Commission of Jurists, founded in the wake of World War II,

provides an additional example of developed research functions and limited publicity. It was staffed by elite lawyers and career diplomats; the organization sought to emulate the Council of Foreign Relations model of creating international organizations that could further American interests. These experts saw little cause for waging their campaigns publicly. The Central Intelligence Agency, through an entity called the American Fund for Free Jurists, covertly provided the International Commission of Jurists with funds. As Howard Tolley notes in his history of the commission, the "directors favored the Council on Foreign Relations approach: the organization of a highly exclusive elite, selected and governed by a small inner circle" (1994, 51).

15. Jebb is said to have disliked fund-raising and not considered herself especially skilled in doing so. Nonetheless, from the outset she recognized the need to lead by example in embracing fund-raising (Mulley 2009).

16. The figures for humanitarian groups are certainly undercounted because they capture only those groups that self-identify as development oriented—merely one pole in the larger field of humanitarian action. On divisions within the humanitarian sector, see Krause 2014.

17. This funding by nation-states has increasingly been dedicated to short-term emergency funding rather than longer-term development assistance. As James Fearon has shown, emergency relief aid has soared dramatically since the 1970s, going from a relatively small portion of overall development assistance in the 1960s (roughly 2 percent) and rising steadily through the 1970s and 1980s to roughly 15 percent of all aid in 2000 (2008, 54).

18. As multiple people reminded me, NGOs have for decades hired people with backgrounds in journalism. The perception that working for an NGO is now a wise career move does seem to be more common, though.

19. Interview with staff member, Mercy Corps, June 2, 2011.

20. Interview with communication director, Save the Children UK, July 14, 2011.

21. Interview with press officer, Amnesty International UK, July 15, 2011.

22. Interview with communication officer, Médecins Sans Frontières, February 18, 2011.

23. Interview with public-relations director, World Vision, July 14, 2011.

24. Interview with press officer, Amnesty International, July 22, 2011.

25. Developing relations with journalists is a theme echoed by most contemporary NGO communication professionals. One person described cultivating social contacts among journalists in her job for Mercy Corps: "You kind of get on people's Rolodex.... The bureau chiefs know you, and ... they say, 'Be sure to look her up.' ... You definitely gain familiarity, and that was a positive thing about covering a region for a while.... People get to know who you are, and then they call you 'cause ... they know you" (interview with press officer, Mercy Corps, June 2, 2011).

26. Interview with press officer, Save the Children UK, July 21, 2011.

27. Interview with communication officer, Médecins Sans Frontières, July 19, 2011.

28. The famine also proves an excellent example of how "successful" messaging is not always successful for the issue itself. As Alex de Waal argues, the publicity about the famine generated lots of donation funds, much of which was not well spent and most of which created the false impression—de Waal calls it the "big lie"—that relief could ameliorate suffering. It instead, he argues, largely allowed the Ethiopian government to remain in power and pursue strategies that furthered the famine in exchange for allowing NGOs access to some areas. In short, he argues, publicity worked to spur donations and mobilize public opinion toward Western action, but the action itself was misguided and ultimately harmful (1998, 106–132).

29. Interview with broadcast-relations manager, Médecins Sans Frontières, July 27, 2011.

30. Interview with communication director, Médecins Sans Frontières, February 18, 2011.

31. Interview with media officer, Mercy Corps, June 2, 2011.

32. Interview with the executive director of external relations, Human Rights Watch, November 29, 2010.

33. Interview with the executive director of external relations, Human Rights Watch, November 29, 2010.

34. Interview with the director of communication, International Crisis Group, July 4, 2011.

35. Interview with media officer, International Crisis Group, April 1, 2011.

36. Interview with media officer, International Crisis Group, April 1, 2011.

37. Interviews with communication officer, Oxfam, February 18, 2011, and researcher, Christian Aid, July 11, 2011.

3. THE PARTIALLY OPENING NEWS GATES

1. As noted in chapter 1, some researchers assume that changes in technology have enabled NGOs to bypass the news media and directly target relevant stakeholders. I investigate this assumption in chapter 4. Here my aim is to investigate whether other factors—that is, changes in journalism, politics, and advocacy, as identified in chapter 1—alter the established scholarly wisdom on NGO news access.

2. Some aspects of this article have been previously published in Matthew Powers, "Opening the News Gates? Humanitarian and Human Rights Groups in the U.S. News Media, 1990–2010," *Media, Culture & Society* 38 (3) (2016): 315–331. This chapter deepens the analysis in that article by exploring the various human rights frames associated with NGOs' appearances in the news.

3. As I noted in chapter 1, human rights and humanitarianism were historically

separate discourses, with the former focused on protecting citizens against state violence and the latter driven primarily to reduce suffering. Since the end of the Cold War, the two have become increasingly intertwined, with both relying on human rights discourses to justify their work (Moyn 2010). One can thus group them together for content-analytic purposes without denying the actual differences in the work the two sets of actors do on the ground.

4. I thank an anonymous reviewer for making this point to me in an earlier version of this chapter. The extent to which humanitarian groups ought to speak publicly about the human rights problems they encounter in their work is a recurrent theme in both the popular literature and the scholarly literature. See, for example, Kennedy 2004, Rieff 2002, and Terry 2002.

5. The division of the press into the broadcast press and the prestige press hardly exhausts the range of available media. In using these two, I draw upon the primary sources of media coverage for most organizations. Future research is needed to explore how and in what ways these findings can be extended to cable, satellite, and digital news providers.

6. NGO prevalence is also likely to vary in accordance with a number of other organizational features (e.g., internal organizational relations between public-relations and research departments, an organization's historical identity, and others) (see Krause 2014; Orgad 2013; Powers 2014). My aim here is simply to adjudicate the main features of the debate on NGO prevalence in the news media.

7. This use of framing is associated with the first of Robert Entman's (1993) four framing "functions"—the selection and emphasis of some aspect of reality to promote a particular "problem definition." My framing analysis does not seek to identify causal claims, moral evaluations, or proposed solutions, which are other legitimate uses of "frame" analysis. I instead use framing to answer an empirical question related to human rights news: Has "human rights" news diversified over time to include problems such as economic deprivation, given the historical tendency for human rights frames to focus on political rights and free expression? For methodological discussions of framing issues, see Gitlin 1980, Reese 2007, and Ryan 1991.

8. This decrease is likely due to a larger number of sources used in news articles over time.

9. Clifford Bob (2006) suggests that the situation of smaller civic groups can be seen as a market for loyalties. Small groups must package their causes and ideals in ways that appeal symbolically, linguistically, and culturally to the larger, typically Western NGOs. For a contrasting perspective, see Engle Merry 2006.

10. This finding dovetails with the research by A. Trevor Thrall, Dominik Stecula, and Diana Sweet (2014), who find that NGOs tend to be mentioned in connection with a small number of countries. In their work, they attribute this problem to the problem of attention—that is, the news media can pay attention to only a

limited number of issues at any one given moment of time. Without denying the validity of this argument, I suggest there may be additional factors at work. See chapters 5 and 6.

11. Interview with press officer, Amnesty International, July 26, 2011.

12. The Make Poverty History campaign had its detractors, who argued that the coalition focused too much on "insider" strategies and thus marginalized more radical criticisms of the causes of poverty. For an overview, see Davis 2007, chapter 8.

13. See Powers 2013 for a longer discussion of the methodology used by NGOs to investigate human rights violations. See Roth 2007 for a discussion of the merits and drawbacks of this approach from the perspective of human rights practitioners.

14. See the photograph "Praying on a Volatile Central Asian Border" (*New York Times* 2005a).

15. Saskia Sassen (2017) makes a similar point in her research on the representation of human rights abuses in Myanmar. She argues that NGO reporting—which the news media largely amplify—frames the problem primarily in terms of religious freedom while sidestepping the business interests (e.g., corporate land grabs) that underlie such efforts.

4. THE STRATEGIC ADVOCATE IN THE DIGITAL STORM

1. My use of the term *publicity* here is deliberately expansive because I intend to capture the multiple ways these groups seek to raise awareness of an issue, organization, or individual. Thus, I do not examine solely how NGOs create digital content to be picked up by the news media, nor do I focus solely on how advocacy groups see digital tools as part of their agenda-building process. I instead asked advocacy professionals how digital tools figure into their everyday practices (see the methods appendix). My hope is that by casting a wide net, I have been able to capture the various ways digital tools are integrated in NGO communication strategies more generally.

2. Andrew Chadwick's (2013) influential notion of a "hybrid" media system differs from the idea of "direct-to-public" communication. In Chadwick's view, media systems contain a mixture of older and newer logics, which advocacy groups seek to exploit. Thus, he argues, the point is not that advocacy groups bypass the news media so much as they integrate with the news media in new ways. His empirical work on advocacy groups, however, stresses that the online environment provides these groups with an important degree of power to put their issues on the news agenda.

3. Interview with media officer, International Crisis Group, April 1, 2011.

4. Field notes, July 2011 and June 2013.

5. As James Grunig has shown, the act of creating content to be picked up by the news media has a long history. Although NGOs' efforts are not precisely forms of "press agentry" (2009, 2), a description that carries connotations of manipulation, they do correspond with a long history of public-relations professionals seeking to influence media coverage.

6. Interview with media officer, Amnesty International, July 22, 2011.

7. Interview with social media manager, CARE, February 17, 2015.

8. The Vulture Club has, for example, criticized the Israeli government's human rights record, criticism that in turn invited criticism from the Israeli government that the lines separating journalists from advocates was thin, if not entirely nonexistent. See Kirell 2013.

9. Interview with social media officer, CARE, February 15, 2015; interview with press officer, Oxfam, February 20, 2011; interview with press officer, Médecins Sans Frontières, June 18, 2013.

10. Interview with social media officer, CARE, February 17, 2015. This response corresponds with the distinction Shani Orgad (2013) identifies in her analysis of the organizational politics that shape visual-messaging strategies at humanitarian organizations. See also Powers 2014.

11. Interview with social media officer, CARE, February 9, 2015.

12. Interview with advocacy officer, Médecins Sans Frontières, March 20, 2015.

13. Interview with press officer, Amnesty International, June 19, 2011.

14. As Erich Sommerfeldt, Michael Kent, and Maureen Taylor (2012) note, most practitioners see organizational websites as passive tools that need to be supplemented with more traditional advocacy approaches, such as mainstream media advocacy. For quantitative data, see Seo, Kim, and Yang 2009.

15. Interview with press officer, Oxfam, February 20, 2011.

16. Interview with social media officer, CARE, February 15, 2015.

17. I pursue these reasons at greater depth in chapter 5.

18. Interview with social media officer, CARE, February 15, 2015.

19. Interview with press officer, Amnesty International, July 15, 2011.

20. Interview with press officer, Médecins Sans Frontières, June 18, 2013.

21. See, for example, the photographs in *Zombietime* 2006. For an overview of this controversy and the criticisms made, see Zuckerman 2006.

22. As Robert Entman (2012) notes, scandal-oriented news coverage is typically not calibrated to notions of corruption, which means that lesser scandals can still generate substantial media attention. It is this knowledge that in part seems to motivate a conservative approach to online publicity by NGOs.

23. Ella McPherson (2015) provides an account of how NGOs are seeking to improve verification issues in their social media reporting. She also highlights the tradeoffs between efficiency and legitimacy, with the two often appearing to advocacy

groups as a zero-sum game, with increases in efficiency seen as frequently result-ing in a loss of legitimacy and vice versa.

24. The term *graft* is my own description for the action observed and heard about through interviews with NGO professionals.

25. Interview with online editor, Human Rights Watch, March 4, 2015.

26. Field notes, Amnesty International Secretariat, London, July 2011. At times, these efforts can take on a humorous dimension. During the summer of 2011, several Amnesty staff joked about finding a "human rights angle" to an ongoing scandal surrounding the now defunct *News of the World*. It was revealed that journalists at the newspaper illegally hacked into phone lines as the basis of their news reporting. The claims at Amnesty International were made in jest and never with a hint of seriousness, but the absurdity stems from their being highly attuned to the news agenda and well acclimated to thinking through news hooks.

27. Interview with head of news unit, Christian Aid, July 11, 2011.

28. Interview with press officer, Save the Children, July 8, 2013.

29. Interview with communication officer, Oxfam, February 11, 2011.

30. Lynn Zoch and Juan-Carlos Molleda (2006) make a parallel argument in their work on organizational framing as a way to build the news agenda in a favorable manner. Adrienne Russell suggests that activists cultivate a "sensibility" for the news agenda that makes it possible to better manipulate the news agenda in their favor (2016, 5).

31. Interview with media officer, Oxfam, February 18, 2011. He continued: "After the first week, people were like 'yeah, yeah, yeah floods.' But I couldn't make it up: There were twenty million people that needed assistance."

32. On the concept of "compassion fatigue," see Susan Moeller's book (1999) featur-ing these words in its main title.

33. This episode is taken from an interview with the senior online editor at Human Rights Watch, March 4, 2015, as well as from the public remarks about the event found in Bogert 2014.

34. The CNN transcript of this episode of *Amanpour* is available at http://edition.cnn.com/TRANSCRIPTS/1402/13/ampr.01.html.

35. Interview with press officer, Oxfam, February 15, 2012.

36. A related criticism is that NGOs erase other potential forms of advocacy. This is the argument, for example, made by those who see large NGOs as removing arguments from the local public spheres in which smaller organizations might be expected to exert an influence (Shivji 2007; Yanacopulos 2015).

5. PUBLICITY'S ENDS

1. An earlier version of this chapter was published as Matthew Powers, "NGO Publicity and Reinforcing Path Dependencies: Explaining the Persistence of

Media-Centered Publicity Strategies," *International Journal of Press/Politics* 21 (4) (2016): 490–507.

2. Simon Cottle and David Nolan (2007) find that leading humanitarian groups are just as interested in garnering mainstream media coverage today as they were in the past. Natalie Fenton similarly argues that these same groups use digital technologies to "clone" the news in an effort to have their copy picked up by cash-strapped news organizations (2010, 156; see also Wright 2016a). Finally, Silvio Waisbord suggests that advocacy groups adapt to what he terms a "journalism logic" that privileges the needs of the news media (2011, 149).

3. To be sure, such an explanation is beyond the scope of Cottle and Nolan's important article, in which they explicitly call on future scholars to provide a much "closer mapping" of the NGO sector's organizational ecology and political economy (2007, 864).

4. An example of this sort of explanation can be found in Waisbord's (2008b) account of the failure of international aid groups to develop "participatory" communication approaches. In that case, NGOs failed to implement participatory approaches not for lack of effort but because they are bureaucratically set up to achieve different communicative aims (i.e., to communicate with elites).

5. *Exogenous shocks* and *critical junctures* are terms used in the new-institutional literature to describe large-scale and often unexpected changes in the political, economic, and social environs in which institutions operate. For a discussion of both concepts, see R. Scott 2014. For an application of the concept of critical junctures in relation to media history, see Starr 2004.

6. Interview with media officer, Oxfam, February 18, 2011.

7. Interview with press officer, Amnesty International UK, July 15, 2011.

8. Interview with the communication director, Médecins Sans Frontières, February 18, 2011.

9. Interview with the deputy executive director of external relations, Human Rights Watch, November 29, 2010. The 70 percent figure has declined since, due partly to grant money that encourages the organization to internationalize its efforts.

10. Interview with media officer, Oxfam, February 18, 2011.

11. Interview with media officer, Amnesty International US, December 14, 2011.

12. Interview with communication director, International Crisis Group, July 4, 2011.

13. Interview with researcher, Amnesty International, June 5, 2013.

14. Interview with researcher, World Vision, July 15, 2011.

15. Interview with advocacy officer, Save the Children, July 15, 2011.

16. Interview with the deputy executive director of external relations, Human Rights Watch, November 29, 2010.

17. Interview with communication director, International Crisis Group, July 4, 2011.

18. Interview with communication officer, Human Rights Watch, May 11, 2013.

19. The literature on how to evaluate the effectiveness of humanitarian and human rights efforts is enormous. For various perspectives, see Kennedy 2004, Krause 2014, Moyn 2010, and Terry 2002.
20. For a discussion of donor views of social media, see McPherson 2015.
21. To be sure, advocacy groups sometimes prefer not to be in the media spotlight (see, e.g., Powers 2014 and Reese 2015). My point is simply that when such groups do want attention, they prefer mainstream media coverage rather than alternative forms of publicity.
22. Interview with advocacy officer, Amnesty International, February 10, 2015.
23. Interview with communication officer, Médecins Sans Frontières, February 18, 2011.
24. Interview with media officer, Oxfam, February 18, 2011.
25. The examples given in the text blur the lines between perception and practice. On the one hand, the idea that government officials cannot ignore NGOs when NGOs are referred to and cited in the *New York Times* is clearly an overstatement, one that is unlikely to hold up to empirical scrutiny (given the fact that government officials regularly eschew advocacy claims broadcast in the news media). On the other hand, the fact that government officials' behavior does (at least sometimes) change when NGO messages appear in the news media indicates that advocacy groups do receive cues that media coverage remains important to political elites.
26. Interview with communication director, International Crisis Group, July 3, 2011.
27. Interview with communication officer, World Vision, October 10, 2013.
28. Interview with press officer, Médecins Sans Frontières UK, July 19, 2011.
29. Interview with the executive director of external relations, Human Rights Watch, November 29, 2010.
30. Interview with the executive director of external relations, Human Rights Watch, November 29, 2010.
31. Interview with communication officer, Amnesty International, December 14, 2011.
32. Interview with news unit producer, Amnesty International, July 22, 2011.
33. Interview with news unit producer, Amnesty International, July 22, 2011.
34. Interview with communication officer, Human Rights Watch, September 4, 2013.
35. Interview with press officer, Save the Children UK, July 21, 2011.
36. Interview with media officer, International Crisis Group, April 1, 2011.
37. Interview with country researcher, Amnesty International, June 19, 2013. In fact, this proximity to reporters is a source of contention for some critical academics. Alex de Waal, for example, argues that because NGOs and journalists share so much socially, reporters are unable to see advocacy groups as anything other than a potential solution to the problems they describe (rather than as potentially part of the problem) (1998, 82–85). As he puts it, "Most journalists do not see anything wrong with this intimacy [between NGOs and reporters]. They tend to believe

that relief works are impartial and humanitarian and that aid work provides a solution to the problems they can see" (83).

38. Interview with the executive director of external relations, Human Rights Watch, November 29, 2010.

39. The Vulture Club, discussed in chapter 4, is a private Facebook group that includes human rights professionals and journalists. Its participants interact to coordinate travel planning and discuss issues of shared concern. When Richard Engel of NBC News was abducted while on a reporting trip in Syria, leaders in the group encouraged members to protest the decision by a *Gawker* reporter to publish information about the kidnapping. For the latter publication, see J. Cook 2012.

40. Interview with press officer, Amnesty International UK, July 26, 2011.

41. Interview with media officer, International Crisis Group, April 1, 2011.

42. Interview with media officer, International Crisis Group, April 1, 2011.

43. In his research on environmental summits, Hartmut Wessler and his collaborators find that such events provide moments where advocacy groups and journalists may temporarily suspend otherwise adversarial relations (Lück, Wozniak, and Wessler 2016).

44. This finding is similar to Rodney Benson's (2013) analysis of a "habitus gap" between national immigration reporters and restrictionist groups. In both cases, shared social worlds make it possible for some groups to interact more easily with one another but to create barriers between others.

45. Interview with news writer, Amnesty International, July 22, 2011.

46. Interview with media officer, Oxfam International, February 17, 2012.

47. Interview with the director of communication, Amnesty International US, December 9, 2011.

6. EXPLAINING THE ENDURANCE OF NEWS NORMS

1. Richard Sambrook, who writes that "NGOs from Oxfam to Amnesty to Open Society now directly contribute to public debate in their areas of concern," takes the news media's openness to advocacy perspectives as given. For him, the ensuing questions are primarily ethical: "In this blurring of boundaries, NGOs need to be clear whether they are acting as reporters or [as] advocates. And if news organizations use NGO material it must be transparently flagged as such" (2010, 35–36).

2. My emphasis here is on the relative durability of news norms, not on disproving extant claims of change. It is possible that different types of NGOs working in different areas (say, environmental organizations working in China) will in fact effect greater changes in news norms, as Stephen Reese (2015) finds in his research. This does not obviate the need to explain durability, which has mostly been downplayed in the available literature on NGO–journalist relations. I return to

questions of generalizability in this chapter's concluding paragraphs as well as in chapter 7.

3. Although Istanbul was geographically speaking the closest bureau, several news outlets also sent reporters from their offices in Cairo for language reasons (i.e., contemporary Turkish is distinct from Syrian Arabic).

4. By December 2016, the official number of registered Syrians living in Turkey was 2.8 million, making Turkey the largest host country. The actual number of Syrians residing in Turkey at the time was likely higher. See http://data.unhcr.org/syrianrefugees/country.php?id=224.

5. Although I did not systematically collect demographic data on the journalists, my impression is that many were relatively young (i.e., younger than forty) and primarily male. This was especially true of freelancers, who overwhelmingly tended to be young and male.

6. Interview with journalist, June 26, 2011.

7. See, for example, Albayrak 2011 and Stack 2011.

8. Interview with journalist, June 26, 2011.

9. Interview with journalist, June 26, 2011.

10. Interview with journalist, July 11, 2011.

11. Field notes, June 25, 2011.

12. It is important to note that these comments reflect journalists' perceptions. NGO professionals may be broadly sympathetic to activists, but their own organizational processes require a degree of skepticism regarding the activists' claims (see Powers 2016a).

13. Interview with journalist, June 25, 2011.

14. Interview with journalist, July 2, 2012.

15. Interview with journalist, June 25, 2011.

16. Interview with journalist, June 25, 2011.

17. Interview with journalist, June 24, 2011.

18. Although the Turkish government hosted many Syrians, it never formally declared them refugees, thus raising questions about the Syrians' security within the country over the long term.

19. Interview with journalist, June 26, 2011.

20. Interview with journalist, June 25, 2011.

21. Interview with journalist, June 22, 2011. Guvecci is a small town in the Hatay region of Turkey.

22. Interview with journalist, June 25, 2011.

23. Field notes, June 25, 2011.

24. Interview with the communication director, International Crisis Group, July 4, 2011; interview with communication officer, Oxfam, February 18, 2011; interview with the communication director, Médecins Sans Frontières, February 18, 2011.

25. Interview with journalist, June 25, 2011.

26. Interview with the deputy executive director for external relations, Human Rights Watch, November 29, 2010.

27. Although I do not discuss them in detail here, there are also one-off relationships between individual NGOs and individual news organizations. Ben Jones (2017), for example, writes about the interplay between an advocacy group and a leading British newspaper (the *Guardian*) in coproducing news about Uganda and finds that the uptake in interactions between the two signals the growing incorporation of news norms into the everyday work of advocacy groups and, in his view, may also make the communication staff more powerful vis-à-vis other units within an NGO.

28. To be sure, not all freelancers are equally interested in working with NGOs. For example, although it is relatively common for photographers and multimedia specialists to work with NGOs, it seems less common for print-based journalists to do so. Moreover, even those who do work with NGOs have different opinions of the relationship. Some, in keeping with Wright's findings, do report feeling "freer" in working with advocacy groups, but others claim that such work constrains the types of reporting they do. One photographer explained to me that although he did sometimes work with NGOs for economic reasons, he much preferred working with news organizations. The former placed constraints on the types of photographs he could produced, whereas the latter had relatively little input (field notes, June 26, 2011).

29. Interview with media officer, Médecins Sans Frontières UK, July 19, 2011.

30. Interview with broadcast-relations manager, Médecins Sans Frontières, July 27, 2011.

31. Interview with researcher, Amnesty International, July 7, 2011.

32. Interview with audio-visual producer, Amnesty International, July 7, 2011.

33. Interview with news unit officer, Amnesty International, July 22, 2011.

34. Interview with news unit, Amnesty International, July 25, 2011.

35. Interview with the deputy executive director for external relations, Human Rights Watch, November 29, 2010.

36. Interview with communication officer, International Medical Corps, April 27, 2011.

37. Interview with researcher, Amnesty International, June 5, 2013.

38. Interview with news unit, Amnesty International, July 25, 2011.

39. Interview with public-relations staffer, Amnesty International, June 5, 2013.

40. The degree to which media publicity is important varies somewhat by organization. See Powers 2014 on this point.

41. Some authors have suggested that local correspondents might pick up the slack, yet existing efforts to link local journalists to large Western news organizations have experienced little pickup. See Zuckerman 2013.

7. THE POSSIBILITIES AND LIMITATIONS OF NGO COMMUNICATION

1. The description of NGOs as "awkward symbols" borrows from a discussion in Calhoun 2010 regarding media coverage of humanitarian emergencies.

2. For a longer discussion about normative theories of public communication as well as about the roles they prescribe for NGOs, see Powers 2017.

3. In *Liberty and the News*, Lippmann (1920) foreshadowed this normative argument in his discussion of "political observatories"—that is, independent organizations that research important public-affairs topics. More recently, Michael Schudson (2010) explicitly refers to Human Rights Watch as a contemporary instantiation of such an observatory. Central to both claims is the status of NGOs as experts.

4. In her discussion of the messages circulated by NGOs in the aftermath of the Haiti earthquake, Lilie Chouliaraki notes that they were "primarily testimonial": rather than convey detailed information about what had happened, they sought to "express compassion with the earthquake victims" (2012, 273).

5. See Kavada 2012 for an account of how Avaaz utilizes digital tools to boost its engagement and overall activism.

6. For an overview of this development in Greenpeace, see Powers 2015d.

7. See my review of this case in Powers 2015b.

8. Interview with communication director, Médecins Sans Frontières, February 18, 2011.

9. The Red Cross response can be found at http://www.redcross.org/news/press -release/American-Red-Cross-Responds-to-Recent-ProPublica-Report-on-Haiti.

References

Aday, Sean, and Steven Livingston. 2009. "NGOs as Intelligence Agencies: The Empowerment of Transnational Advocacy Networks and the Media by Commercial Remote Sensing in the Case of the Iranian Nuclear Program." *GeoForum* 40 (4): 514–522. doi:10.1016/j.geoforum.2008.12.006.

Albayrak, Ayla. 2011. "Refugees Urge Action in Syria." *Wall Street Journal*, June 16.

Amnesty International. 2005. *Annual Report on the State of Human Rights*. New York: Amnesty International. https://www.amnesty.org/download/Documents/POL 1000012005ENGLISH.PDF.

——. 2012. "Homs at Gunpoint: Satellites Track Assault on Syrian Cities." Blog post, March 3. http://blog.amnestyusa.org/middle-east/homs-at-gunpoint-satellites -trackassault-on-syrian-cities/.

Anderson, C. W. 2013. *Rebuilding the News: Metropolitan Journalism in the Digital Age*. Philadelphia: Temple University Press.

Appiah, Kwame Anthony. 2006. *Cosmopolitanism: Ethics in a World of Strangers*. New York: Norton.

Barnett, Michael. 2011. *Empire of Humanity: A History of Humanitarianism*. Ithaca: Cornell University Press.

Bartlett, Rachell. 2011. "Amnesty International Launches News Service." *Journalism*, April 14. http://www.journalism.co.uk/news/-media140-amnesty-international -launchesnews-service/s2/a543699/.

Beck, Ulrich. 2006. *Cosmopolitan Vision*. Cambridge: Polity.

Becker, Jo. 2013. *Campaigning for Justice: Human Rights Advocacy in Practice*. Stanford: Stanford University Press.

Beckett, Charlie. 2008. "NGOs and Journalists: Not Communicating?" Blog post, May 29. http://eprints.lse.ac.uk/78375/1/blogs.lse.ac.uk-NGOs%20and%20Journalists%20not%20communicating%20Polis%20at%20Harvard%20II.pdf.

Bennett, W. Lance. 1990. "Toward a Theory of Press–State Relations in the United States." *Journal of Communication* 40 (2): 103–125. doi:10.1111/j.1460–2466.1990.tb02265.x.

——. 1996. "An Introduction to Journalism Norms and Representations of Politics." *Political Communication* 13 (4): 373–384. doi:10.1080/10584609.1996.9963126.

——. 2003. "Communicating Global Activism: Strengths and Vulnerabilities of Networked Politics." *Information, Communication, & Society* 6 (2): 143–168. doi:10.1080/1369118032000093860.

Bennett, W. Lance, Regina Lawrence, and Steven Livingston. 2007. *When the Press Fails: Political Power and the News Media from Iraq to Katrina*. Chicago: University of Chicago Press.

Bennett, W. Lance, and Jarol B. Mannheim. 2006. "The One-Step Flow of Communication." *Annals of the American Academy of Political and Social Science* 608 (1): 213–232. doi:10.1177/0002716206292266.

Bennett, W. Lance, and Alexandra Segerberg. 2013. *The Logic of Connective Action: Digital Media and the Personalization of Contentious Politics*. Cambridge: Cambridge University Press.

Benson, Rodney. 2009. "Normative Theories of Journalism." In *The Blackwell International Encyclopedia of Communication*, edited by Wolfgang Donsbach, 2591–2597. New York: Blackwell.

——. 2013. *Shaping Immigration News: A French–American Comparison*. Cambridge: Cambridge University Press.

Benson, Rodney, and Erik Neveu, eds. 2005. *Bourdieu and the Journalistic Field*. Cambridge: Polity.

Benthall, Jonathan. 1993. *Disasters, Relief, and the Media*. London: I. B. Tauris.

Black, Maggie. 1992. *A Cause for Our Times: Oxfam, the First Fifty Years*. Oxford: Oxfam.

Bob, Clifford. 2006. *The Marketing of Rebellion: Insurgents, Media, and International Activism*. Cambridge: Cambridge University Press.

Boczkowski, Pablo. 2010. *News at Work: Imitation in an Age of Information Abundance*. Chicago: University of Chicago Press.

Bogert, Carroll. 2012. "Look Who's Talking: Non-profit Newsmakers in the Digital Age." Talk given at MIT, September 10. http://www.media.mit.edu/events/2012/09/10/media-lab-conversations-series-carroll-bogert-look-whos-talking-non-profit-newsmakers-new-media-age.

——. 2014. "The Information Marketplace." *Vimeo*, n.d. https://vimeo.com/105688348.

Bortolotti, Dan. 2004. *Hope in Hell: Inside the World of Doctors Without Borders*. Richmond Hill, Canada: Firefly Books.

Bourdieu, Pierre. 1993. *The Field of Cultural Production*. New York: Columbia University Press.

——. 1996. *The Rules of Art: Genesis and Structure of the Literary Field*. Stanford: Stanford University Press.

Bowley, Graham. 2005. "European Commission Seeks Faster Repatriation of Some Migrants." *New York Times*, September 2. http://www.nytimes.com/2005/09/02/world/europe/european-commission-seeks-faster-repatriation-of-some-migrants.html.

Breckenridge, Bryan, and Anne Maloney. 2015. "Why Fund Tech for Nonprofits." http://www.techsoup.org/SiteCollectionDocuments/blog-why-fund-tech-for-nonprofits-white-paper-pdf.pdf .

Breed, Warren. 1955. "Social Control in the Newsroom: A Functional Analysis." *Social Forces* 33 (4): 326–335. doi:10.2307/2573002.

Briones, Rowena, Beth Kuch, Brooke Fisher Liu, and Yan Jin. 2011. "Keeping Up with the Digital Age: How the American Red Cross Uses Social Media to Build Relationships." *Public Relations Review* 37 (1): 37–43. doi:10.1016/j.pubrev.2010.12.006.

Bristol, Nellie, and John Donnelly. 2011. *Taking the Temperature: The Future of Global Health Journalism*. Kaiser Family Foundation Report. Menlo Park, CA: Kaiser Family Foundation. https://kaiserfamilyfoundation.files.wordpress.com/2013/01/8135.pdf.

Buchanan, Tom. 2002. "'The Truth Will Set You Free': The Making of Amnesty International." *Journal of Contemporary History* 37 (4): 575–597. doi:10.1177/0022009402037004050.1.

Calhoun, Craig. 2008. "The Imperative to Reduce Suffering." In *Humanitarianism in Question*, edited by Thomas Weiss and Michael Barnett, 73–97. Ithaca: Cornell University Press.

——. 2010. "The Idea of Emergency." In *Contemporary States of Emergency*, edited by Didier Fassin and Mariella Pandolfi, 29–58. New York: Zone.

Campbell, John L. 2004. *Institutional Change and Globalization*. Princeton: Princeton University Press.

Campbell, Wallace J. 1990. *The History of CARE: A Personal Account*. Berkeley: University of California Press.

Carroll, Jill. 2007. "Foreign News Coverage: The News Media's Undervalued Asset." Working Paper Series, Joan Shorenstein Center on the Press, Politics, and Public Policy. https://shorensteincenter.org/wp-content/uploads/2012/03/2007_01_carroll.pdf.

Castells, Manuel. 2009. *Communication Power*. New York: Oxford University Press.

Chadwick, Andrew. 2013. *The Hybrid Media System: Power and Politics*. New York: Oxford University Press.

Chivers, C. J. 2005. "Rights Report Details Uzbek Crackdown After Uprising in May." *New York Times*, September 20.

Christians, Clifford, Theodore Glasser, Denis McQuail, Kaarle Nordenstreng, and Robert A. White. 2009. *Normative Theories of the Media: Journalism in Democratic Societies*. Urbana: University of Illinois Press.

Chouliaraki, Lilie. 2007. *The Spectatorship of Suffering*. London: Sage.

——. 2012. "Re-mediation, Inter-mediation, Trans-mediation." *Journalism Studies* 14 (2): 267–283. doi:10.1080/1461670X.2012.718559.

——. 2013. *The Ironic Spectator: Solidarity in the Age of Post-humanitarianism*. London: Polity.

Clark, Ann Marie. 2001. *Diplomacy of Conscience: Amnesty International and Changing Human Rights Norms*. Princeton: Princeton University Press.

Clemens, Elisabeth. 1997. *The People's Lobby: Organizational Innovation and the Rise of Interest Group Politics in the United States, 1890–1925*. Chicago: University of Chicago Press.

Cmiel, Kenneth. 1999. "The Emergence of Human Rights Politics in the United States." *Journal of American History* 86 (3): 1231–1250. doi:10.2307/2568613.

Cohen, Dara Kay, and Amelia Hoover Green. 2012. "Dueling Incentives: Sexual Violence in Liberia and the Politics of Human Rights Advocacy." *Journal of Peace Research* 49 (3): 445–458. doi:10.1177/0022343312436769.

Conrad, David. 2015. "The Freelancer–NGO Alliance: What a Story of Kenyan Waste Reveals About Contemporary Foreign News Production." *Journalism Studies* 16 (2): 275–288. doi:10.1080/1461670X.2013.872418.

Cook, John. 2012. "Fifteen Ways of Looking at the Media Blackout of Richard Engel's Abduction, Vol. 1: For." *Gawker*, December 12. http://gawker.com/5969842/fifteen-ways-of-looking-at-the-media-blackout-of-richard-engels-abduction-vol-i-for.

Cook, Timothy. 1998. *Governing with the News: The News Media as a Political Institution*. Chicago: University of Chicago Press.

Cooley, Alexander, and James Ron. 2002. "The NGO Scramble: Organizational Insecurity and the Political Economy of Transnational Action." *International Security* 27 (1): 5–39. doi:10.1162/016228802320231217.

Cooper, Glenda. 2009. "When Lines Between NGO and News Organizations Blur." *NiemanLab*, December 21. http://www.niemanlab.org/2009/12/glenda-cooper-when-lines-between-ngo-and-news-organization-blur/.

——. 2011. *From Their Own Correspondents? News Media and the Changes in Disaster Coverage*. Oxford: Reuters Institute for the Study of Journalism.

Cottle, Simon. 2000. "Rethinking News Access." *Journalism Studies* 1 (3): 427–448. doi:10.1080/14616700050081768.

——. 2009. *Global Crisis Reporting: Journalism in the Global Age*. Maidenhead, UK: Open University Press.

Cottle, Simon, and David Nolan. 2007. "Global Humanitarianism and the Changing Aid–Media Field: 'Everyone Was Dying for the Footage.'" *Journalism Studies* 8 (6): 862–878. doi:10.1080/14616700701556104.

Cowell, Alan. 2000. "A Call to Put Social Issues on Corporate Agendas." *New York Times*, April 6.

Curran, James. 2005. "What Democracy Requires of the Media." In *The Press: Institutions of American Democracy*, edited by Geneva Overholser and Kathleen Jamieson, 120–140. New York: Oxford University Press.

Dale, Stephen. 1996. *McLuhan's Children: Greenpeace's Message and the Media*. Toronto: Between the Lines.

Darnton, Andrew, with Martin Kirk 2011. *Finding Frames: New Ways to Engage the UK Public in Global Poverty*. Oxfam white paper. Oxford: Oxfam. http://finding-frames.org/Finding%20Frames%20New%20ways%20to%20engage%20the%20 UK%20public%20in%20global%20poverty%20Bond%202011.pdf.

Davis, Aeron. 2002. *Public Relations Democracy: Public Relations, Politics, and the Mass Media in Britain*. Manchester: Manchester University Press.

——. 2007. *The Mediation of Power: A Critical Introduction*. New York: Routledge.

Dawes, James. 2007. *That the World May Know: Bearing Witness to Atrocity*. Cambridge, MA: Harvard University Press.

Dean, Jodi, Jon W. Anderson, and Geert Lovink. 2004. *Reformatting Politics: Information Technology and Global Civil Society*. London: Routledge.

DeMars, William E. 2005. *NGOs and Transnational Networks: Wild Cards in World Politics*. London: Pluto.

De Waal, Alex. 1998. *Famine Crimes: Politics and the Disaster Relief Industry in Africa*. Bloomington: Indiana University Press.

Dewey, John. 1927. *The Public and Its Problems*. New York: Henry Holt.

Dezalay, Yves, and Bryant Garth. 2002. *The Internationalization of Palace Wars: Lawyers, Economists, and the Contest to Transform Latin American States*. Chicago: University of Chicago Press.

DiMaggio, Paul, and W. W. Powell. 1983. "The Iron Cage Revisited: Institutional Isomorphism and Collective Rationality in Organizational Fields." *American Sociological Review* 48 (2): 147–160.

——. 1991. Introduction to *The New Institutionalism in Organizational Analysis*, edited by Paul DiMaggio and W. W. Powell, 1–38. Chicago: University of Chicago Press.

Dogra, Nandita. 2012. *Representations of Global Poverty*. New York: I. B. Tauris.

Downing, John. 2001. *Radical Media: Rebellious Communication and Social Movements*. New York: Polity.

Drezner, Daniel. 2017. *The Ideas Industry*. New York: Oxford University Press.

Elliot, Justin, and Laura Sullivan. 2015. "How the Red Cross Raised Half a Billion Dollars for Haiti and Built Six Homes." ProPublica, June 3. https://www.propublica .org/article/how-the-red-cross-raised-half-a-billion-dollars-for-haiti-and-built -6-homes.

Elsbach, Kimberly D., and Robert I. Sutton. 1992. "Acquiring Organizational Legitimacy

Through Illegitimate Actions: A Marriage of Institutional and Impression Management Theories." *Academy of Management Journal* 35 (4): 699–738. doi:10.2307/256313.

Engle Merry, Sally. 2006. *Human Rights and Gender Violence: Translating International Law Into Local Justice.* Chicago: University of Chicago Press.

Ennals, Martin. 1982. "Amnesty International and Human Rights." In *Pressure Groups in the Global System*, edited by Peter Willets, 63–83. New York: St. Martin's Press.

Entman, Robert. 1993. "Framing: Toward Clarification of a Fractured Paradigm." *Journal of Communication* 43 (4): 51–58. doi:10.1111/j.1460-2466.1993.tb01304.x.

——. 2012. *Scandal and Silence: Media Responses to Presidential Misconduct.* Cambridge: Polity.

Faris, Stephan. 2012. "The Hackers of Damascus." *Bloomberg Businessweek*, November 15. https://www.bloomberg.com/news/articles/2012-11-15/the-hackers-of-damascus.

Fearon, James. 2008. "The Rise of Emergency Relief Aid." In *Humanitarianism in Question: Politics, Power, Ethics*, edited by Thomas Weiss and Michael Barnett, 49–72. Ithaca: Cornell University Press.

Fenton, Natalie. 2010. "NGOs, New Media, and the Mainstream News." In *New Media, Old News: Journalism and Democracy in the Digital Age*, edited by Natalie Fenton, 153–168. London: Sage.

Ferree, Myra Marx, William Anthony Gamson, Jürgen Gerhards, and Dieter Rucht. 2002. *Shaping Abortion Discourse: Democracy and the Public Sphere in Germany and the United States.* New York: Cambridge University Press.

Fligstein, Neil, and Doug McAdam. 2012. *A Theory of Fields.* New York: Oxford University Press.

French, Howard. 1995. "62 Slain in Raid on Village near Liberia Port." *New York Times*, April 19. http://www.nytimes.com/1995/04/19/world/62-slain-in-raid-on-village-near-liberia-port.html.

Friedland, Lewis. 1996. "Electronic Democracy and the New Citizenship." *Media, Culture, & Society* 18 (2): 185–212. doi:10.1177/016344396018002002.

Friedland, Lewis, and Thomas B. Hove. 2016. "Habermas' Account of Truth in Political Communication." In *Truth in the Public Sphere*, edited by Jason Hannan, 23–40. New York: Lexington.

Galtung, Johan, and Mari Holmboe Ruge. 1965. "The Structure of Foreign News: The Presentation of the Congo, Cuba, and Cyprus Crises in Four Norwegian Newspapers." *Journal of Peace Research* 2 (1): 64–91.

Gandy, Oscar. 1982. *Beyond Agenda Setting: Information Subsidies and Agenda Setting.* Norwood, NJ: Ablex.

Gans, Herbert J. 1979. *Deciding What's News: A Study of CBS Evening News, NBC Nightly News, Newsweek, and Time.* New York: Pantheon.

——. 2003. *Democracy and the News*. New York: Oxford University Press.

Gill, Peter. 1986. *A Year in the Death of Africa: Politics, Bureaucracy, and the Famine*. London: Paladin.

Gillmor, Dan. 2014. "In Praise of the Almost-Journalists." *Slate*, March 28. http://www.slate.com/articles/technology/future_tense/2014/03/human_rights_watch_and_other_advocacy_groups_doing_great_journalism.html.

Gitlin, Todd. 1980. *The Whole World Is Watching: Mass Media in the Making and Unmaking of the New Left*. Berkeley: University of California Press.

Graves, Lucas. 2016. *Deciding What's True: The Rise of Fact Checking in American Journalism*. New York: Columbia University Press.

Grayson, Louise. 2014. "The Role of Non-governmental Organizations (NGOs) in Practicing Editorial Photography in a Globalized Media Environment." *Journalism Practice* 8 (5): 632–645. doi:10.1080/17512786.2014.883124.

Greenberg, Josh, Graham Knight, and Elizabeth Westersund. 2011. "Spinning Climate Change: Corporate and NGO Public Relations Strategies in Canada and the United States." *International Communication Gazette* 73 (1–2): 65–82. doi:10.1177/1748048510386742.

Grunig, James. 2009. "Paradigms of Global Public Relations in an Age of Digitalization." *Prism* 6 (2): 1–19.

Guilhot, Nicolas. 2005. *The Democracy Makers: Human Rights and the Politics of Global Order*. New York: Columbia University Press.

Habermas, Jürgen. 1998. *Between Facts and Norms: Contributions to a Discourse Theory of Law and Democracy*. Cambridge, MA: MIT Press.

Hall, Stuart, Chas Critcher, Tony Jefferson, John Clarke, and Brian Roberts. 1978. *Policing the Crisis: Mugging, the State, and Law and Order*. London: MacMillan.

Hamilton, John Maxwell. 2009. *Journalism's Roving Eye: A History of American Foreign Reporting*. Baton Rouge: Louisiana State University Press.

Hannerz, Ulf. 2004. *Foreign News: Exploring the World of Foreign Correspondence*. Chicago: University of Chicago Press.

Harrison, Paul, and Robin Palmer. 1986. *News out of Africa: Biafra to Band Aid*. London: Hilary Shipman.

Heins, Volker. 2008. *Non-governmental Organizations in International Society: Struggles Over Recognition*. New York: Palgrave.

Herscher, Andrew. 2011. "From Target to Witness: Architecture, Satellite Surveillance, Human Rights." In *Architecture and Violence*, edited by Bechir Kenzari, 123–144. Barcelona: Actar.

Hess, Stephen. 1996. *International News and Foreign Correspondents*. Washington, DC: Brookings Institution Press.

Hiebert, Ray E. 2005. "Commentary: New Technologies, Public Relations, and Democracy." *Public Relations Review* 31 (1): 1–9. doi:10.1016/j.pubrev.2004.11.001.

Hopgood, Stephen. 2006. *Keepers of the Flame: Understanding Amnesty International*. Ithaca: Cornell University Press.

Human Rights Watch. 2005. *Bullets Were Falling Like Rain: The Andijan Massacre*. New York: Human Rights Watch, June 6. https://www.hrw.org/report/2005/06/06/bullets-were-falling-rain/andijan-massacre-may-13-2005.

——. 2006a. *Fatal Strikes: Israel's Indiscriminate Attacks on Civilians*. New York: Human Rights Watch, August. http://www.hrw.org/reports/2006/lebanon0806/.

——. 2006b. *The Hoax That Wasn't: The July 23 Qana Ambulance Attack*. Background Briefing no. 1. New York: Human Rights Watch. http://www.hrw.org/legacy/backgrounder/mena/qana1206/index.htm.

——. 2012. "Syria: New Satellite Images Show Homs Shelling." News release, March 3. https://www.hrw.org/news/2012/03/02/syria-newsatellite-images-show-homs-shelling.

Hurst, Mark. 2016. *British Human Rights Organizations and Soviet Dissent, 1965–1985*. London: Bloomsbury Academic.

Institute for War and Peace Reporting. 2005. "No Requiem for the Dead." May 16. https://iwpr.net/global-voices/no-requiem-dead.

International Crisis Group. 2005. "Uzbekistan: The Andijon Uprising." May 25. https://www.crisisgroup.org/europe-central-asia/central-asia/uzbekistan/uzbekistan-andijon-uprising.

Jacobs, Ronald, and Daniel Glass. 2002. "Media Publicity and the Voluntary Sector: The Case of Nonprofit Organizations in New York." *Voluntas: International Journal of Voluntary and Nonprofit Organizations* 13 (3): 235–252. doi:10.1023/A:1020337425782.

Jacoby, Tamar. 1986. "The Reagan Turnaround on Human Rights." *Foreign Affairs* 64:1066–1086.

Jones, Ben. 2017. "Looking Good: Mediatization and International NGOs." *European Journal of Development Research* 29 (1): 176–191. doi:10.1057/ejdr.2015.87.

Karpf, Dave. 2012. *The MoveOn Effect: The Unexpected Transformation of American Political Advocacy*. New York: Oxford University Press.

——. 2016. *Analytic Activism: Digital Listening and the New Political Strategy*. New York: Oxford University Press.

Kavada, Anastasia. 2012. "Engagement, Bonding, and Identity Across Multiple Platforms: Avaaz on Facebook, YouTube, and MySpace." *Media Kultur* 28 (52): 28–48. doi:10.7146/mediekultur.v28i52.5486.

Keck, Margaret, and Kathryn Sikkink. 1998. *Activists Beyond Borders: Advocacy Networks in International Politics*. Ithaca: Cornell University Press.

Keller, Bill. 2013. "It's the Golden Age of News." *New York Times*, November 4. http://www.nytimes.com/2013/11/04/opinion/keller-its-the-golden-age-of-news.html?_r=0.

Kennedy, David. 2004. *The Dark Side of Virtue: Reassessing International Humanitarianism*. Princeton: Princeton University Press.

Keys, Barbara. 2014. *Reclaiming American Virtue: The Human Rights Revolution of the 1970s*. Cambridge, MA: Harvard University Press.

Kirell, Andrew. 2013. "Journalists and Human Rights Officials Blast Israel in Private Facebook Group." *MEDIAite*, May 22. http://www.mediaite.com/online/journalists-and-human-rights-officials-blast-israel-in-private-facebook-group/.

Klutz, Daniel, and Neil Fligstein. 2016. "Varieties of Sociological Field Theory." In *Handbook of Contemporary Sociological Theory*, edited by Seth Abrutyn, 185–204. Basel: Springer.

Kondracke, Morton. 1988. "Broken Watch." *New Republic*, August 22, 8–11.

Korey, William. 1998. *NGOs and the Universal Declaration of Human Rights: A Curious Grapevine*. New York: Palgrave.

Krause, Monika. 2014. *The Good Project: Humanitarian Relief NGOs and the Fragmentation of Reason*. Chicago: University of Chicago Press.

Kreiss, Daniel. 2012. *Taking Our Country Back: The Crafting of Networked Politics from Howard Dean to Barack Obama*. New York: Oxford University Press.

Kumar, Priya. 2011. "Shrinking Foreign Coverage." *American Journalism Review*, December–January. http://ajrarchive.org/article.asp?id=4998.

Lang, Sabine. 2013. *NGOs, Civil Society, and the Public Sphere*. Cambridge: Cambridge University Press.

Larsen, Engon. 1978. *A Flame in Barbed Wire: The Story of Amnesty International*. London: MW Books.

Larson, James. 1982. "International Affairs Coverage on U.S. Evening News Networks." In *Television Coverage of International Affairs*, edited by William C. Adams, 15–39. Norwood, NJ: Alex Publishing.

Lebon, Nathalie. 1996. "Professionalization of Women's Health Group in Sao Paolo: The Troublesome Road Towards Organizational Diversity." *Organization* 3 (4): 588–609. doi:10.1177/135050849634016.

Lippmann, Walter. 1920. *Liberty and the News*. Princeton: Princeton University Press.

——. 1922. *Public Opinion*. New York: Harcourt, Brace.

Livingston, Steven, and W. Lance Bennett. 2003. "Gatekeeping, Indexing, and Live-Event News: Is Technology Altering the Construction of News?" *Political Communication* 20 (4): 363–380. doi:10.1080/10584600390244121.

Lück, Julia, Antal Wozniak, and Hartmut Wessler. 2016. "Networks of Coproduction: How Journalists and Environmental NGOs Create Common Interpretations of the UN Climate Change Conferences." *International Journal of Press/Politics* 21 (1): 25–47. doi:10.1177/1940161215612204.

Madianou, Mirca. 2013. "Humanitarian Campaigns in Social Media: Network

Architectures and Polymedia Events." *Journalism Studies* 14 (2): 249–266. doi:10
.1080/1461670X.2012.718558.

Malkin, Elisabeth, and Randal C. Archibold. 2010. "US Withholds Millions in Mexico Antidrug Aid." *New York Times*, September 4. http://www.nytimes.com/2010
/09/04/world/americas/04mexico.html.

Martin, John Levi. 2003. "What Is Field Theory?" *American Journal of Sociology*
109:1–49. doi:10.1086/375201.

Mawad, Dalal. 2012. "Syria: Too Much Information?" *Columbia Journalism Review*,
February 24. http://www.cjr.org/behind_the_news/syria_too_much_information
.php.

McChesney, Robert, and John Nichols. 2010. *The Death and Life of American Journalism*. Philadelphia: Nation Books.

McNair, Brian. 2000. *Journalism and Democracy*. New York: Routledge.

McPherson, Ella. 2015. "Advocacy Organization's Evaluation of Social Media Information for NGO Journalism: The Evidence and Engagement Models." *American Behavioral Scientist* 59 (1): 124–148. doi:10.1177/0002764214540508.

Medvetz, Thomas. 2012. *Think Tanks in America*. Chicago: University of Chicago
Press.

Meyers, Steven Lee. 2005. "At Least 10 Die as Conflict Erupts in Restive Uzbek Area."
New York Times, May 14.

Moeller, Susan. 1999. *Compassion Fatigue: How the Media Sell Disease, Famine, War,
and Death*. New York: Routledge.

Moon, Ruth. 2017. "Getting Into Living Rooms: NGO Media Relations Work as Strategic Practice." *Journalism: Theory, Practice, & Criticism*, February 17 (early
online publication). doi:10.1177/1464884917691542.

Moyn, Samuel. 2010. *The Last Utopia: Human Rights in History*. Cambridge, MA:
Harvard University Press.

Mulley, Clare. 2009. *The Woman Who Saved the Children: A Biography of Eglantyne
Jebb*. London: One World Publications.

Murrell, Colleen. 2014. "The Vulture Club: International Newsgathering Via Facebook." *Australian Journalism Review* 36 (1): 15–27.

Nafplpioti, Alexandros. 2005. *The British Labour Government's Policy Towards the
Greek Colonels, 1967–1968*. London: Department of International History, London
School of Economics and Political Science. http://www.lse.ac.uk/europeanInsti
tute/research/hellenicObservatory/pdf/2nd_Symposium/Alexandros_Nafpli
otis_paper.pdf.

Naudé, Annelie, Johannes Froneman, and Roy Atwood. 2004. "The Use of the Internet by Ten South African Non-governmental Organizations—a Public Relations
Perspective." *Public Relations Review* 30 (1): 87–94. doi:10.1016/j.pubrev.2003.11
.008.

Neier, Aryeh. 2003. *Taking Liberties: Four Decades in the Struggle for Rights*. New York: Public Affairs.

——. 2012. *The International Human Rights Movement: A History*. Princeton: Princeton University Press.

New York Times. 2000. "What Meat Means." February 6.

——. 2005a. "Praying on a Volatile Central Asian Border" (photograph). May 21.

——. 2005b. "World Briefing: Uzbekistan: Rare Protest." May 12.

Nichols, Bill. 2000. "No Action on China Resolution: Activists Point Fingers at Clinton." *USA Today*, April 19.

Nielsen, Rasmus Kleis. 2012. *Ground Wars: Personalized Communication in Political Campaigns*. Princeton: Princeton University Press.

Nolan, David, and Akina Mikami. 2013. "'The Things That We Have to Do': Ethics and Instrumentality in Humanitarian Communication." *Global Media and Communication* 9 (1): 53–70. doi:10.1177/1742766512463040.

Orgad, Shani. 2013. "Visualizers of Solidarity: Organizational Politics in Humanitarian and International Development NGOs." *Visual Communication* 12 (3): 295–314. doi:10.1177/1470357213483057.

Orgad, Shani, and Bruna Irene Seu. 2014. "Intimacy at a Distance in Humanitarian Communication." *Media, Culture, & Society* 36 (7): 916–934. doi:10.1177/0163443714536077.

Packer, George. 2010. "Exiled." *New Yorker*, October 18. http://www.newyorker.com/magazine/2010/10/18/exiled.

Pew Research Center. 2009. *An Annual Report on American Journalism*. Washington, DC: Pew Research Center. http://www.stateofthemedia.org/2009/index.htm.

Pickard, Victor. 2014. *America's Battle for Media Democracy: The Triumph of Corporate Libertarianism and the Future of Media Reform*. Cambridge: Cambridge University Press.

Pierson, Paul. 1994. *Dismantling the Welfare State?* Cambridge: Cambridge University Press.

——. 2000. "Increasing Returns, Path Dependence, and the Study of Politics." *American Political Science Review* 94 (2): 251–267. doi:10.2307/2586011.

Platon. 2011. "Facing Power." Video file, September 12. http://www.youtube.com/watch?v=8mmTJBxugfM.

Pollock, John. 2014. "Illuminating Human Rights: How Demographics Drive Media Coverage." *Atlantic Journal of Communication* 22 (3–4): 141–159.

Power, Jonathan. 2001. *Like Water on Stone: The Story of Amnesty International*. London: Penguin Press.

Powers, Matthew. 2013. "Humanity's Publics: NGOs, Journalism, and the International Public Sphere." PhD diss., New York University.

——. 2014. "The Structural Organization of NGO Publicity: Explaining Divergent

Publicity Strategies at Humanitarian and Human Rights Organizations." *International Journal of Communication* 8:90–107. doi:1932–8036/20140005.

——. 2015a. "Contemporary NGO–Journalist Relations: Reviewing and Evaluating an Emergent Area of Research." *Sociology Compass* 9 (6): 427–437.

——. 2015b. "Does It Matter That Greenpeace Journalists Lied in Order to Expose Academics for Hire?" *The Conversation*, December 16. https://theconversation .com/does-it-matter-that-greenpeace-journalists-lied-in-order-to-expose -academics-for-hire-52192.

——. 2015c. "NGOs as Journalistic Entities: The Possibilities, Promises, and Limits of Boundary Crossing." In *The Boundaries of Journalism: Professionalism, Practices, and Participation*, edited by Matt Carlson and Seth Lewis, 184–198. New York: Sage.

——. 2015d. "When Greenpeace Hires Journalists, It's a Double-Edged Sword." *The Conversation*, September 16. https://theconversation.com/when-greenpeace-hires -journalists-its-a-double-edged-sword-47398.

——. 2016a. "The New Boots on the Ground: NGOs in the Changing Landscape of International News." *Journalism: Theory, Practice, & Criticism* 17 (4): 401–416. doi:10.1177/1464884914568077.

——. 2016b. "A New Era of Human Rights News? Contrasting Two Paradigms of Human Rights News Making." *Journal of Human Rights* 15 (3): 314–329.

——. 2016c. "NGO Publicity and Reinforcing Path Dependencies: Explaining the Persistence of Media-Centered Publicity Strategies." *International Journal of Press/ Politics* 21 (4): 490–507.

——. 2016d. "Opening the News Gates? Humanitarian and Human Rights Groups in the U.S. News Media, 1990–2010." *Media, Culture, & Society* 38 (3): 315–331. doi:10 .1177/0163443715594868.

——. 2017. "Beyond Boon or Bane: Using Normative Theories to Evaluate the Newsmaking Efforts of NGOs." *Journalism Studies* 18 (9): 1070–1086.

Ramos, Howard, James Ron, and Oskar Thoms. 2007. "Shaping the Northern Media's Human Rights Coverage, 1986–2000." *Journal of Peace Research* 44 (4): 385–406. doi:10.1177/0022343307078943.

Reese, Stephen. 2007. "The Framing Project: A Bridging Model for Media Research Revisited." *Journal of Communication* 57 (1): 148–154. doi:10.1111/j.1460-2466.2006 .00334.x.

——. 2010. "Journalism and Globalization." *Sociology Compass* 4 (6): 344–353.

——. 2015. "Globalization of Mediated Spaces: The Case of Transnational Environmentalism in China." *International Journal of Communication* 9:2263–2281. doi:1932–8036/20150005.

Reimann, Kim. 2006. "A View from the Top: International Politics, Norms, and the Worldwide Growth of NGOs." *International Studies Quarterly* 50 (1): 45–67. doi:10.1111/j.1468–2478.2006.00392.x.

Richey, Lisa Ann, and Stefano Ponte. 2011. *Brand Aid: Shopping Well to Save the World*. Minneapolis: University of Minnesota Press.

Rieff, David. 1999. "The Precarious Triumph of Human Rights." *New York Times*, August 8. http://www.nytimes.com/1999/08/08/magazine/the-precarious-triumph -of-human-rights.html.

——. 2002. *A Bed for the Night: Humanitarianism in Crisis*. New York: Simon & Schuster.

Ron, James, Howard Ramos, and Kathleen Rodgers. 2005. "Transnational Information Politics: NGO Human Rights Reporting, 1986–2000." *International Studies Quarterly* 49 (3): 557–588. doi:10.1111/j.1468-2478.2005.00377.x.

Rootes, Christopher, and Clare Saunders. 2007. "The Global Justice Movement in Great Britain." In *The Global Justice Movement: Cross-National and Transnational Perspectives*, edited by Donatella della Porta, 128–156. New York: Paradigm.

Rosanvallon, Pierre. 2008. *Counter-Democracy: Politics in an Age of Distrust*. Cambridge: Cambridge University Press.

Roth, Kenneth. 2007. "Defending Economic, Social, and Cultural Rights." In *Ethics in Action: The Ethical Challenges of International Human Rights Nongovernmental Organizations*, edited by Daniel Bell and Jean-Marc Coicaud, 169–180. Cambridge: Cambridge University Press.

Rothmyer, Karen. 2011. "Hiding the Real Africa: Why NGOs Prefer Bad News." *Columbia Journalism Review*, March–April, 18–20.

Russell, Adrienne. 2013. "Innovation in Hybrid Spaces: 2011 UN Climate Summit and the Expanding Journalism Landscape." *Journalism: Theory, Practice, & Criticism* 17 (4): 904–920. doi:10.1177/1464884913477311.

——. 2016. *Journalism as Activism: Recoding Media Power*. Cambridge: Polity.

Ryan, Charlotte. 1991. *Prime Time Activism: Media Strategies for Grassroots Organizing*. Boston: South End Press.

Ryfe, David. 2011. *Can Journalism Survive? An Inside Look in American Newsrooms*. Cambridge: Polity.

——. 2016. *Journalism and the Public*. Cambridge: Polity.

Sambrook, Richard. 2010. *Are Foreign Correspondents Redundant? The Changing Face of International News*. Oxford: Reuters Institute for the Study of Journalism. http://reutersinstitute.politics.ox.ac.uk/sites/default/files/Are%20Foreign%20 Correspondents%20Redundant%20The%20changing%20face%20of%20international%20news_0.pdf.

Sassen, Saskia. 2017. "Is Rohingya Persecution Caused by Business Interests Rather Than Religion?" *Guardian*, January 4. https://www.theguardian.com/global -development-professionals-network/2017/jan/04/is-rohingya-persecution -caused-by-business-interests-rather-than-religion.

Scammell, Margaret. 2014. *Consumer Democracy: The Marketing of Politics*. Cambridge: Cambridge University Press.

Schubert, Misa. 2006. "Downer Attacks Lebanon Coverage." *The Age* (Australia), September 1. http://www.theage.com.au/news/national/downer-attacks-lebanon -coverage/2006/08/31/1156817031818.html.

Schudson, Michael. 2008. *Why Democracies Need an Unlovable Press*. Cambridge: Polity.

——. 2010. "Political Observatories, Databases, and the News." *Daedalus*, Spring, 100–109.

——. 2011. *The Sociology of News*. 2nd ed. New York: Norton.

——. 2015. *The Rise of the Right to Know: Politics and the Culture of Transparency, 1945–1975*. Cambridge, MA: Harvard University Press.

Scoble, Harry, and Laurie Wiseberg. 1974. "Human Rights and Amnesty International." *Annals of the Academy of Political and Social Science* 413 (1): 11–26. doi:10 .1177/000271627441300103.

Scott, Martin. 2014. *Media and Development*. London: Zed Books.

Scott, Richard. 2014. *Institutions and Organizations: Ideas, Interests, and Identities*. 4th ed. London: Sage.

Seo, Hyunjin, Ji Young Kim, and Sung-Un Yang. 2009. "Global Activism and New Media: A Study of Transnational NGOs' Online Public Relations." *Public Relations Review* 35 (2): 123–126. doi:10.1016/j.pubrev.2009.02.002.

Shaer, Matthew. 2015. "The Media Doesn't Care What Happened Here." *New York Times*, February 18. https://www.nytimes.com/2015/02/22/magazine/the-media -doesnt-care-what-happens-here.html.

Shephard, Ben. 2008. "Becoming Planning Minded: The Theory and Practice of Relief, 1940–1945." *Journal of Contemporary History* 43 (3): 405–419. doi:10.1177/0022 009408091820.

Shivji, Issa. 2007. *Silences in NGO Discourse: The Role and Future of NGOs in Africa*. Oxford: Fahamu.

Silverstone, Roger. 2007. *Media and Morality: On the Rise of the Mediapolis*. Cambridge: Polity.

Smith, Brian G. 2010. "Socially Distributing Public Relations: Twitter, Haiti, and Interactivity in Social Media." *Public Relations Review* 36 (4): 329–335. doi:10.1016 /j.pubrev.2010.08.005.

Sobieraj, Sarah. 2011. *Soundbitten: The Perils of Media-Centered Activism*. New York: New York University Press.

Sommerfeldt, Erich J., Michael Kent, and Maureen Taylor. 2012. "Activist Practitioner Perspectives of Website Public Relations: Why Aren't Activist Websites Fulfilling the Dialogic Promise?" *Public Relations Review* 38 (2): 303–312. doi:10.1016 /j.pubrev.2012.01.001.

Stack, Liam. 2011. "Activists Using Video to Bear Witness." *New York Times*, June 18.

Starr, Paul. 2004. *The Creation of the Media: Political Origins of Modern Communications*. New York: Basic Books.

Sternberg, Steve. 2000. "AIDS Activists Discount Big Drug Makers' Gifts." *USA Today*, July 11.

Stroup, Sarah. 2012. *Borders Among Activists: International NGOs in the United States, Britain, and France.* Ithaca: Cornell University Press.

Suchman, Mark. 1995. "Managing Legitimacy: Strategic and Institutional Approaches." *Academy of Management Review* 20 (3): 571–610. doi:10.5465/AMR.1995.950 8080331.

Terry, Fiona. 2002. *Condemned to Repeat? The Paradox of Humanitarian Action.* Ithaca: Cornell University Press.

Thelen, Kathleen. 2002. *How Institutions Evolve: The Political Economy of Skills in Germany, Britain, the United States, and Japan.* Cambridge: Cambridge University Press.

Thompson, John B. 2000. *Political Scandal: Power and Visibility in the Media Age.* Oxford: Polity.

Thrall, A. Trevor. 2006. "The Myth of the Outside Strategy: Mass Media News Coverage of Interest Groups." *Political Communication* 23 (4): 407–420. doi:10.1080 /10584600600976989.

Thrall, A. Trevor, Dominik Stecula, and Diana Sweet. 2014. "May We Have Your Attention Please? Human-Rights NGOs and the Problem of Global Communication." *International Journal of Press/Politics* 19 (2): 135–159. doi:10.1177/19401612 13519132.

Tolley, Howard. 1994. *The International Commission of Jurists: Global Advocates for Human Rights.* Philadelphia: University of Pennsylvania Press.

Trenz, Hans-Jörg. 2004. "Media Coverage on European Governance: Exploring the European Public Sphere in National Quality Newspapers." *European Journal of Communication* 19 (3): 291–319. doi:10.1177/0267323104045257.

Van Leuven, Sarah, Annelore Deprez, and Karin Raeymaeckers. 2013. "Increased News Access for International NGOs? How Médecins Sans Frontières Press Releases Built the Agenda of Flemish Newspapers (1995–2010)." *Journalism Practice* 7 (4): 430–445. doi:10.1080/17512786.2013.802479.

Van Leuven, Sarah, and Stijn Joye. 2014. "Civil Society Organizations at the Gates? A Gatekeeping Study of News Making Efforts by NGOs and Government Institutions." *International Journal of Press/Politics* 19 (2): 160–180. doi:10.1177/1940 161213514615.

Volkmer, Ingrid. 2014. *The Global Public Sphere: Public Communication in an Age of Reflective Interdependence.* Cambridge: Polity.

Waisbord, Silvio. 2008a. "Advocacy Journalism in a Global Context: The 'Journalist' and the 'Civic' Model." In *Handbook of Journalism Studies*, edited by Karin Wohl-Jorgensen and Thomas Hanitzsch, 371–385. New York: Routledge.

——. 2008b. "The Institutional Challenge to Participatory Communication in International Aid." *Social Identities* 14 (4): 505–522. doi:10.1080/13504630802212009.

——. 2011. "Can NGOs Change the News?" *International Journal of Communication* 5:142–165. doi:1932–8036/20110142.

——. 2013. *Reinventing Professionalism: Journalism and News in Global Perspective.* Cambridge: Polity.

Walker, Ed. 2015. *Grassroots for Hire: Public Affairs Consultants in American Democracy.* Cambridge: Cambridge University Press.

Weber, Max. 1947. "Bureaucracy." In *Max Weber: Essays in Sociology*, edited by H. H. Gerth and C. Wright Mills, 196–244. New York: Oxford University Press.

Wells, Chris. 2015. *The Civic Organization and the Digital Citizen: Communicating Engagement in a Networked Age.* New York: Oxford University Press.

Wessler, Hartmut. 2008. "Investigating Deliberativeness Comparatively." *Political Communication* 25 (1): 1–22. doi:10.1080/10584600701807752.

White, Lyman Cromwell. 1951. *International Non-governmental Organizations: Their Purposes, Methods, and Accomplishments.* New Brunswick, NJ: Rutgers University Press.

Willets, Peter. 2011. *Non-governmental Organizations in World Politics: The Construction of Global Governance.* Milton Park, UK: Routledge.

Williams, Bruce, and Michael Delli Carpini. 2011. *After Broadcast News: Media Regimes, Democracy, and the New Information Environment.* Cambridge: Cambridge University Press.

Williams, Randall. 2010. *The Divided World: Human Rights and Its Violence.* Minneapolis: University of Minnesota Press.

Wilson, Francesca. 1944. *In the Margins of Chaos: Recollections of Relief Work in and Between Three Wars.* London: Macmillan.

Wolfsfeld, Gadi. 2011. *Making Sense of Media and Politics.* New York: Routledge.

Wood, Tim. 2017. "The Many Voices of Business: Framing the Keystone Pipeline in the US and Canadian News." *Journalism: Theory, Practice, & Criticism*, July 7 (early online publication). doi:10.1177/1464884917717536.

Wozniak, Antal, Hartmut Wessler, and Julia Lück. 2016. "Who Prevails in the Visual Framing Contest About the United Nations Climate Change Conferences?" *Journalism Studies*, November 25 (early online publication). doi:10.1080/1461670X.2015.1131129.

Wright, Kate. 2016a. "Moral Economies: Interrogating the Interactions of NGOs, Journalists, and Freelancers." *International Journal of Communication* 10:1510–1529. doi:1932-8036/20160005.

——. 2016b. "These Grey Areas: How and Why Freelance Work Blurs INGOs and News Organizations." *Journalism Studies* 17 (8): 989–1009. doi:10.0.4.56/1461670X.2015.1036904.

Yanacopulos, Helen. 2015. *International NGO Engagement, Advocacy, and Activism: The Faces and Spaces of Change.* Basingstoke, UK: Palgrave Macmillan.

Zald, Mayer, and John McCarthy. 1987. *Social Movements in an Organizational Society: Collected Essays*. New Brunswick, NJ: Transaction.

Zaller, John, and Dennis Chiu. 1996. "Government's Little Helper: U.S. Press Coverage of Foreign Policy Crises, 1945–1991." *Political Communication* 13:385–405. doi:10.1080/10584609.1996.9963127.

Zoch, Lynn M., and Juan-Carlos Molleda. 2006. "Building a Theoretical Model of Media Relations Using Framing, Information Subsidies, and Agenda Building." In *Public Relations Theory II*, edited by Carl Botan and Vincent Hazleton, 279–309. Mahwah, NJ: Lawrence Erlbaum Associates.

Zombietime. 2006. "The Red Cross Ambulance Incident: How the Media Legitimized an Anti-Israel Hoax and Changed the Course of a War." N.d. http://www .zombietime.com/fraud/ambulance/.

Zuckerman, Ethan. 2004. "Using the Internet to Determine Patterns of Foreign Coverage." *Nieman Reports*, Fall, 51–53.

——. 2006. "Rebunking the Lebanese Ambulance Story." *My Heart's in Accra*, December 20. http://www.ethanzuckerman.com/blog/2006/12/20/rebunking-the-leba nese-ambulance-story/.

——. 2013. *Rewire: Digital Cosmopolitans in an Age of Constant Connection*. New York: Norton.

Index

grafting advocacy reporting into news flows, 85, 91, 99–104, 186n24; growth of, 6; Human Rights Watch's use of, 3–4; information-gathering supplemented by, 49–51, 98; information management strategies, 23–24; interaction with journalists via, 93, 123–24, 185n8, 189n39; to interact with citizens, 87; to monitor news and mimic news norms, 84–85, 88–89, 91–94, 102, 104–6, 159; NGOs reluctant to embrace, 165; NGOs' use of (generally), 4–6, 8, 10–11, 12, 15–16, 23, 104–6 (*see also specific organizations*); NGO websites, 48, 84, 95–96, 101, 184n14, 185n14; opposing views on NGOs' use of, 84–85, 86–89; pragmatic use of, 15–16, 90, 105; protecting legitimacy/reputation/brand, 89, 91, 106; and protest organization and publicity, 101; and public criticisms/negative publicity, 23, 85, 96–99, 124; and public engagement by NGOs, 85, 95–96, 124; security concerns, 50; types used by NGOs, 48–50. *See also* social media, NGOs use of; *and specific tools and technologies*

DiMaggio and Powell, 178n15
discursive tradition, NGOs and, 158–59
displaced persons (as term), 32
Doctorow, E.L., 44
Doctors Without Borders. *See* Médecins Sans Frontières
donors: digital tools and, 93–94, 95, 117, 161–62; incentivizing changes in NGO communications, 127, 161–62; information communicated to, 7, 95; media coverage valued by, 5, 17, 24, 107–8, 109, 114–18, 115t, 125, 161; negative publicity and, 99; reasons for funding NGOs, 154. *See also* fund-raising

ECC (European Economic Community), 46
economic issues, NGOs and, 76–81
Economist, 116
Elsbach, Kimberly, 89–90
emergency relief aid, 181n17. *See also specific emergencies, by country*
emergency situations, exploitation of, 39–40, 158, 182n28. *See also* Ethiopian famine
Engel, Richard, 189n39
Ennals, Martin, 180n8
Entman, Robert, 183n7, 185n22
Ethiopian famine, 41, 45–47, 182n28
"European Commission Seeks Faster Repatriation of Some Migrants" *(New York Times)*, 71
European Economic Community (ECC), 46

Facebook. *See* social media, NGOs use of; Vulture Club
Fatal Strikes (Human Rights Watch), 96–98
Fearon, James, 181n17
Fenton, Natalie, 11, 58–59, 110, 178n11, 187n2
field diffusion, 17, 24–25, 130, 133–34, 143–50
field inertia, 24, 127–28, 130, 133–34, 137–43, 149–50
fields, institutional. *See* institutional fields
Ford Foundation, 33, 44

foundations, prominence of, 39

framing analysis, 59–60, 64, 183n7

freelance journalists: contracted by NGOs, 47–48, 93, 105–6, 144–45, 147–49, 191n28; increasingly common, 7, 55; and reporting on Syrian refugees, 137, 143, 190n5; subject to editorial decisions, 140–41, 143

Friedman, Milton and the "Chicago Boys," 33

fund-raising: digital tools and, 93–94, 95, 110, 117, 161–62; exploitation of emergencies for, 39–40, 158; media coverage and, 5, 17, 24, 40, 41, 110, 114–18, 115t; NGO communication efforts and, 5, 36–43, 51–52, 158. *See also* donors; *and specific organizations*

Geldof, Bob, 40–41, 47

Glass, Daniel, 164

Goldberg, Arthur, 33

Golden, Lewis, 37

Grayson, Louise, 145, 147–48

Greece, 31, 36, 37, 45

Greenpeace, 165–66

Griswold, Erwin, 180n9

Grunig, James, 185n8

Guantánamo Bay, 68

Guinea stadium massacre, 49

Habermas, Jürgen, 10

Haiti earthquake, 68–69, 74, 169, 192n4

Hannerz, Ulf, 7

Harrison, George, 40

Hepburn, Audrey, 41

Hopgood, Stephen, 41–42

humanitarianism: humanitarian frames for human rights issues, 74–75; and human rights advocacy, 19–20, 55, 182–83n3 (*see also* human rights; human rights organizations)

humanitarian organizations: dual role, 74–76; government funding for, 39, 181n17; growth of, 38–39, 181n16; and the Haiti earthquake, 68–69, 192n4; and human rights advocacy, 19–20, 55, 58, 183n4; information-gathering strategies, 32, 180nn7–9; institutionalization and professionalization of, 30, 167–68 (*see also* professionalization of NGOs); news access, 53–54, 58, 60–70, 67t (*see also* news access); and the primacy of political/civil rights violations, 74–77, 81; public and official acceptance of, 55–56. *See also* NGOs; *and specific organizations*

human rights: in American policy discourse, 65–66, 65t (*see also* Human Rights Watch); American politics and, 33–34, 68; Chinese record on, 100–101; humanitarianism and, 19–20, 55, 182–83n3 (*see also* humanitarianism; humanitarian organizations); human rights frames, 59–60, 64, 74–77, 75t; increase in human rights discourses, 55–56; location of human rights news stories, 72–74, 82, 109 (*see also* story location); in Myanmar, 1–4, 99, 100; narrative journalism and, 83; primacy of political/civil violations, 23, 59–60, 74–77, 81; world events and news coverage of, 68–69, 82–83. *See also specific countries and peoples* human rights organizations: dual role, 74–76; focus broadened to include social/cultural/economic rights, 59–60; government funding for, 39, 181n17; growth of, 38; and humanitarianism, 19–20; institutionalization and professionalization of, 30, 167–68 (*see also* professionalization of NGOs); news access, 53–54, 58, 60–70, 67t (*see also* news access); and the primacy of political/civil rights violations, 74–77, 81; public and official acceptance of, 55–56. *See also* NGOs; *and specific organizations*

Human Rights Watch: ambulance attack report, 96–98; on the American meatpacking industry, 76–77; beheading story found incorrect, 50–51, 98; in the Central African Republic, 102–4; credibility established, 30, 34; early information strategies, 33–34; fact-checking for journalists, 142; founding (formation) of, 31, 33, 44, 160, 180n10; fund-raising strategies, 116; and H. Clinton's campaign, 99, 100; included in news access study, 61–62; journalists hired by, 144; media savvy, 57, 66–67, 82, 103–4; on Mexican human rights and U.S. funding, 76; multimedia content produced, 48, 120, 121; name, 177n4; news access, 57, 66–67, 72, 74; and Olympic protests over Chinese human rights violations, 101; and photojournalists, 1–4, 47–48, 103–4, 105, 177nn1–3; policy makers' news consumption studied, 120–21; as

"political observatory," 192n3; professionalization, 35; reasons for seeking media coverage, 116; reasons for studying, 20; response to public criticism, 96–98, 124; satellite imagery used, 50; social media used, 103; and Syrian refugees in Turkey, 137; and Uzbekistan, 74, 80

impartiality (objectivity; fairness), 131, 146, 156–57

inertia: and path dependence, 16–17, 111–12, 127–28. *See also* field inertia

information-gathering. *See* research by NGOs

information technologies, 49–50. *See also* digital tools and strategies

institutional fields: NGOs and journalism as interacting institutional fields, 14–18, 178nn12–13; theory, 14, 16–17, 111–12, 178n12, 178n15

International Commission of Jurists, 180–81n14

International Crisis Group, 20, 49, 61–62, 80, 91, 119

International Medical Corps, 20

international news: changes and cutbacks in reporting/coverage, 6–7, 55, 58, 61, 68, 151, 177–78n7, 178n8; story location (countries), 59, 63, 72–74, 82, 109, 183–84n10. *See also* journalism and journalists; news access; news media; news norms; *and specific countries, news organizations, and events*

International Yearbook of Organizations, 38

interviews, 20–22, 109, 129–30, 134–36,
171–72
Invisible Children, 120
Israel-Lebanon War (2006), 96–98

Jacobs, Ronald, 164
Jebb, Eglantyne, 38, 181n15
Jolie, Angelina, 41
Jones, Ben, 143, 191n27
journalism and journalists: author's
interviews with, 129–30 (see also
Syrian refugees, in Turkey; and
specific topics); changes in
journalism, 6–7, 29, 55, 132,
177–78n7, 178n8, 189n1; and civic
engagement, 158; economic
constraints on, 55, 130 (see also
international news); editors' impact
on content/coverage, 139–41, 143;
and the Ethiopian famine, 45–47;
fact-checking, 141–42; field
diffusion and news norms, 24–25,
130, 133–34, 143–50; field inertia
and news norms, 24, 127–28, 130,
133–34, 137–43, 149–50; freelance
journalists, 7, 47–48, 55, 93, 105–6,
144–45, 147–49, 190n5, 191n28;
journalism seen as ally by NGOs,
24, 108, 122, 123, 125; journalists
switching to advocacy, 143–44 (see
also NGO-journalist relations:
journalists hired by NGOs); NGOs
and journalism as interacting
institutional fields, 14–18, 43–44,
178nn12–13; normative orders
(values), 131; objectivity and
fairness, 131, 146, 156; oversight of
NGOs needed, 168–69; primacy of
political/civil violations for, 23,
59–60, 74–77; rise of narrative

journalism, 83; Syrian refugees
reporting, 134–35, 137–43, 190nn3,
5, 12; verbatim use of NGO
materials, 49, 58, 63, 72. See also
international news; news access;
news media; news norms; NGO-
journalist relations; and specific
news organizations and individuals

Karpf, Dave, 10, 87
Keck, Margaret, 10
Kent, Michael, 184n14
Kondracke, Morton, 34
Kony, Joseph, 120
Kouchner, Bernard, 40. See also
Médecins Sans Frontières

Lang, Sabine, 12, 55, 88, 161
Lebanon, 96–98
legitimacy of NGOs: digital tools and,
89, 91, 106; political legitimacy
through media attention, 118–22,
188n25; preserving, 89, 96–98, 106.
See also credibility of NGOs
Liberia, 75
Lippmann, Walter, 192n3
Live Aid (concert), 47. See also Geldof,
Bob
Livingston, Steven, 10
location. See story location

Make Poverty History campaign, 77,
184n12
Mandela, Nelson, 35
McPherson, Ella, 87, 165, 185–86n23
Médecins Sans Frontières (Doctors
Without Borders): on civilian
injuries in Liberia's civil war, 75;
digital tools and strategies, 96; drug
companies criticized, 77; founding

news access (*cont.*)
  professionalization of NGOs);
  prominence of NGOs within news
  articles, 58–59, 63, 69–74, 70t, 71t,
  73t, 81, 83; real-world events and,
  68–69; story location and, 59,
  72–74, 73t, 82, 109, 183–84n10;
  unevenly distributed, 57, 66–67, 82;
  US legacy news media and, 60–61,
  139; verbatim use of NGO materials,
  49, 58, 63, 72. *See also* news media;
  NGO-journalist relations
news media: broadcast vs. prestige
  media, 58, 64–65, 67–68, 67t, 183n5;
  challenge of getting stories into,
  139; challenging the news media
  agenda, 125–26; changes/cutbacks
  in international reporting, 6–7, 55,
  58, 61, 68, 151, 177–78n7, 178n8,
  191n41; changing media landscape,
  NGO communication in, 43–51;
  economic issues sidelined by, 77–78
  (*see also* economic issues, NGOs
  and); editors' impact on coverage/
  content, 139–41, 143; efficiency and
  profitability, 131; government
  sources, 13, 54–55, 59, 69–71, 70t,
  109, 136; grafting advocacy
  reporting into news flows, 23–24,
  85, 91, 99–104, 129, 186nn24, 26,
  30–31; Human Rights Watch's
  relationship with, 2–4; and "hybrid"
  media system, 151, 161, 184n2;
  integration of news considerations
  by NGOs, 44–47, 122–23 (*see also*
  news norms: NGO adaptation to);
  legacy news media, 60–61, 139;
  monitoring of news by NGOs,
  91–92, 100, 102, 104; news coverage
  and NGO funding, 5, 17, 24, 40, 41,

107–9, 114–18, 125; news cycle, 121;
  NGO communication as boon/
  bane, 9–11 (*see also under* NGO
  communication efforts); NGOs as
  experts for, 156–57, 192n3; NGOs'
  coverage more exhaustive than,
  86–87; online vs. legacy editions,
  139; primacy of political/civil
  violations in human rights
  coverage, 23, 59–60, 74–77,
  81; scandal-oriented news
  coverage, 185n22; seen as ally
  by NGOs, 24, 108, 122, 123, 125;
  sensationalization/distortion of
  NGO messages, 109–10; story
  location (countries), 59, 63, 72–74,
  82, 109, 183–84n10; verbatim use of
  NGO materials, 49, 58, 63, 72. *See
  also* digital tools and strategies;
  international news; journalism and
  journalists; news access; news
  norms
news norms: adaptation of NGOs to,
  87–88, 92–93, 100, 105–6, 121,
  129–33, 143–49, 159–60, 191n27;
  case study (Syrian refugee
  reporting), 134–36 (*see also* Syrian
  refugees, in Turkey); changes in,
  132, 189n1; drama and human
  interest, 83, 139, 146; endurance of
  (generally), 24–25, 127–28, 129–31,
  149–50 (*see also* field inertia);
  explaining continuity amid change,
  131–34, 149–50; field diffusion and
  the endurance of, 17, 24–25, 130,
  133–34, 143–50; field inertia and the
  endurance of, 24, 127–28, 130,
  133–34, 137–43, 149–50; imbrication
  of advocacy and journalism, 132,
  189n1; NGO news access limited by,

131, 138–39, 142–43; normative orders (values), 131; objectivity and fairness, 131, 146, 156; potential for change, 150–51; reinforced by editors, 136, 139–41, 143, 149, 151; timeliness, 11, 133, 139, 145–46, 147. *See also* news media

NGO communication efforts (*cont.*)
See also digital tools and strategies; journalism and journalists; news access; NGO-journalist relations; NGOs; publicity strategies of NGOs; public relations and marketing; social media; *and specific organizations and strategies*

NGO-ization, 179(n17)

NGO-journalist relations: and the Ethiopian famine, 46–47; field diffusion and, 24–25, 130, 133–34, 143–50; field inertia and, 24, 130, 133–34, 137–43, 149–50; and integration of news considerations by NGOs, 44–47, 122–23 (*see also* news access); journalism and NGOs as interacting fields, 14–18, 43–44, 178nn12–13; journalism seen as ally by NGOs, 24, 108, 122, 123, 125; journalists' access to sources facilitated, 83, 140; journalists hired/contracted by NGOs, 24, 44, 47–48, 92–93, 105–6, 122, 133, 143–49, 181n18, 191n28 (*see also* photojournalists and NGOs); journalists' perceptions of NGOs' contributions to news, 16, 24, 43–44, 135, 136, 139–42, 163; journalists' use of NGOs limited, 138–39; mix of factual reporting and advocacy claims provided by NGOs, 75–76; NGOs as experts, 156–57; online interactions between journalists and NGO professionals, 93, 96; photojournalists and NGOs, 1–4, 47–48, 103–4, 105, 147–48, 177nn1–3, 191n28; press releases expected from NGOs, 95–96; social proximity, 16, 93, 122–25, 181n25,

188–89n37, 189nn39, 43–44; suggestions for improvement, 163–64; on the Turkey-Syria border, 137–43; verbatim use of NGO materials by news media, 49, 58, 63, 72. *See also* journalism and journalists; news access; news media; NGO communication efforts; *and specific organizations and journalists*

NGOs: accountability, in donors' eyes, 161–62; advocacy role, 157–58; appearance in the news (*see* news access); as "boots on the ground," 18, 22, 29, 51, 164; and civic engagement, 8, 10, 158–59, 162–63; credibility of (*see* credibility of NGOs); as critics, 159–60; definition and role of, 18–19, 178–79n16, 179n18; digital-first groups, 106; as dominant form of civil society organization, 18, 179(n17); engagement between, 162; as experts, 156–57; as facilitators, 158–59; government funding for, 39, 181n17; growing competition among, 21, 22, 29, 51, 148; growth of, 38–39; historical scholarship lacking, 27–28, 179n3; influence of, 23, 178n9; as information providers, 6–9 (*see also* NGO communication efforts); institutionalization and professionalization of, 7–8, 21, 26–27, 29–36, 56, 130 (*see also* advocacy, professionalization of; professionalization of NGOs); journalistic oversight needed, 168–69; in the news (*see* news access; news media); organizational needs of, 11, 178n10; organizational slowness, 147; other forms of advocacy erased by large NGOs, 186n36; posssibility of change within, 127; as "proxy publics," 88; public and official acceptance of, 55–56; roles of, vis-a-vis public communications theories, 156–60; state functions devolved to, 39; and Syrian refugees news reporting, 137–38; transnational advocacy networks, 10. *See also* NGO communication efforts; NGO-journalist relations; *and specific topics and organizations*

Nolan, David, 11–12, 88, 110, 187nn2–3

nongovernmental organizations. *See* NGOs

NPR (National Public Radio), 134–35, 169

NRC Handelsblad (Dutch newspaper), 103

Olympics (2008), 100–101

Orgad, Shani, 184n10

organizational analysis (institutional theory), 15–16, 89–90

Oxfam: clothing drives, 38; contemporary communications efforts, 27; credibility of, 31; digital tools and strategies, 95; early communication efforts, 31; and the Ethiopian famine, 45–47; founding (formation) of, 27, 30; fund-raising and branding strategies (PR and marketing), 37–40, 116; growth of, 39–40; information-gathering strategies, 4, 32; and the Make Poverty History campaign, 77; Make Trade Fair campaign, 162; news access, 61–62, 67–68; news

strategies, 100, 102, 104, 113–14, 125, 186n31; reasons for seeking media coverage, 116, 119; reasons for studying, 20; self-reflection within, 168; and WWII-era Greece, 31, 36

El País, 134–35

Papo Reto (Straight Talk), 165

participatory democratic tradition, NGOs and, 156, 157–58

path dependence: defined and explained, 16, 108, 126–27; exogenous shocks and critical junctures explained, 112, 187n5; of government officials, 118–22, 188n25; inertia and, 16–17, 111, 127–28 (*see also* field inertia); and the persistence of media-centric publicity strategies, 109–13; and the possibility of change, 127–28; reinforcing path dependencies, 17, 24, 109, 112–27, 115t

philanthropy. *See* donors; fund-raising

photojournalists and NGOs, 1–4, 47–48, 103–4, 105, 147–48, 177nn1–3, 191n28

Pinochet, Augusto, 33

Platon (photographer), 1–3, 177nn1–2

podcasts, 49, 124

political elites. *See* political officials

political legitimacy of NGOs, 118–22. *See also* legitimacy of NGOs; political officials

"political observatories," 192n3

political officials (government officials): information materials produced for, 7; media consumption by, 103, 116, 118–22, 127–28; as news sources, 13, 54–55, 59, 69–71, 70t, 109, 136;

radical democratic traditions, NGOs and, 159–60

Ramos, Howard, 63

Red Cross, 96–98, 169

Reese, Stephen, 10

Reimann, Kim, 39

Remnick, David, 2

representative liberal tradition, NGOs and, 156–57

reputation, protection of NGOs', 89, 95. *See also* branding; credibility of NGOs

research by NGOs: development of research functions, 26–27, 30–32, 35–36; incorrect information, 50–51, 98–99, 124; journalistic approach, 123; researchers and news reporting, 137–38; supplemented by information technologies, 49–50, 87, 98; tensions between PR and marketing and, 41–43; verification of information, 49–51, 87, 95, 96–98, 124, 141–42, 185–86n23

Rohingya, 99

Ron, James, 63

roving correspondents, for NGOs, 48

Russell, Adrienne, 9, 86, 186n30

Ryfe, David, 132–33

Sambrook, Richard, 189n1

San Francisco, Olympic protests in, 101

Sassen, Saskia, 184n15

satellite imagery, 10, 50

Saudi Arabia, 146

Save the Children: and the Ethiopian famine, 45; founding (formation) of, 30, 38; fund-raising and branding strategies, 37–38, 40, 181n15; and the Make Poverty History campaign, 77; news access, 61–62,

67; news monitored by, 100; reasons for studying, 20; relations with journalists, 44

Scammell, Margaret, 180n5

Schudson, Michael, 132, 192n3

Segerberg, Alexandra, 17, 87

Sikkink, Kathryn, 10

social criticism, NGOs and, 159–60

social media, NGOs' use of: for communicating with public/supporters, 93–94; for fund-raising, 93–94; generally, 5, 10–11, 48, 84, 86–87; Human Rights Watch's use of, 103; to interact with journalists, 123–24; and Olympic protests over Chinese human rights violations, 101; raising awareness through, 120; smaller organizations, 165; Twitter, 91, 94, 103; used to attract journalists' attention, 96. *See also* digital tools and strategies

Sommerfeldt, Erich, 184n14

Stecula, Dominik, 164–65, 183–84n10

story location: coding for, in study, 63 (*see also* news access); and NGOs in the news, 72–74, 82, 109, 183–84n10; as term, 59

Sutton, Robert, 89–90

Sweet, Diana, 164–65, 183–84n10

Syria, 50–51, 98, 138, 189n39

Syrian refugees, in Turkey, 21–22, 130, 134–35, 137–43, 190nn3–5, 12, 18

Taylor, Maureen, 184n14

Thompson, John, 97

Thoms, Oskar, 63

Thrall, A. Trevor, 164–65, 183–84n10

Tibet, 100–101

Tolley, Howard, 181n14

transnational advocacy networks, 10

Turkey, 137, 140, 190n4. *See also* Syrian refugees

Twitter, 91, 94, 103. *See also* social media

Uganda, 120, 121, 191n27

United Fruit Company, 37

United Nations: cited in news articles, 71–72; Climate Summit, NGO coverage of, 9; and humanitarian and human rights issues, 34; media consumption by UN officials, 103, 116, 119, 120–21

United States: and Afghanistan, 119; American politics and human rights, 33–34 (*see also* Human Rights Watch); human rights discussions among policymakers, 63, 65–66, 65t; meatpacking industry labor violations, 76–77; and Mexico, 76; and Uzbekistan, 79; "war on terror" and human rights abuses by, 68. *See also* political officials

USA Today, 61, 68, 72, 75–76, 79, 82

Uzbekistan, 74, 78–80

videos and audio-visual materials, 47, 50–51, 83, 146

vocabularies, expert, 32

volunteers, 26–27, 31, 35–36

Vulture Club, 93, 185n8, 189n39

Waisbord, Silvio, 11, 59, 187nn2, 4

Walker, Ed, 166–67

Wall Street Journal, 138

Warren, Robert Penn, 44

Washington Post, 49, 119–20, 134–35

websites of NGOs: generally, 48, 84, 184n14, 185n14 (*see also* digital tools and strategies); informational purpose of, 95–96; issue-specific websites, 101, 151; NGO websites, 117, 151

Wells, Chris, 165

Wessler, Hartmut, 189n44

Wilson, Francesca, 180n7

Witness (human rights group), 165

Wood, Tim, 167

World Vision, 20, 61–62, 67

Wright, Kate, 47–48, 105–6, 145, 148

YouTube, 103

Zoch, Lynn, 186n30

Zuckerman, Ethan, 9